NYC
STOREFRONTS

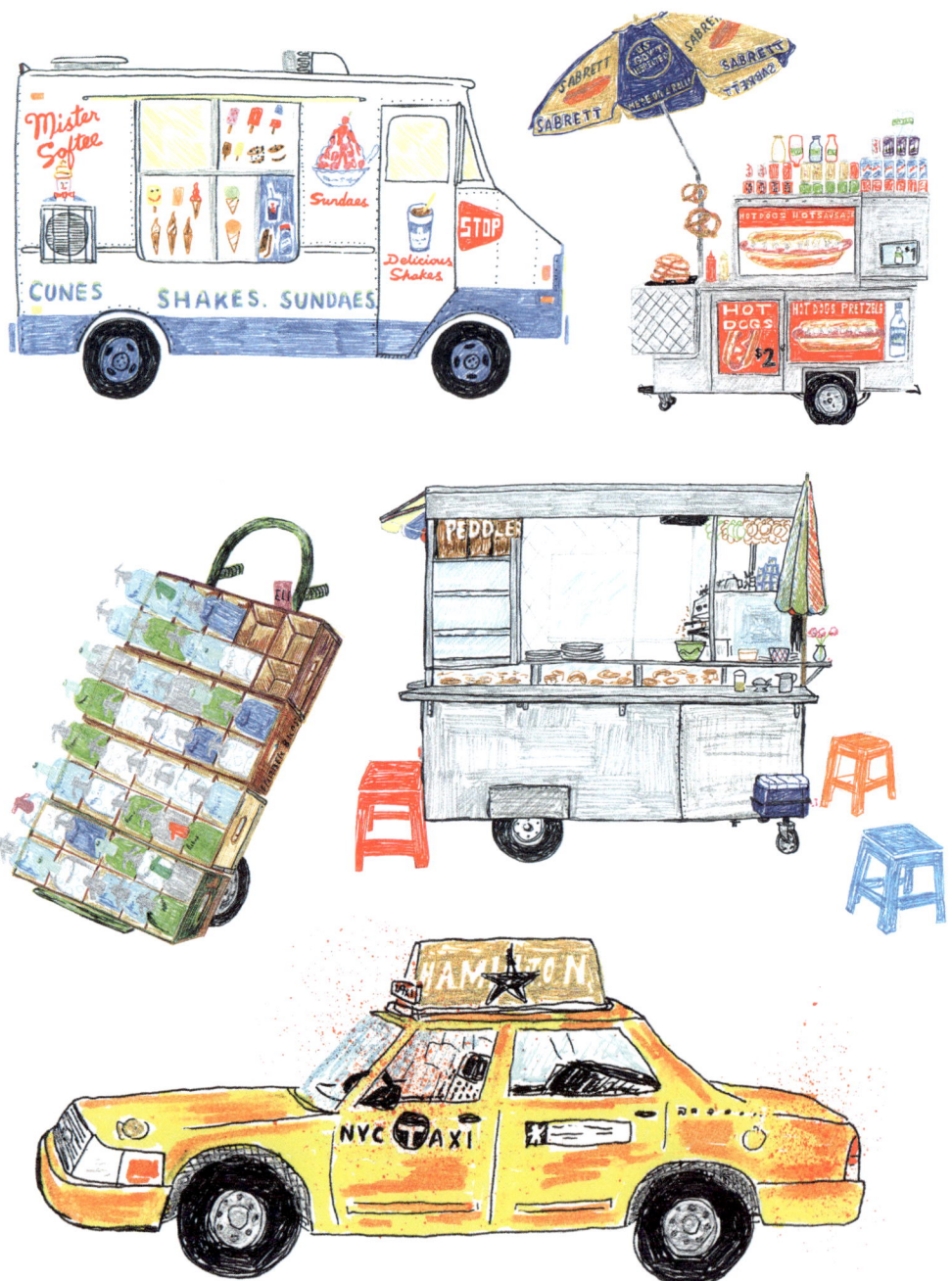

NYC
STOREFRONTS

ILLUSTRATIONS OF THE BIG APPLE'S BEST-LOVED SPOTS

—

JOEL HOLLAND

words by **DAVID DODGE**

foreword by **NICOLAS HELLER**

AKA NEW YORK NICO

PRESTEL

Munich • London • New York

CONTENTS

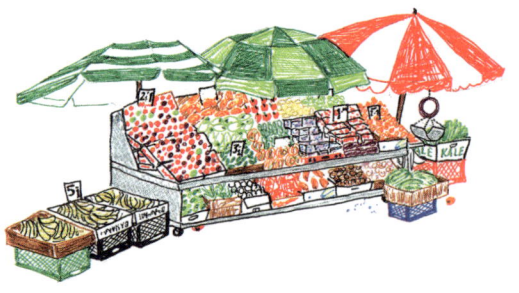
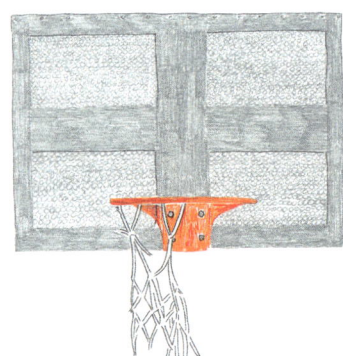
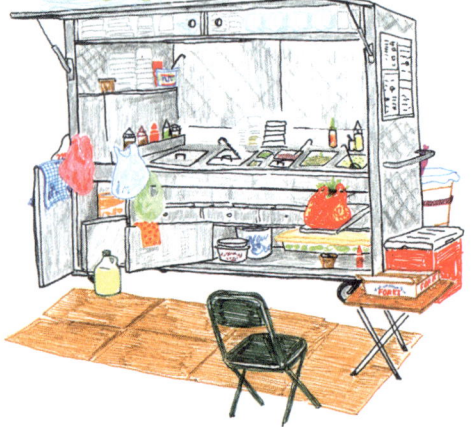
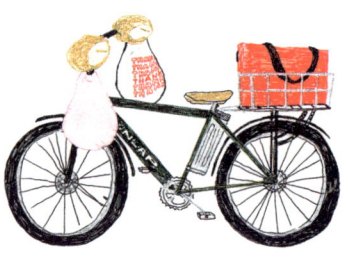
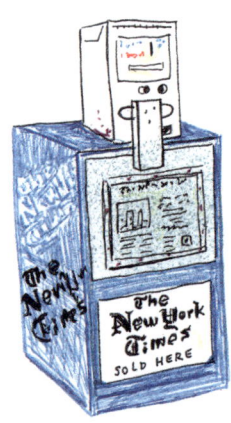
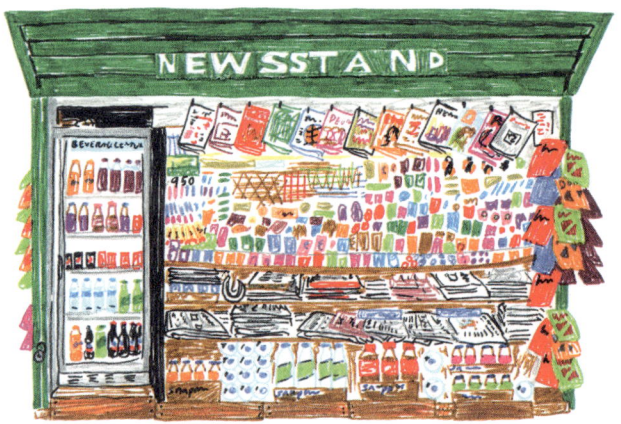

FOREWORD

NiCOLAS HELLER AKA NEW YORK NiCO

———

New York is the greatest city on earth. Hands down, no contest. What sets it apart from any other city? Simple. It's the people and the small businesses. Where else will you find specialty shops like Chess Forum, Casey Rubber Stamps, or Punjabi Deli? Sure, there might be a few places in other cities that sell similar things, but they don't have the same types of individuals running them that we have here.

As a filmmaker, I travel around the city every day meeting exciting New Yorkers and highlighting small, local businesses on Instagram. The most fascinating people I have ever met are shop owners—like Big Mike, who runs Astor Place Hairstylists, or Jamal, who runs Village Revival Records. These are so much more than just stores to me. They are spots where I can go and hang out with good people.

Joel Holland's illustrations capture these storefronts beautifully. His style is so unique, and I always look forward to seeing new pieces from him. More importantly, the owners of the places he draws take pride in these depictions. Many of my favorite businesses have his illustrations front and center when you walk in. In fact, Joel and I first met when I recommended that he draw Artful Posters on Bleecker Street to help its owners promote the store. They were thrilled with the result (see page 120 of this book).

There are lots of amazing places included here, and it feels impossible to choose a personal favorite. But pro tip: order the New York Nico Special at La Bonbonniere.

With NYC rents soaring, it is so important to keep supporting these establishments. If New York loses its local butchers, bakeries, record stores, barber shops, etcetera, then it might as well be any other city.

Nicolas Heller is a filmmaker who was born and raised in NYC. Known as the "unofficial talent scout of New York City," he uses his popular Instagram account (@newyorknico) to highlight charismatic citizens, including local business owners. He also spearheads fund-raising campaigns to help keep them in operation. His first book, New York Nico's Guide to NYC, was published in 2024.

INTRODUCTiON

My family moved into a new apartment on March 13, 2020—during the same week that New York City shut down due to the Covid-19 pandemic. The move had excited me for many reasons, despite it being only two blocks (long blocks!) west of our old place. We'd now be closer to my daughter's school, some friends, Ralph's Ices, Mohammed's fruit stand, convenient bus stops, the Epiphany Library, and family too. But with quarantines and closures, all that turned moot.

This is when I decided to start drawing storefronts. It began mostly as a way for me to visit, in some small way, my favorite places and businesses—like a visual love letter. It was my method of grabbing tight to New York and squeezing. Hard.

Economy Candy on Rivington Street (open since 1937!) was the first of these illustrations. I drew it for my two daughters as a rain check for not being able to go there. It proved sufficient ... though my personal stash of Swedish Fish did seem to disappear rather quickly, until they started shipping again.

The project took on new meaning for me after news broke that an East Village staple, Gem Spa—maker of the best egg creams and the only place around to buy Hav-a-Hank bandannas—was closing. After surviving a yearslong battle with their landlord, they simply couldn't win the war against the coronavirus. I drew the store and posted it to Instagram along with my rendering of Economy Candy, and the immediate enthusiastic response compelled me to continue. It was gratifying and, more importantly, gave me a way to send good vibes to the businesses themselves. Maybe it would even help drive custo-mers to them.

During this process, George Floyd was murdered at the hands of the police, and people took to the streets. Meanwhile, Asian Americans were being targeted and senselessly attacked, and New Yorkers rallied in support. Restaurants reopened, closed again, then opened outdoor seating, then closed portions of indoor seating—and on and on. Some places closed for good. Some merged with other establishments. Some relocated.

The determination of what to illustrate started as mine, but over time family, friends, and people online began suggesting places to draw too. I haven't intentionally focused on locations that are off the beaten path, but sort of (it's Manhattan; there is no unbeaten path here). They are drawings of storefronts that I treasure: the shops I see while riding the southbound M9 bus to play basketball on Mondays. Or the infinite stores seen during Chinatown walks.

This book isn't meant to capture every storefront that keeps New York moving. These are just a few of the places that act like glue, holding a seemingly endless number of different communities together as one great city. Some of these establishments have recently closed, but I wanted to draw them anyhow. Others may have shuttered or moved since *NYC Storefronts* was published, so make sure you double-check before heading out somewhere.

Whether your favorite spot is included here or not, hopefully you will be inspired to visit the places that make New York such a great place to live or visit. And if you're too busy, you can always order takeout.

Go for a walk. Ride the bus. Look up. And over. And keep going.

Peace,
Joel Holland

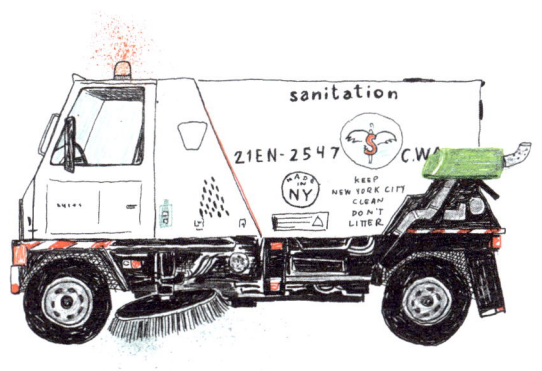

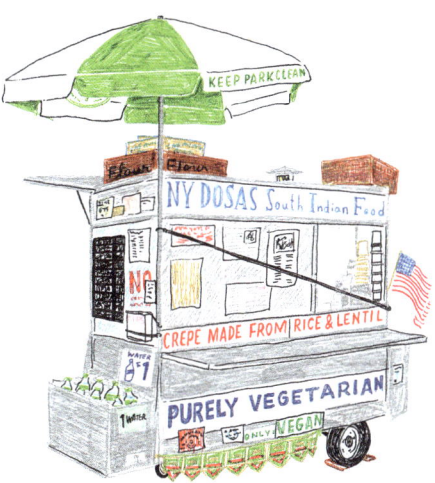

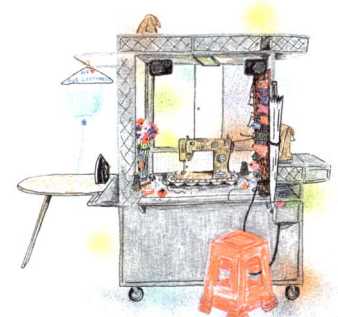

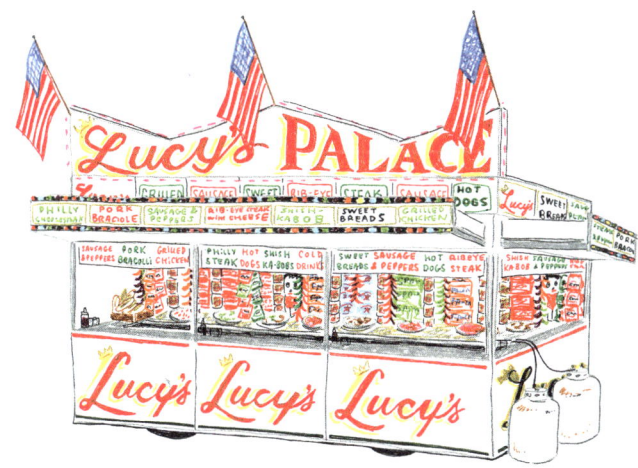

NOTE TO THE READER

New York is known for many things—among them, constant change. Care has been taken to provide current addresses for the storefronts in this book, but some may have since moved or closed. Certain illustrations depict places that have permanently closed. In these cases, the old address is provided, and the text notes that the business has shuttered. Other shops changed locations after the illustration was made, during the process of creating this book. For these, the old storefront is depicted, but the new address is provided to direct readers to the current location (to help keep it open there).

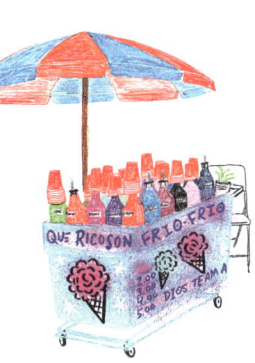

La Bonbonniere

Open since the 1930s, this West Village eatery has developed an incredibly loyal following, including famous folks like Molly Shannon and Ethan Hawke. But despite its name, La Bonbonniere is not a fancy French restaurant requiring a coat and tie (quite the opposite, in fact). So if you're searching for a truffle omelet with pule donkey cheese, best look elsewhere. But it is precisely for this reason that the greasy spoon, which offers nothing but the basics—coffee, pancakes, and eggs—is a breath of fresh air in a neighborhood drowning in bottomless brunches.

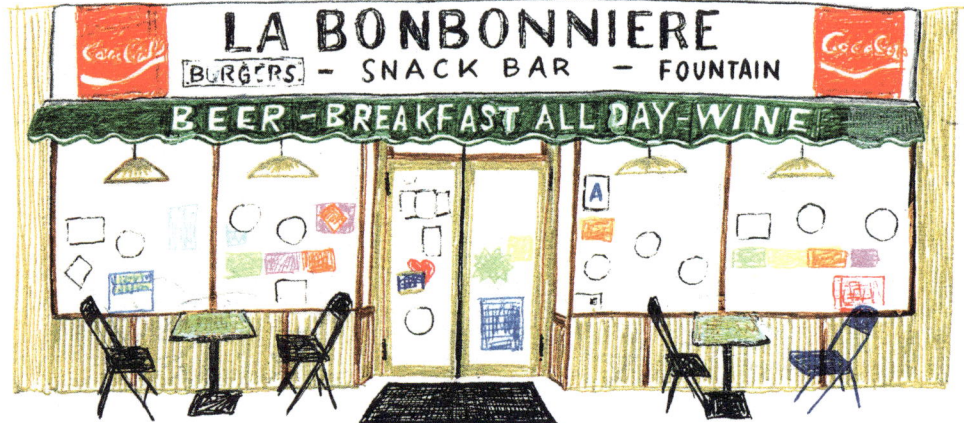

Casa Magazines

In 2012 the *New York Times* deemed this shop's then owner, Mohammed Ahmed, the "last king of print"—and it's not hard to see why. Casa Magazines sells every mag on the market you can think of, tallying to around two thousand titles. For this reason, on any given day, it's not a surprise to find some of the city's top editors, stylists, and writers there.

In 2024 Mohammed retired and sold the business to his friend Hemal Sheth, the proprietor of Iconic Magazines who operates several small magazine shops in Lower Manhattan. While longtime customers worried what new ownership might mean for Casa, Mohammed told the website Curbed that the store would remain largely unchanged. "It will be in good hands," he said. In late 2024 the business expanded, with the book and coffee shop Casa Next Door opening—you guessed it—next door.

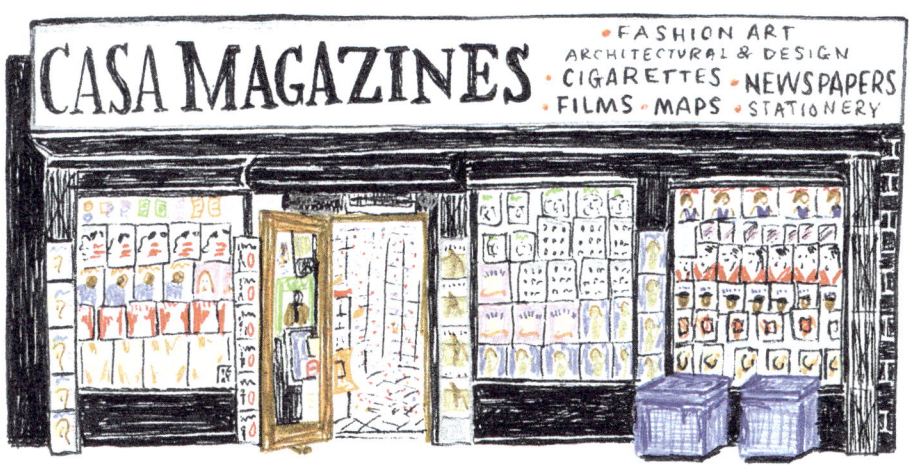

Fanelli Cafe

It's hard to miss Fanelli Cafe thanks to the old-school neon sign hanging on the corner of Prince and Mercer proclaiming its name. But regulars of this space, which has been around since 1847, need no reminder: some have visited daily for decades. In recent years it has become equally as popular with tourists, who swarm the surrounding streets of SoHo during the day and pop into the restaurant for a quick reprieve between bouts of shopping. As a result, mornings tend to be the "sweetest, most local time," as proprietor Sasha Noe told the *New York Times* in a 2019 profile.

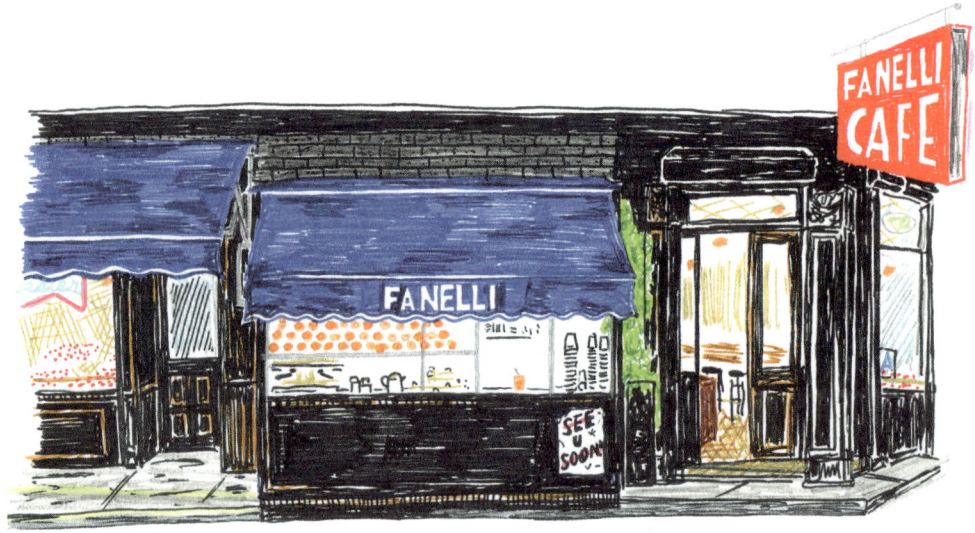

Nom Wah Tea Parlor

The doors of this tea parlor opened on Doyers Street in 1920, making it the oldest dim sum spot in Chinatown. In 1974 Wally Tang, who worked in the restaurant from the age of sixteen, bought the space. In 2011 Wilson Tang, Wally's nephew, abandoned his career as an investment banker for the chance to take over when his uncle decided to retire. Wilson opened new locations but left the original almost entirely untouched, from the classic red booths to the checkered tablecloths. Thanks to this preserved old-world feel (and, of course, the incredible dumplings), regulars and tourists alike line up for hours for a table.

After a half century the Tangs still run Nom Wah. But where there are families there are often feuds: citing internal disagreements, Wilson stepped away from operating the Doyers Street restaurant, but remains involved with their outposts in NoLita and Pier 57.

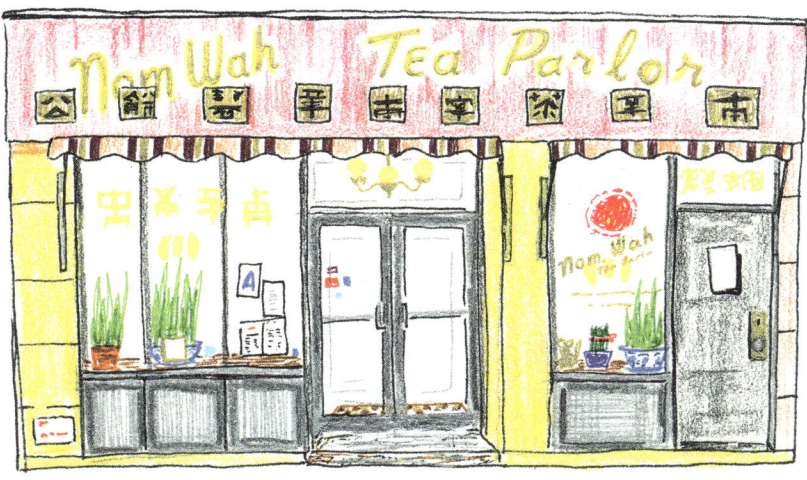

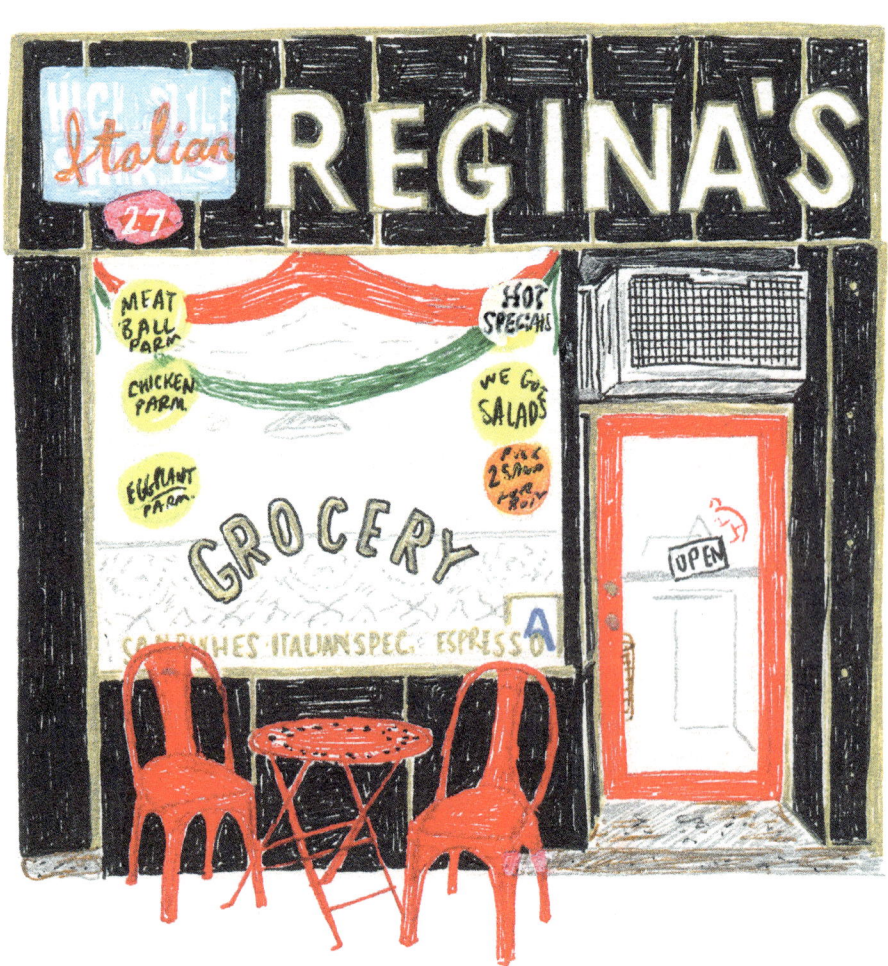

Regina's Grocery

Roman Grandinetti, founder of the downtown creative agency CNNCTD (whose clients include Bob Dylan and A$AP Ferg), opened this sandwich shop located on the border of Chinatown and the Lower East Side in 2017.

While Roman may have friends in high places in the advertising world, he freely admits the store's popularity is thanks almost entirely to the traditional Italian sandwiches—each based on a recipe from his mother, Regina, and named after a member of their family.

The most popular of these, he says, is the Uncle Jimmy, made with prosciutto, fresh mozzarella, and hot sopressata. But plenty of people pop into the tiny establishment (it can fit ten to twelve customers at one time, maximum) just to buy some of Regina's signature Calabrian pepper spread, which the family bottles and sells separately. Too long of a wait to snag your favorite sandwich? Check out the store's other locations in NoLita, the Upper East Side, and Bed-Stuy.

Joe's Bar

This East Village dive bar closed in 2012 when its owner, Joe Vajda, passed away. That same year, Kirk Marcoe and Rich Corton, the owners of two other beloved drinkeries nearby (Mona's [see page 50] and Sophie's), took over the business and renamed it Josie's. By saving the bar, the new proprietors helped continue the space's legacy as a watering hole, which it had been since the 1910s.

Kirk and Rich decided to give the bar a bit of a facelift but were cautious to stay true to Joe's divey roots. They replaced its cigarette smoke–stained wallpaper, for instance, but used the exact same print. "You have to do it within the context of what the East Village was, is, and represents," Kirk told a local paper at the time. "We love this neighborhood. We're not here to make a quick buck, we're here because Joe died and we liked to drink in this bar."

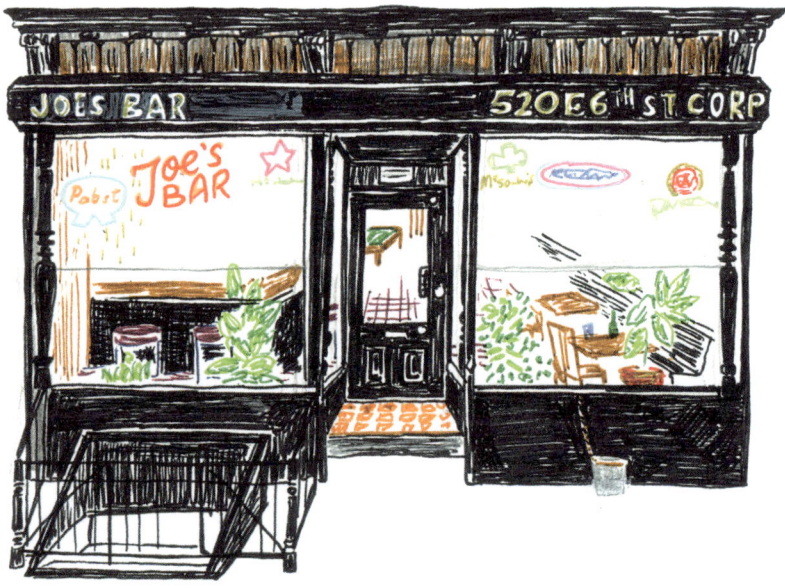

Lucien

Everyone from Lady Gaga to Tilda Swinton has walked through this French bistro's doors, and many of these encounters with the world's entertainment class are documented in pictures that adorn its walls. The owner, Moroccan-born Lucien Bahaj, who died in 2019, was known as a demanding boss with a colorful vocabulary—but also as someone who cared deeply for the neighborhood that kept his restaurant afloat since 1998. For example, he provided free meals to cash-strapped artists in the area.

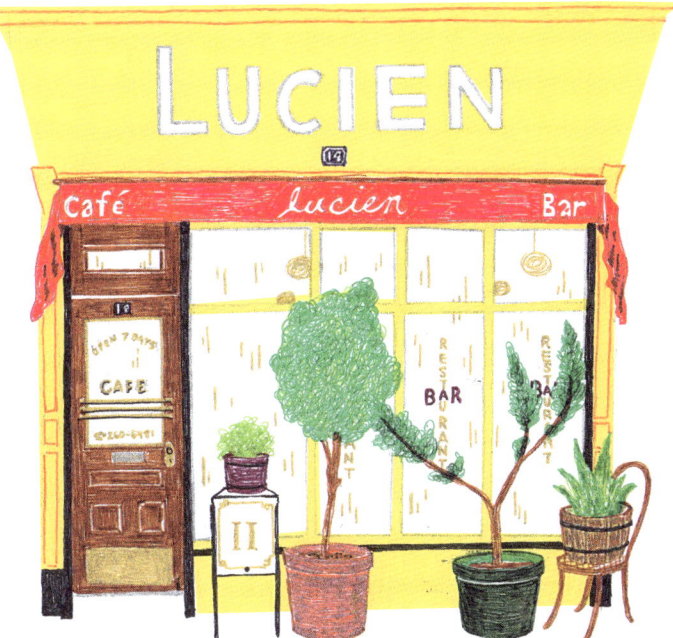

Happy Bones Coffee

Founded by a trio of New Zealanders, this tiny Little Italy coffee shop is now closed. It was known as much for its coffee as for its rotating displays of art from around the globe. Some stopped in just to purchase the shop's trademark tortoise shell–patterned spoons, which were so popular they often sold out.

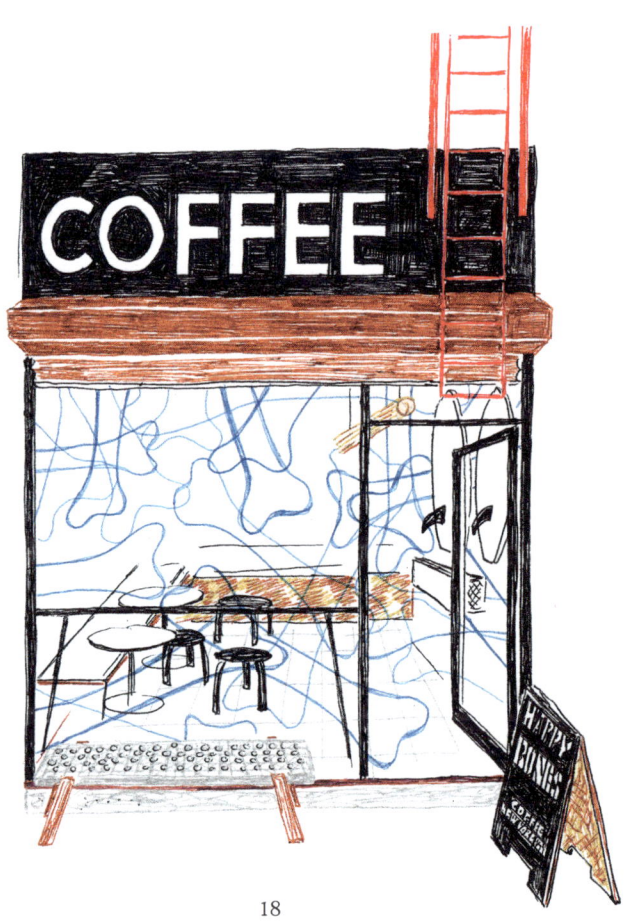

Jing Fong

The dim sum restaurant Jing Fong first opened on Elizabeth Street in Chinatown in 1978 with just one hundred fifty seats. Fifteen years later, it moved to a new twenty-thousand-square-foot space on the same street (which is the location depicted below). There, it became one of the city's best-known banquet halls, serving ten thousand customers a week.

Hundreds of people, including staff and neighbors, rallied to keep it open when it was struggling during the Covid-19 pandemic. Unfortunately, negotiations with the landlord failed, and the downtown restaurant closed in March 2021. Luckily, the owners found a new, though much smaller, location on Centre Street. In 2017 they had also opened a second spot on the Upper West Side. With these two storefronts, the legacy of this beloved dim sum spot is sure to continue well into the future.

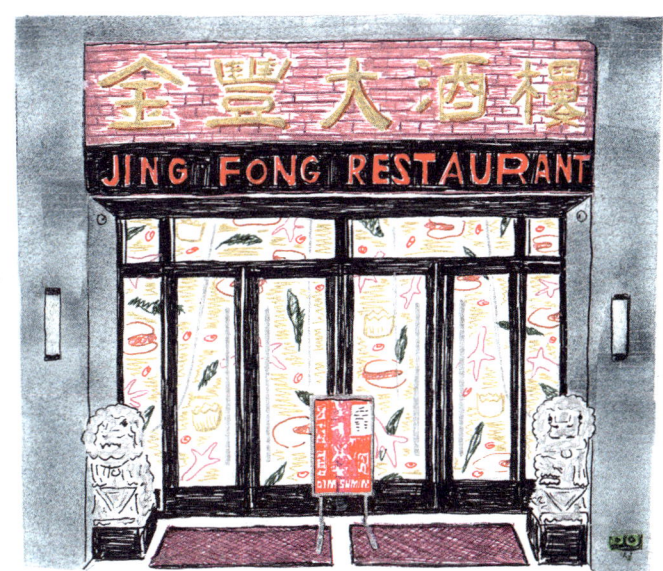

93 1st Ave. #2
between E. 5th and 6th Sts.

Panna II

———

For decades, if you happened by this pair of Indian and Bangladeshi restaurants on First Avenue—Milon (to the left) and Panna II (to the right)—you'd be greeted by two menu-brandishing men, enthusiastically arguing with you, and one another, about which establishment you should choose for dinner. The cuisine of the two spots was nearly identical, as was the decor: a mess of chili-pepper and Christmas lights hanging from the ceiling. (Pros knew to tell the staff it was their birthday, even if it wasn't, for a chance to see what those pepper lights can really do.)

According to urban legend, the restaurants were owned by the same people, who used the performative arguments outside to create a sort of tourist attraction—a dinner-and-a-show type of gimmick.

Those rumors came to an end in 2020, however, when Milon went out of business.

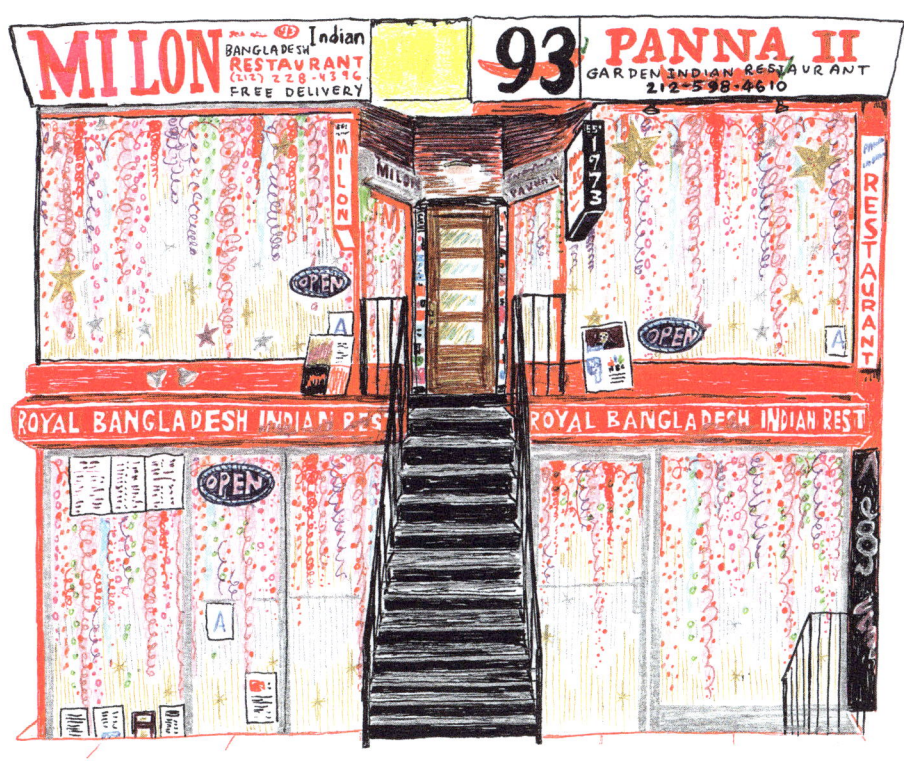

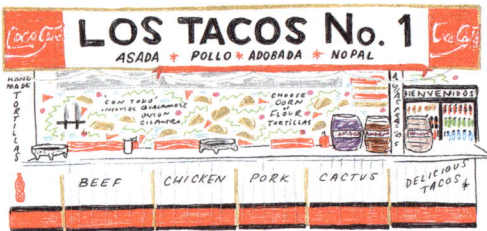

229 W. 43rd St.
between 7th and 8th Aves.

Los Tacos No.1

True to its name, this spot is top of the list for New York taco enthusiasts, particularly those with an appetite for authentic Mexican food. Expect a line—especially at its Hell's Kitchen or Chelsea Market locations—but the wait is worth it.

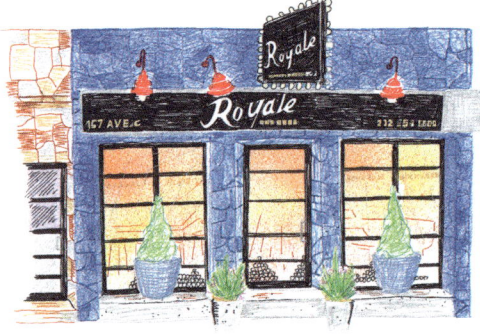

157 Ave. C
between E. 9th and 10th Sts.

Royale

You could easily miss this unassuming watering hole (and its backyard patio) amid all the fancy cocktail bars and restaurants that have sprung up on Avenue C in recent years—but the burgers here are the stuff of Alphabet City lore.

85 Ave. A
between E. 5th and 6th Sts.

Juicy Lucy's

In a city where a blended fruit drink can cost you a cool twenty bucks, the offerings at this East Village hut—which include pressed juices and fresh smoothies, some for under ten dollars—are refreshing in more ways than one.

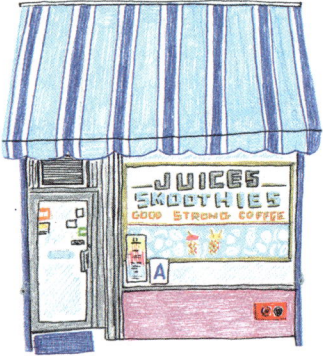

71½ Mulberry St.
between Bayard and Canal Sts.

Asia Market Corp.

This market in Chinatown sources hard-to-find fruits and vegetables—and what one online reviewer referred to as a "dizzying assortment of soy sauces"—from across Southeast Asia. The options may be overwhelming, but searching for what you need is half the fun.

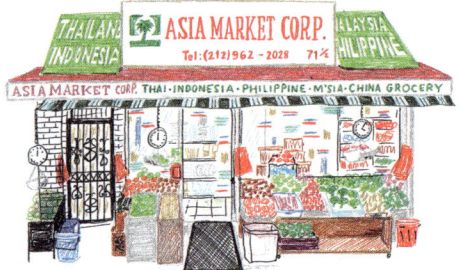

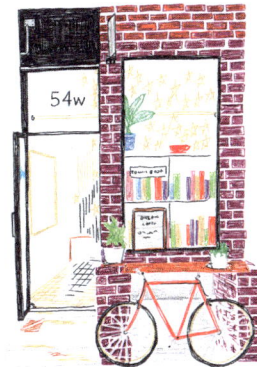

54W Henry St.
between Catherine and Market Sts.

Dreamers Coffee House

The co-owners of this Chinatown coffee shop describe themselves as *jook-sings*, meaning someone of Chinese descent born in the West. They opened this spot to counter the displacement of Chinese-owned businesses catering to the local community.

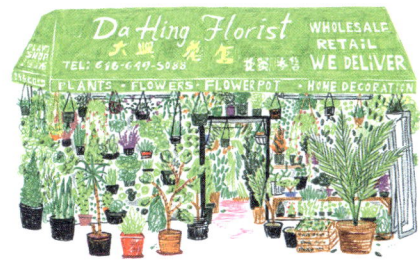

289 Grand St.
at Eldridge St.

Da Hing Florist

This shop is known for delivering plants within NYC's five boroughs and upstate—as well as to parts of New Jersey and Providence, Rhode Island. Not sure whether to spring for that fiddle-leaf fig you've been eyeing? Fear not, Da Hing's online quiz can help you decide.

206 Mercer St.
between W. Houston and Bleecker Sts.

Mercer St. Books

Since the 1990s, this literary institution in Greenwich Village has been a go-to spot for hard-to-find and out-of-print books—and the perfect place to kill time before the start of an indie flick at the Angelika Film Center, located just down the street.

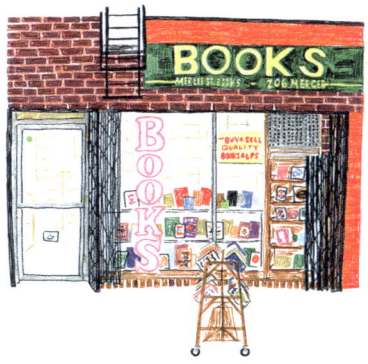

356 E. 19th St. #2
between 2nd and 1st Aves.

Wu Cleaners

Regulars at this Gramercy-area laundry focus their praise as much, if not more, on Mr. Wu himself—a chatty, affable man with a personality that warms his small, unassuming storefront—as on his impeccable alterations.

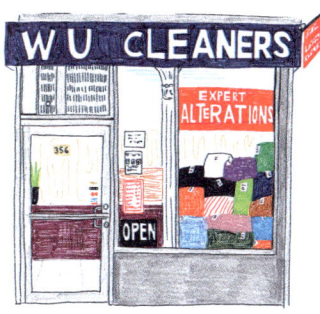

Marie's Crisis Cafe

This historic West Village building has had many lives since it was built in 1839, one of which was as a brothel. In its current incarnation, people flock from all over the world for the chance to belt out show tunes shoulder-to-shoulder with strangers, who are just as likely to be Broadway legends as they are Midwestern tourists.

The site is also notable for another reason: it was once home to American Revolutionary and philosopher Thomas Paine; he lived there until his death in 1809. In fact, "Crisis" was added to the bar's name in homage to Paine's series of pamphlets that urged the public to support the Revolutionary War.

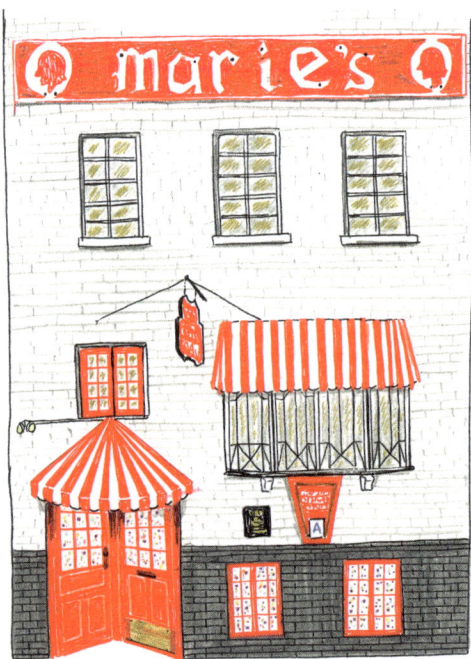

Jimmy's Corner

Jimmy Glenn, the late owner of this Times Square bar, was once an amateur boxer who fought (and lost) against heavyweight champion Floyd Patterson. After retiring from the sport, he opened his own gym, the Times Square Boxing Club, where he trained many well-known athletes, including Jameel McCline.

Though Jimmy's boxing gym didn't survive (closing after fifteen years), the bar that bears his name serves as an enduring ode to his love of the sport. The walls are covered with photos of famous boxers and other remembrances from his years as an athlete and trainer. Don't leave without peeping the shot of Jimmy with Muhammad Ali.

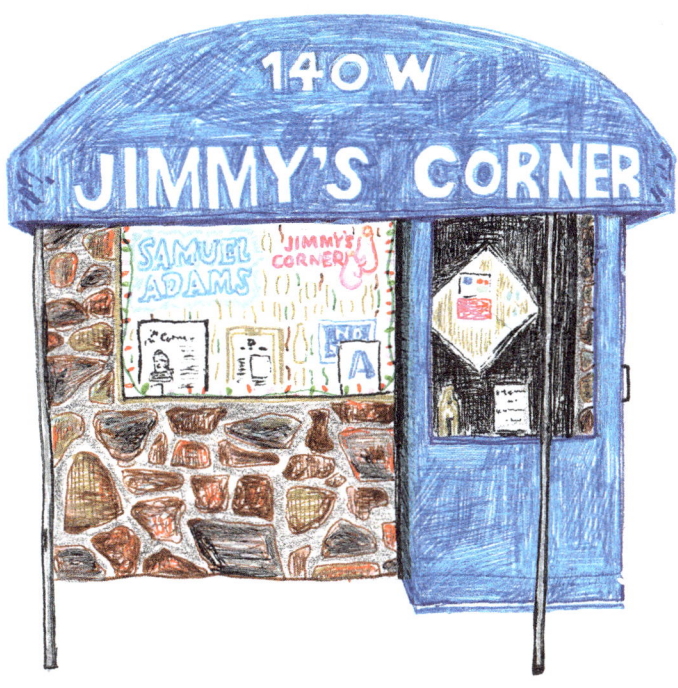

Winnie's Bar

For almost thirty years, this Chinatown karaoke bar coexisted downtown next to the Manhattan Detention Complex, better known as "The Tombs." After closing the bar in 2015 due to rent increases, owner Winnie Mui searched high and low for a new location before finally settling on the second floor of this East Broadway building. Today, the spot once again plays host to the area's peculiar mix of city employees, hedge-fund managers, and tourists as they belt out questionable renditions of Journey's "Don't Stop Believing," among other hits.

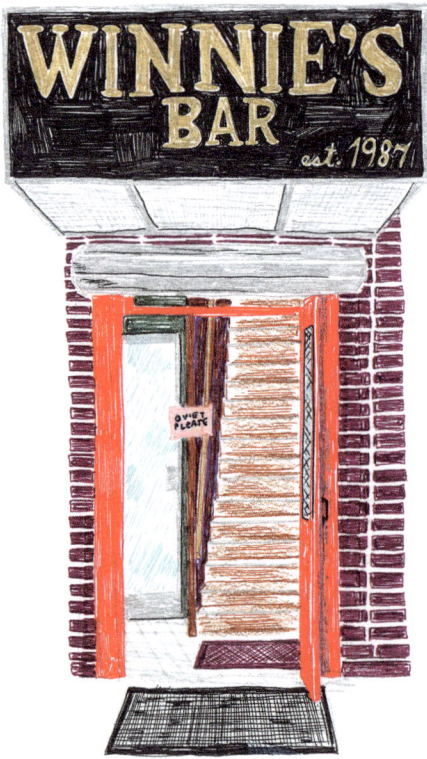

Pearl Diner

One of the few remaining classic New York greasy spoons in the Wall Street area, Pearl Diner has been flipping burgers and serving triple-decker sandwiches since 1962. The single-story building, complete with a retro neon sign, stands out in the best possible way among its Financial District neighbors—some of the tallest skyscrapers in the city.

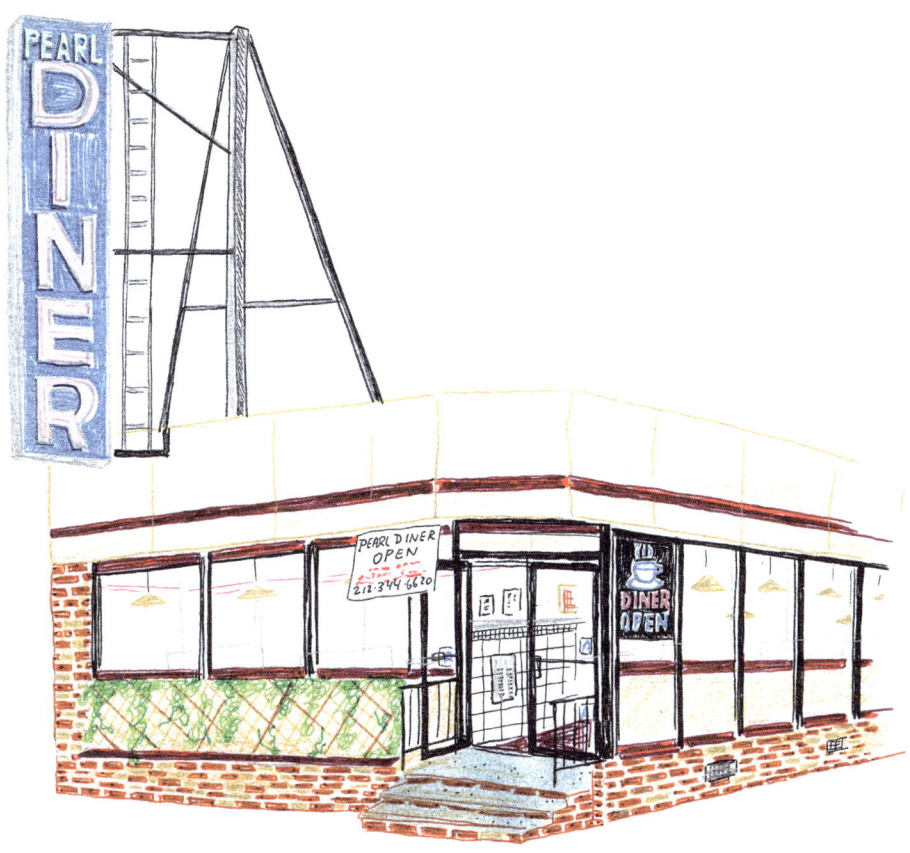

The 4th Street Photo Gallery

Alex Harsley got his start in 1958 as the first Black photographer for the New York City district attorney's office. Over the years he has taken photos of many historical figures, including Shirley Chisholm, Muhammad Ali, and John Coltrane, as well as events like Wigstock, Lady Bunny's outdoor drag festival that started in the city in 1984.

Despite his own accomplishments in the photography world, Alex may be best known for his efforts to champion other artists. In 1971, working out of his apartment, he founded Minority Photographers Inc., a nonprofit meant to showcase up-and-coming Black and brown photographers. He moved the operation to the current space, this small gallery in the East Village, two years later.

Alex has since provided opportunities for David Hammons, Jean-Michel Basquiat, and others to exhibit their work (before their names were made).

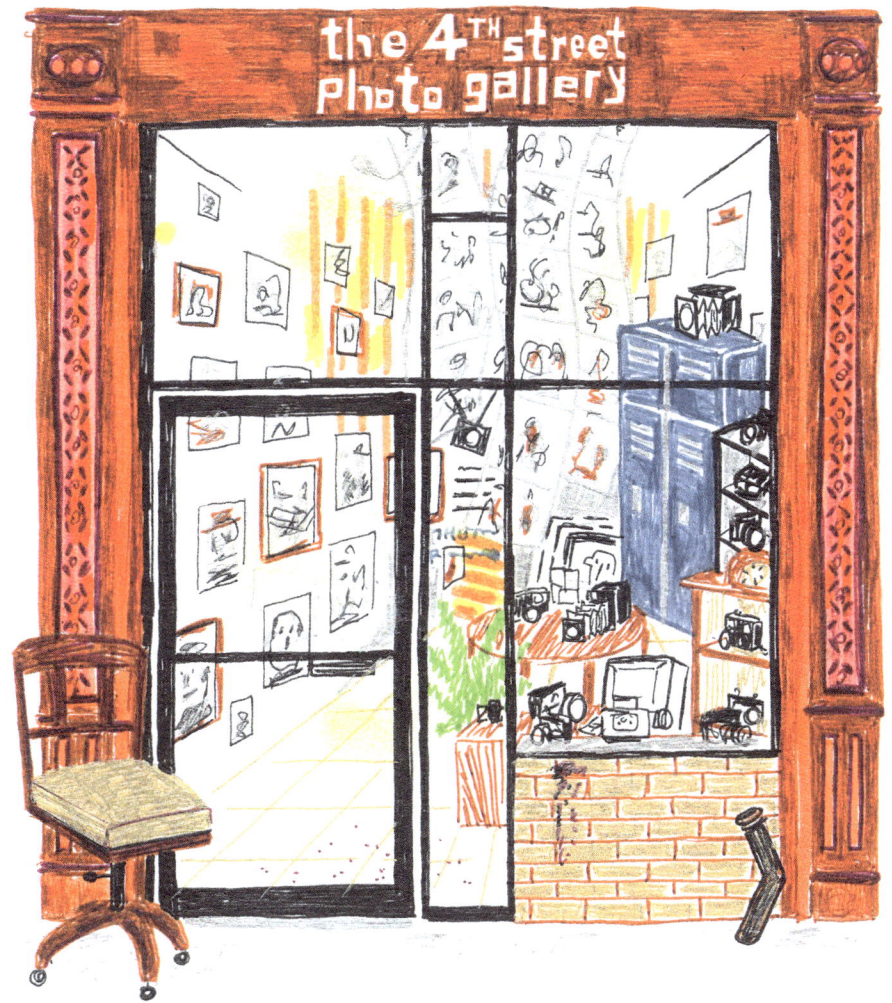

47 Division Street Trading Inc.

During the height of the coronavirus pandemic in 2020, some eagle-eyed Reddit observers—including one *Wall Street Journal* reporter—noticed a user, going by the handle "meat boy," offering insanely low prices at his Chinatown butcher shop (which has a name that seems more appropriate for a Wall Street brokerage firm). "Sup y'all, it's your favorite local meat boy," he wrote. "Let your poor and broke ass friends know that they don't need to starve in times like this."

The generosity of 47 Division Street Trading Inc. owner Jefferson Li's message (combined with his colorful turns of phrase) helped the post go viral, drawing customers from all over the city and keeping the store afloat.

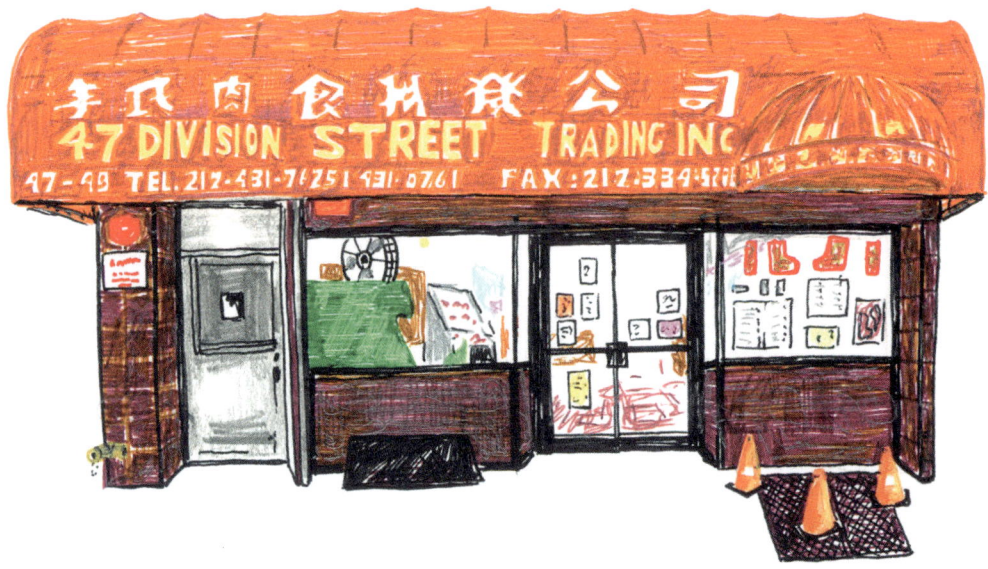

Chess Forum

Billing itself as a place for "smart people not smart phones," this chess shop, opened in 1995, has a range of games for sale, from backgammon to mahjong. It's also a venue where enthusiasts can meet, discuss, and play their favorite games until the store's midnight closing time—"or much later," their website says, "if the games continue."

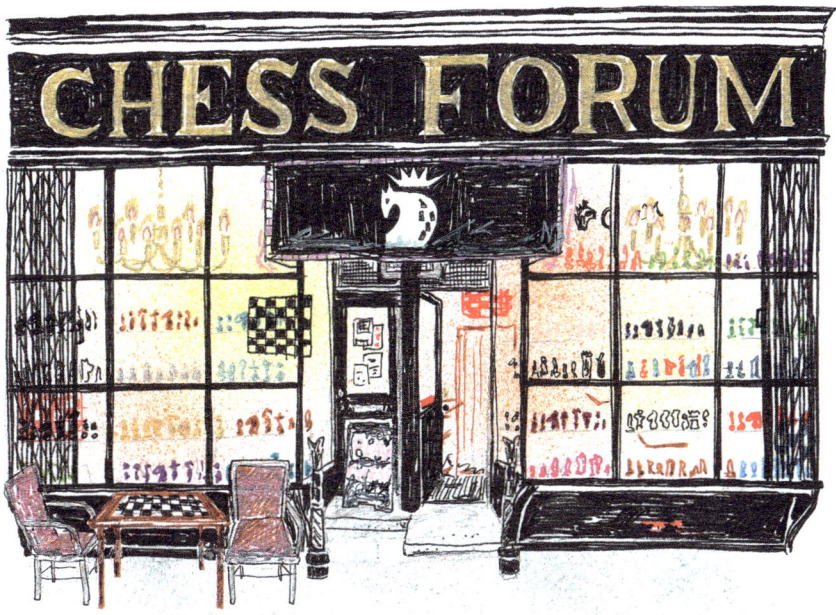

Caffe Reggio

Founded in 1927, this Italian café (whose claim to fame is being the first in the United States to serve a cappuccino) is one of the oldest continuously operating coffee shops in the city. Its original owner, Domenico Parisi, worked as a barber for forty years before saving enough money to purchase a $1,000 espresso machine and have it shipped from Italy. The machine is no longer in use but is still on display in the shop.

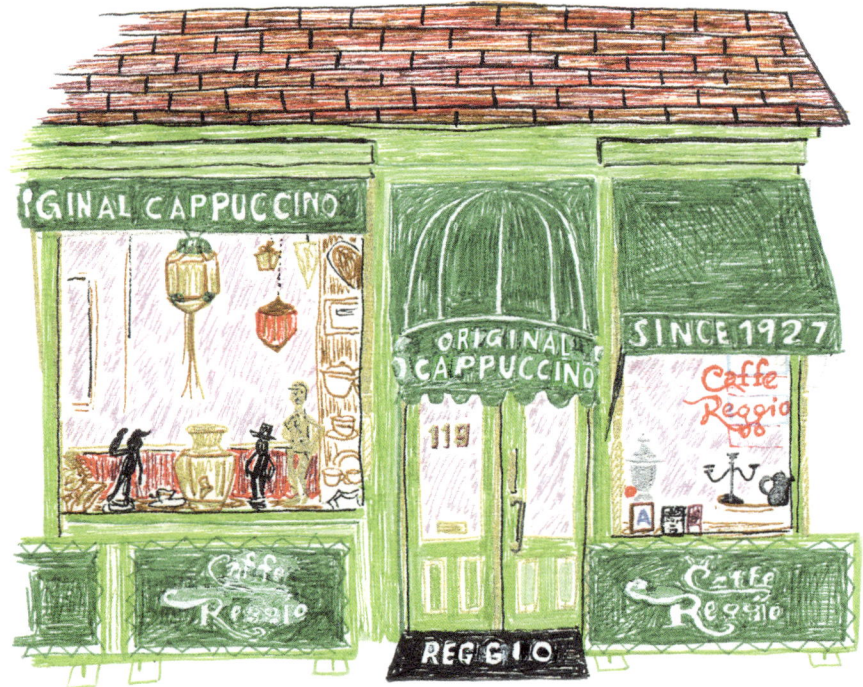

Yonah Schimmel Knish Bakery

This Lower East Side bakery has been cooking up knishes since 1910, making it the oldest still-operating knishery in NYC. Traditionally filling their knishes with potato, onion, and seasoning, all wrapped in baked dough (never fried), Yonah Schimmel has recently gotten more creative with their offerings, with options like cherry cheese and jalapeño cheddar. According to its website, the store has catered to many famous fans over the years, from Eleanor Roosevelt to Barbra Streisand.

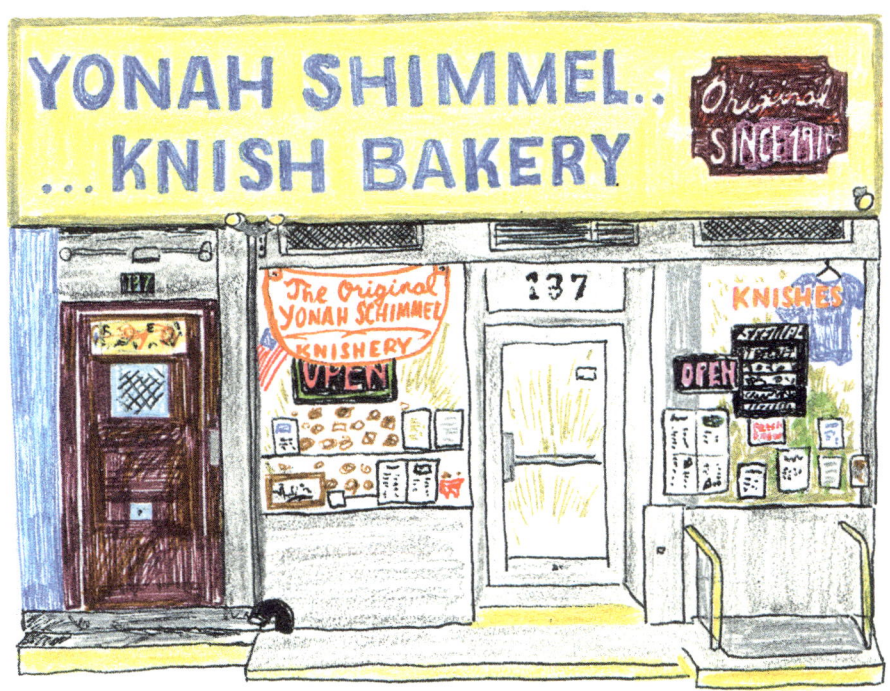

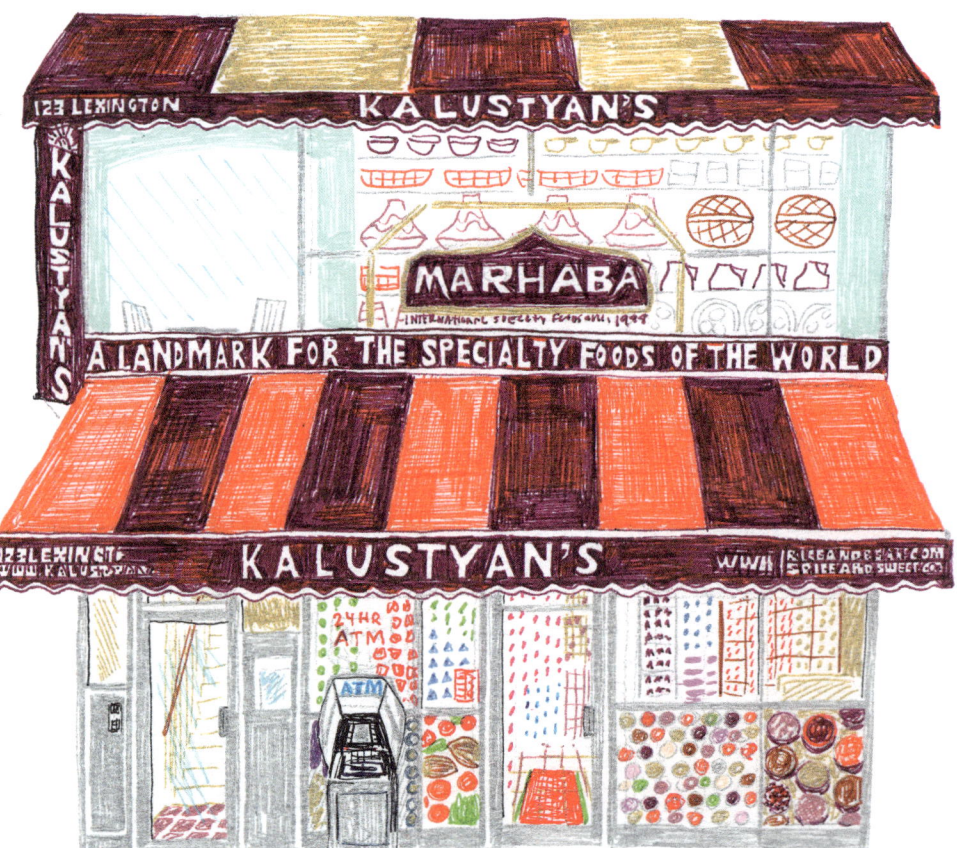

Kalustyan's

Many of New York's home cooks—and very likely *all* of the city's professional chefs—are well acquainted with this specialty grocery store in Kips Bay.

It's known as the place to go to for that one ingredient (likely a spice) that you can't find anywhere else, regardless of the type of cuisine. Opened in 1944 by Kerope Kalustyan, an Armenian Turkish immigrant, the store originally carried mostly Middle Eastern staples. Though it's now sometimes referred to as an Indian market, Kalustyan's has come to carry most (if not all) of the spices you might find in the countries represented on the "It's a Small World" ride at Disneyland.

Lest you think this claim hyperbolic, consider: Kalustyan's sources from 80 countries, from which it procures 300 different spice blends, 100 kinds of salt and just as many types of chilis, and 40 types of rice. Famous foodies, from Martha Stewart to Padma Lakshmi, have been known to frequent the store regularly for this reason. Aziz Osmani, one of the current co-owners of the market, summed up its ethos in a 2021 *New York Times* profile like this: "We don't like to say no, so if it exists, we try to have it, or we'll create a blend, or we'll get it from no matter where."

104 Ave. B
between E. 6th and 7th Sts.

S.O.S. Chefs

———

The staff at this Alphabet City store refers to everyone who walks in as "chef"— and treats them as such. Call ahead to see what spices or freshly foraged fungi they have in stock. And if they don't have what you're looking for, ask: owner Atef Boulaabi loves a challenge.

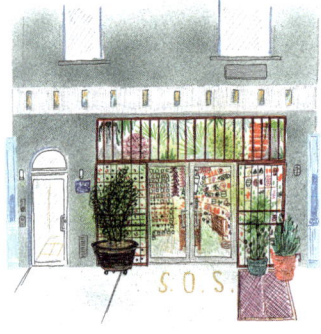

223 1st Ave.
between E. 13th and 14th Sts.

Mee Noodle Shop & Grill

———

Known for its consistent, affordable, and delicious options, this East Village noodle shop is a no-frills favorite for quick delivery or takeout.

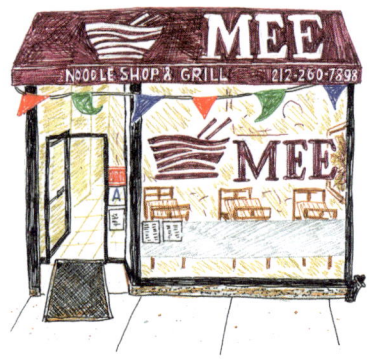

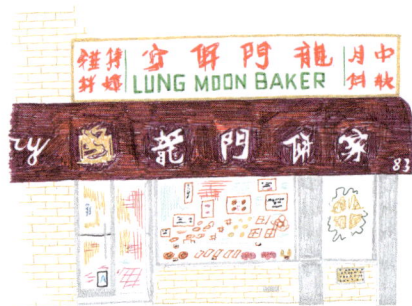

83 Mulberry St.
between Bayard and Canal Sts.

Lung Moon Bakery

———

This Chinatown bakery was a casualty of the Covid-19 pandemic but will forever be remembered for its wide selection of mooncakes and egg custards—which were so popular the owners had to cap the number available to each customer.

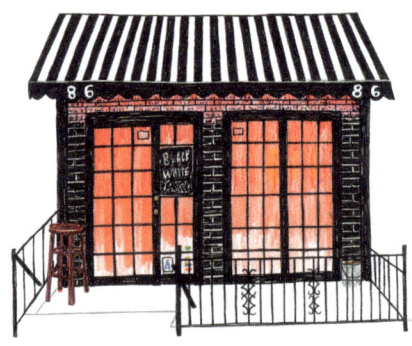

86 E. 10th St.
between 4th and 3rd Aves.

Black and White

———

For twenty-one years, this East Village institution beckoned patrons in with its unofficial tagline "grab a friend and grab a drink." The deeply loved dive bar served up stiff cocktails and loud beats to locals until it closed in October 2020.

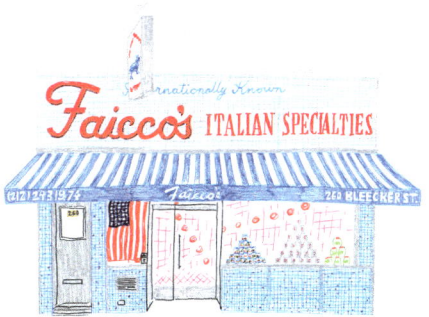

Faicco's Italian Specialties

This Greenwich Village deli has been around since the turn of the century— as in, the nineteenth century. Faicco's opened in 1900 and has been run by the same Italian American family the entire time. It offers some of the best sandwiches in the city.

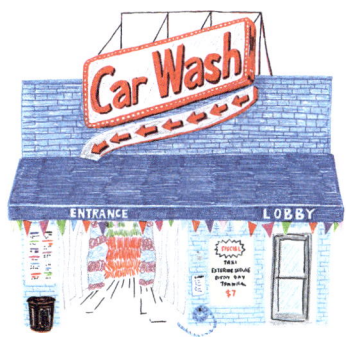

Manhattan Car Wash

The majority of Manhattan's residents are carless, so they likely walk, bike, or scoot on by this Chelsea business without noticing. Those that drive, however, know this spot as one of downtown's last remaining places to clean your car.

Canal Plastics Center

For decades this shop has been supplying New Yorkers with all their acrylic needs— including the quirky comedian Julio Torres, whose HBO special *My Favorite Shapes* featured dozens of tiny plastic creations he conceived of and crafted with the help of the store's staff.

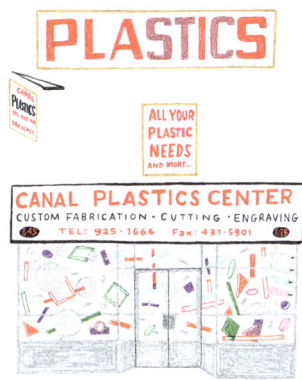

Canal Rubber

"If it's in rubber, we have it," proclaims the bright yellow sign outside this shop, which has been in business at this location since 1954.

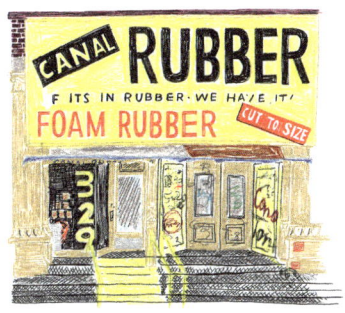

The Roost

———

Opened in 2013, this since-closed Alphabet City spot—which still has a location in Hoboken, New Jersey—was an unassuming coffee shop by day. By night its spacious back room transformed into a bar, where you could find a sizable selection of local craft beers on draft, even more types of beer in bottles and cans, a long list of bourbons and other whiskeys, and cocktails that included house barrel-aged Manhattans and negronis. The bar also offered specials each night of the week. For example, Thursdays were "cheap date night," featuring two-for-one cocktails.

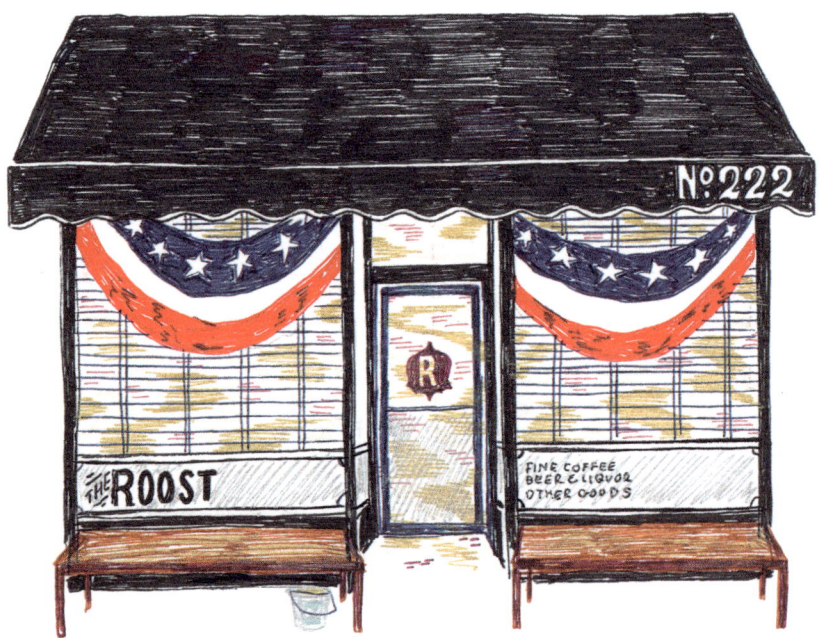

Astor Place Hairstylists

This no-frills Greenwich Village institution, which opened in 1947, has counted everyone from Robert De Niro to former Mayor Bill de Blasio as loyal customers. In October 2020, however, it looked like the barber shop would succumb to the financial pressures caused by the coronavirus pandemic, putting forty hair-stylists (including a man who famously cut Hilary Swank's locks for her role in the film *Boys Don't Cry*) out of a job. But lifelong customer Nicolas Heller—author of the foreword to this book— stepped in, using his popular Instagram account, @newyorknico, to help bring attention to the shop's closure. His advocacy caught the attention of wealthy donors, who bought Astor Place Hairstylists and saved it.

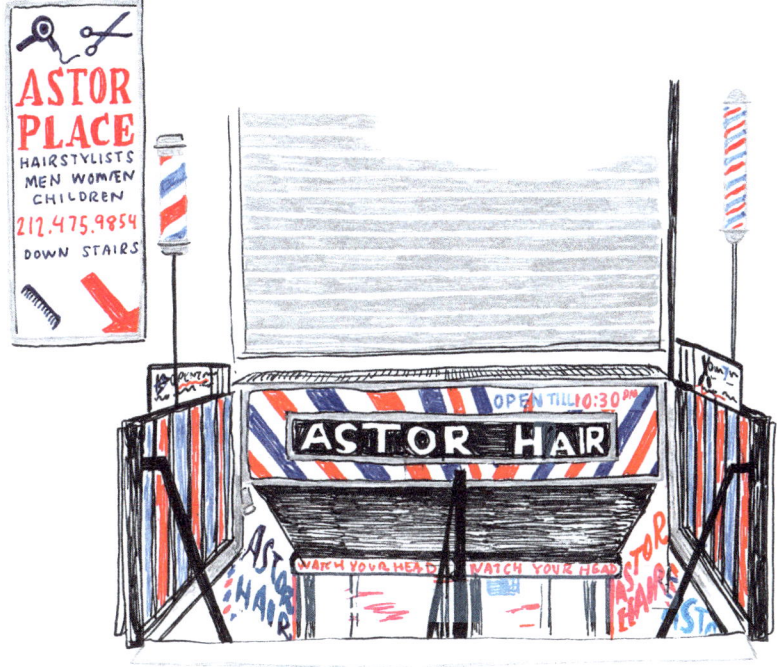

Pepe Rosso

This storied Greenwich Village spot's new location has a few more seats for patrons than its original, now-shuttered address in SoHo (where, as the sign illustrated here indicates, they served most of their food to go). Still, during busy hours, you'll be lucky if you can snag a chair. While the restaurant may be small, its portions are anything but: expect to have lunch the next day from a single order of penne vodka or fettuccine cacio e pepe. With most of its dishes costing under twenty dollars, you'll be hard pressed to find cheaper, quality Italian anywhere nearby.

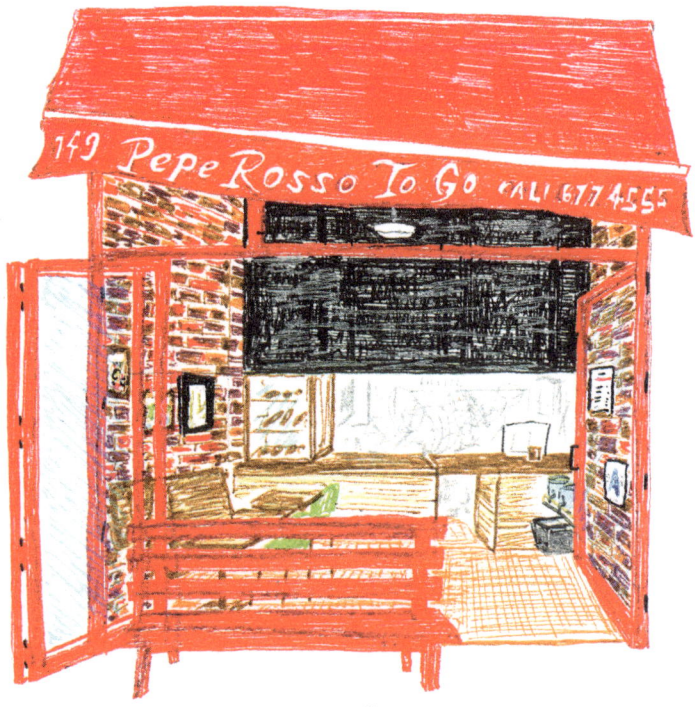

Eisenberg's Sandwich Shop

Eisenberg's Sandwich Shop, which had been open since 1929, gave its loyal regulars a scare in 2020 when it abruptly closed. The following spring, Eric Finkelstein and Matt Ross, owners of the Brooklyn-based Court Street Grocers and fans of the legendary luncheonette, announced plans to prevent the place from becoming yet another Midtown 7-Eleven. They changed the name to S&P Lunch—the spot's name before it was Eisenberg's—and the exterior signage, but they kept the food and interiors, including the red vinyl stools held together by tape, close to the same. The menu is only "slightly better" than before, according to a 2022 *New York Times* review (which is meant as a compliment), and the shop retains the original's "quirky, deadpan spirit."

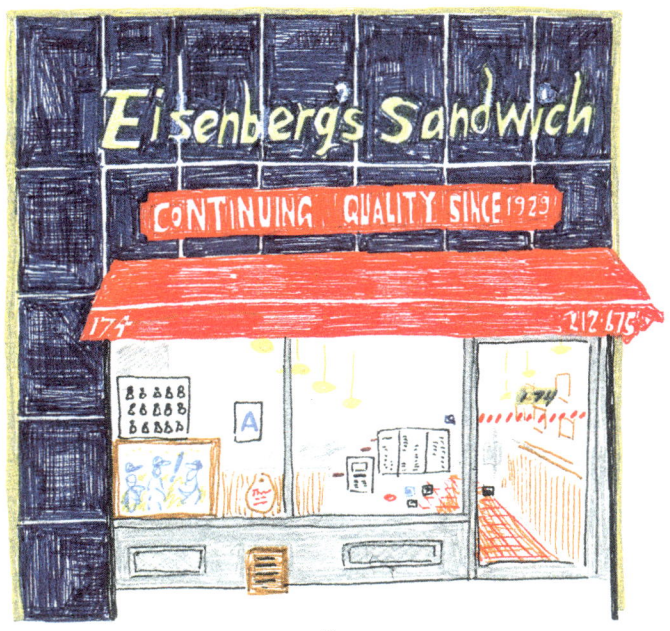

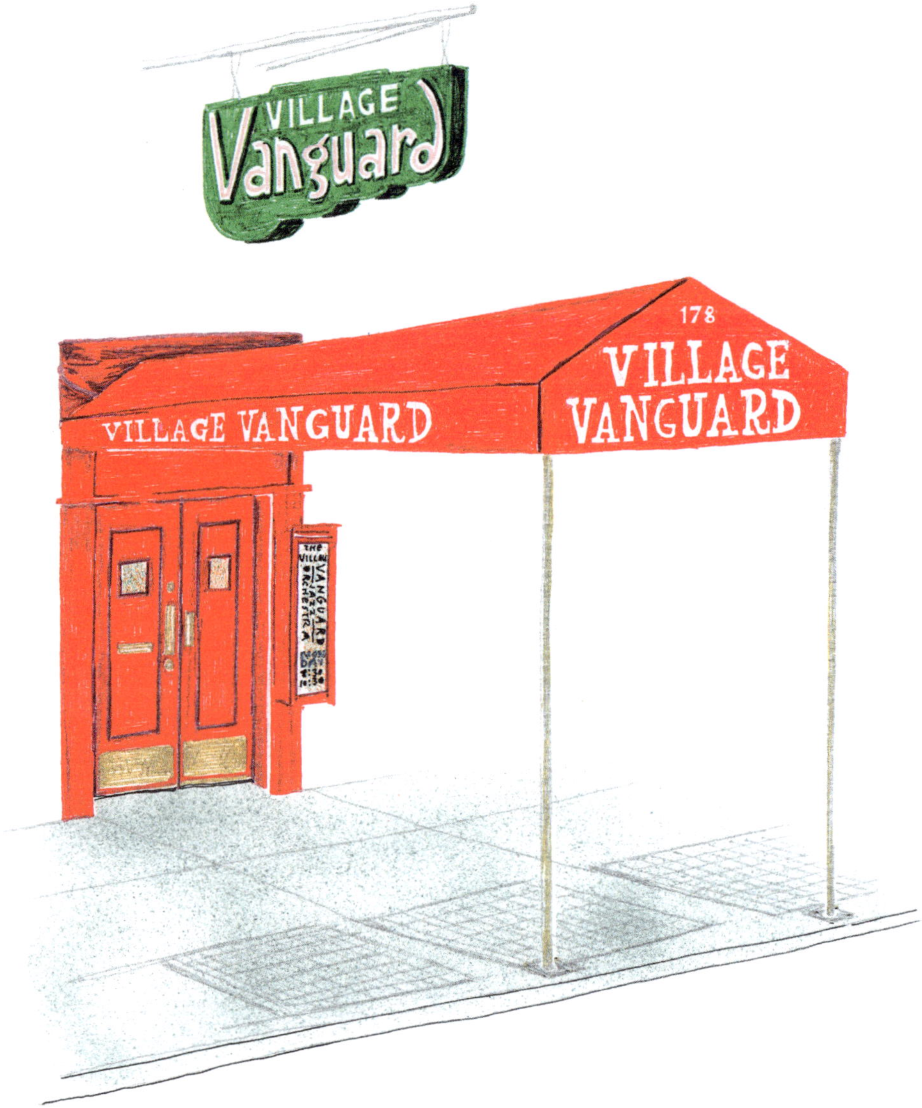

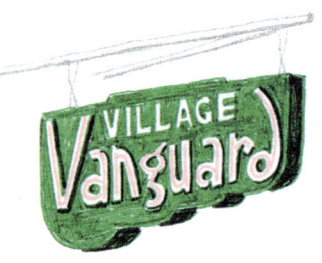

Village Vanguard

Founded in 1935 by producer Max Gordon of Blue Note Records fame, this basement-level West Village jazz club is the oldest of its kind in New York. It has hosted nearly all the greats over the years, including Louis Armstrong, John Coltrane, Miles Davis, Bill Evans, and Thelonious Monk. Thanks to the space's impressive acoustics, the Vanguard may be best known across the globe for the over one hundred live recordings that have taken place here featuring some of the biggest names in the genre.

The club is small, pie-shaped, and seats no more than 123 people, guaranteeing guests an intimate evening with the headliner on any given night.

Though it's hard to imagine, in its earliest incarnation, the Vanguard wasn't solely devoted to jazz: Max originally booked musicians of many different backgrounds, from folk to calypso. He also hosted comedians, including Lenny Bruce. By the late 1950s, however, he had found his groove, and instituted something of a "jazz-only" policy.

Max ran the club up until his death in 1989, when his wife, Lorraine Gordon, took over ownership. When faced with any decision about the space, she would wonder what her late husband would do, "then I'd do the opposite," she once joked. Lorraine died in 2018, but the Vanguard is still in the family: the couple's daughter Deborah now runs the club and is committed to keeping it relevant within the world of jazz, just as her parents did.

Blue Note Jazz Club

Founded in 1981, this legendary club has played host to Dave Brubeck, Dizzy Gillespie, Sarah Vaughan, and Stevie Wonder, making it one of the most famous and beloved venues for jazz in the world. Blue Note's presence now extends far beyond Manhattan, with locations across the globe in cities including Tokyo, Rio de Janeiro, and Honolulu.

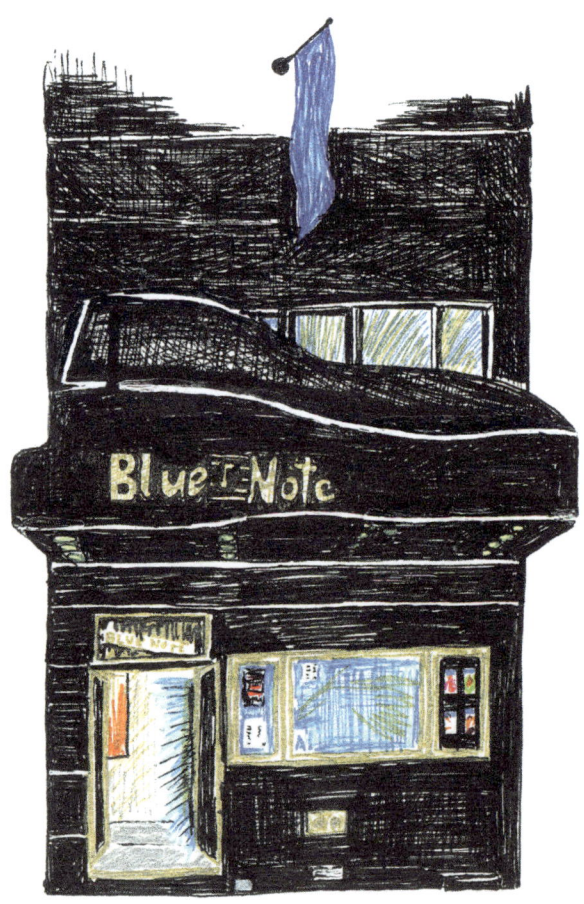

B&H Dairy

———

This old-school kosher lunch counter has been serving up the same offerings of borscht, cheese blintzes, potato pancakes (with applesauce *and* sour cream, of course), and more since it first opened in 1938. Though its menu—and interior—have remained the same for the better part of a century, B&H has been quick to embrace change in many other ways. The staff uniform now includes a shirt with the words "Challah, por favor!" emblazoned across the chest, blending new and old demographic trends in the neighborhood.

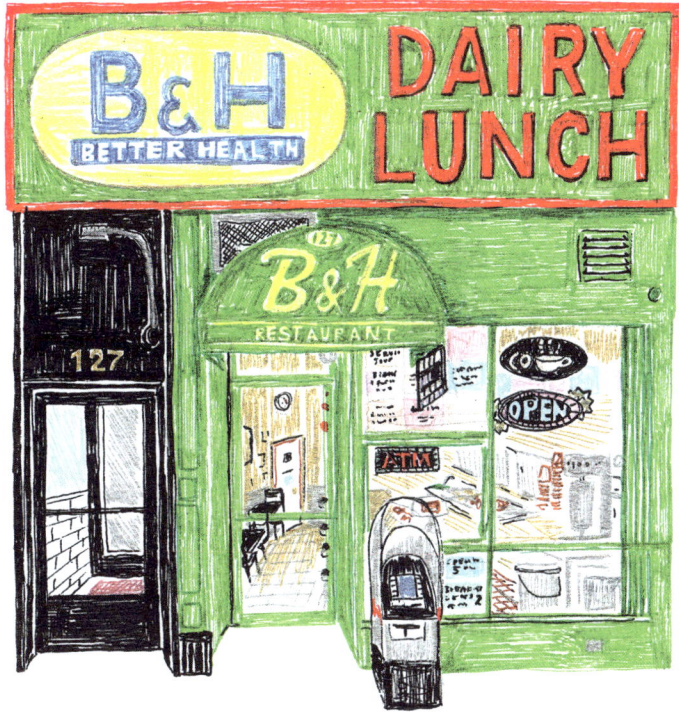

Chef Restaurant Supply

Featured on a 2011 episode of the late Anthony Bourdain's TV show *The Layover*, this kitchen-supply shop is geared more toward restaurateurs, not home cooks—but the store will definitely have whatever obscure item you're looking for, along with many others you didn't even know you needed. You might walk in searching for a simple sauté pan, but be prepared to leave with a forty-eight-blade meat tenderizer, an industrial-grade fly zapper, and a handful of paring knives in various sizes and colors.

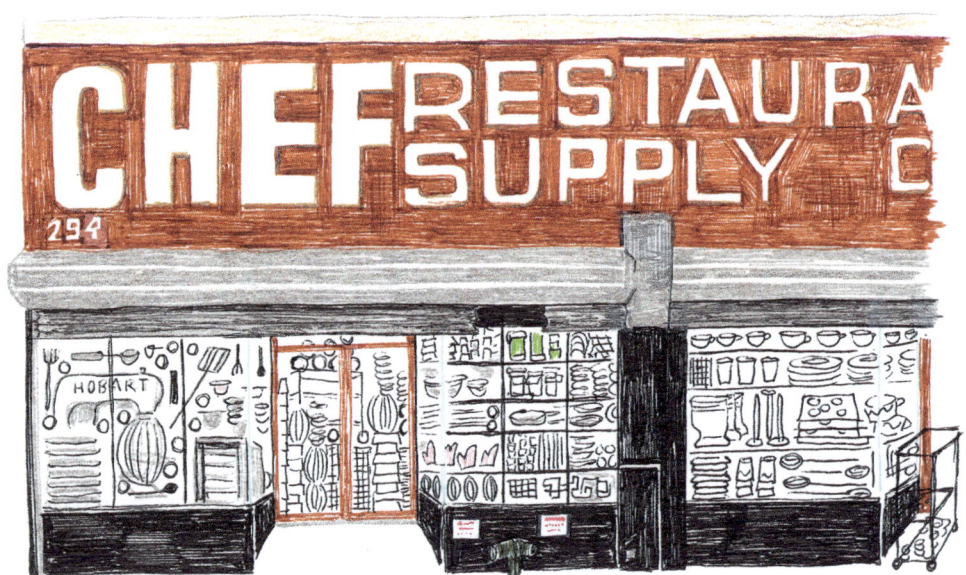

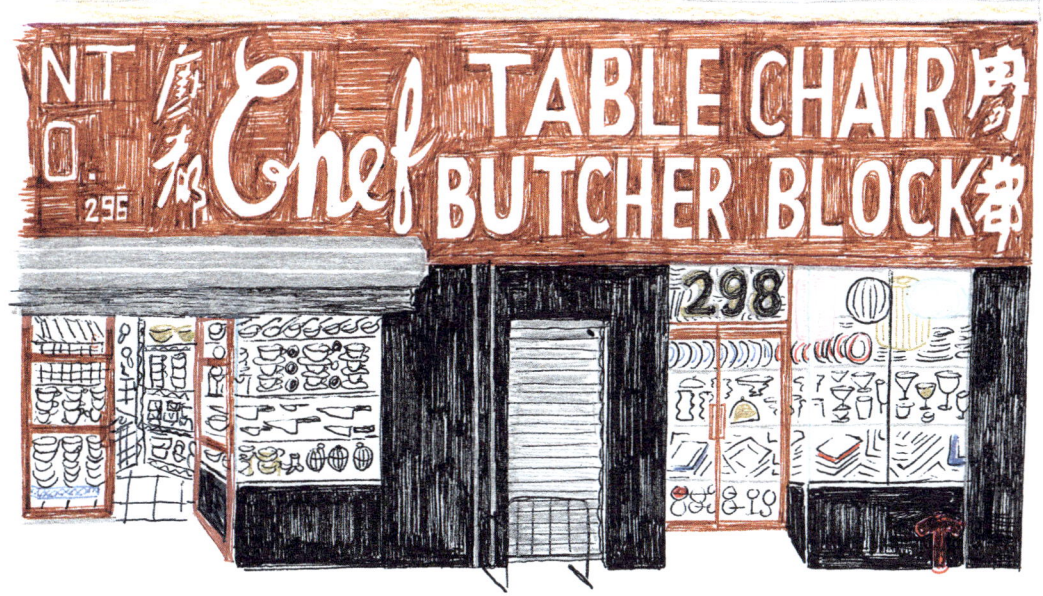

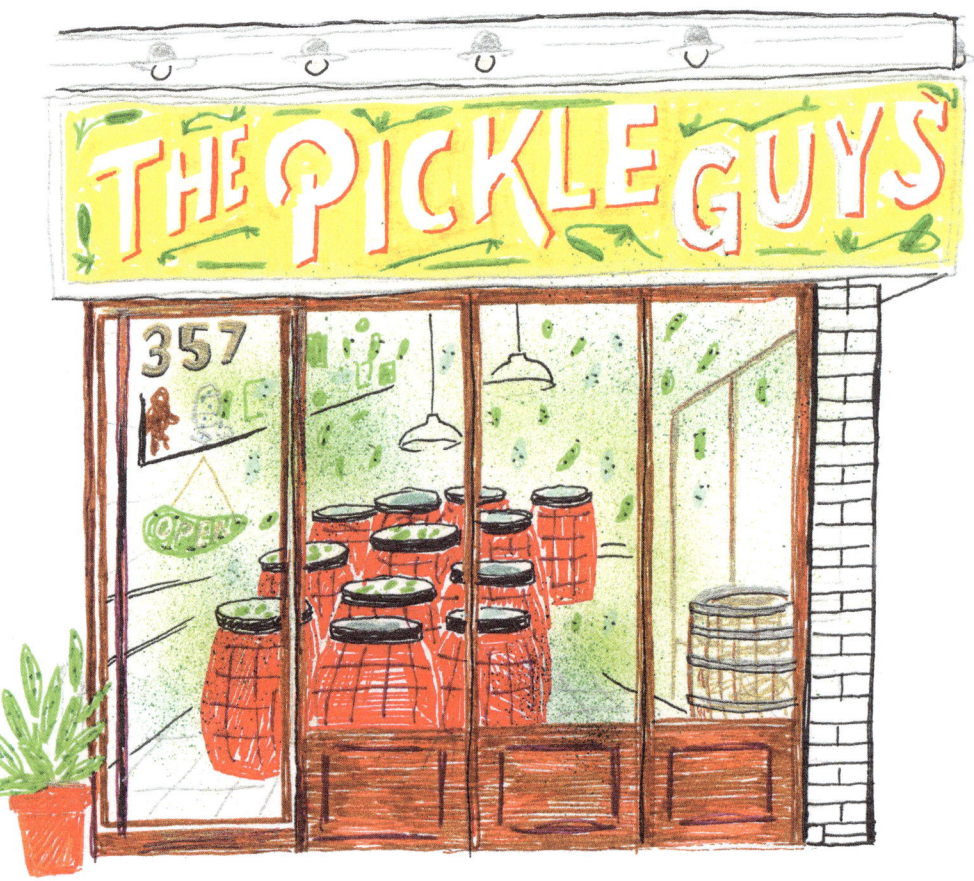

The Pickle Guys

———

In the early twentieth century, Essex Street on the Lower East Side was known as Pickle Alley. Some estimate there were over eighty vendors on this street alone, out of more than three hundred in the city. In 2006, after eighty-five years in business, Guss' Pickles picked up shop and moved its pickling empire out of Manhattan.

The Pickle Guys has since been the sole merchant carrying on the area's briny legacy, proudly offering over thirty types of pickled treats, including sauerkraut, watermelon, and pineapple.

The pickles here are made according to an old Eastern European recipe involving a brine created with a combination of salt, garlic, and spices. The goods are left to cure in this mixture for anywhere between a single day to six months. Owner Alan Kaufman refers to Tuesdays, when a truck drops off thousands of cucumbers to the store, as "pickling day." The shop's brine is available for sale in jars—which feature the company's logo, a grinning pickle wearing a baseball cap and sunglasses—so you can try your hand at pickling from the comfort of your own home.

Every year, a couple weeks before Passover, The Pickle Guys set up a station outside the shop where they grind horseradish from freshly peeled roots from morning to night. Tourists and locals alike flock there to buy this seder staple, and the line often wraps around the block.

280 Mulberry St.
between Prince and E. Houston Sts.

Cafe Belle

———

Regulars of this Italian pasticceria, located on the northern edge of Little Italy, recommend its rainbow cookies—which you'll enjoy amid floral prints plastered to the ceiling and walls, as well as covering the seats of old-school diner chairs.

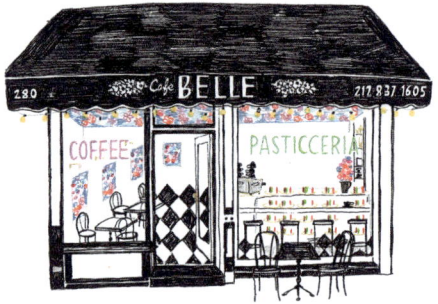

6 Delancey St.
between Bowery and Chrystie St.

Bowery Ballroom

———

Founded in 1998 by the same trio who started the nearby Mercury Lounge, the Bowery Ballroom has been graced by such musical legends as Lou Reed, Tony Bennett, and Arcade Fire.

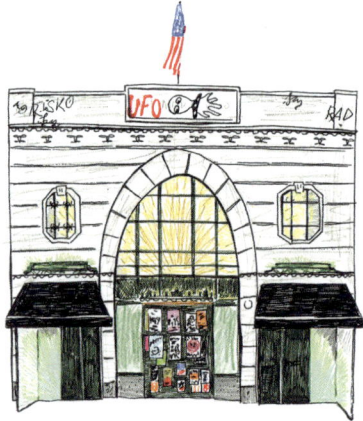

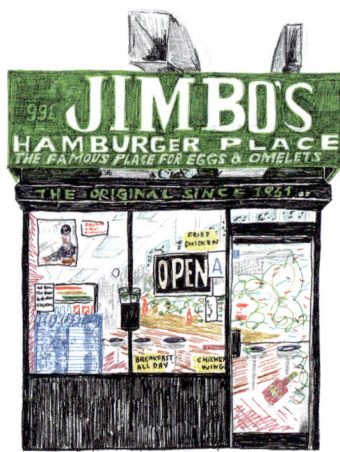

991 1st Ave.
between E. 54th and 55th Sts.

Jimbo's Hamburger Place

———

You can smell the sizzling burgers halfway down the block from this classic Midtown East restaurant. It's the sort of place you can refer to as a "joint" without blushing.

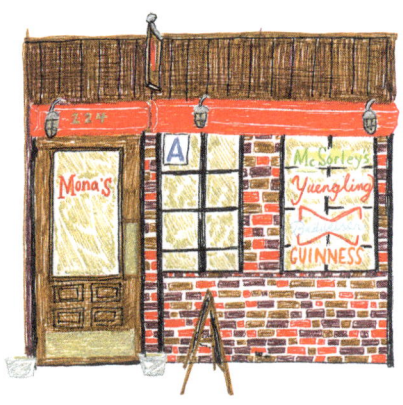

224 Ave. B
between E. 13th and 14th Sts.

Mona's

———

Come to this East Village dive bar for cheap drinks and live jazz or bluegrass; stay for the pool table and Skee-Ball.

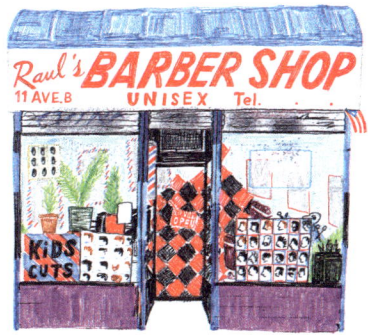

11 Ave. B #1
between E. Houston and 2nd Sts.

Raul's Barber Shop

Raul Velez offered fades and shaves at this Avenue B institution, noted for its trademark black-and-red checkered floors, from 1961 until the shop closed in 2022.

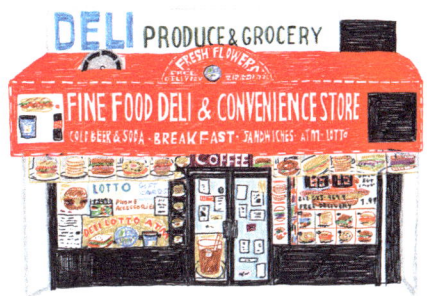

411 2nd Ave.
between E. 23rd and 24th Sts.

Fine Food Deli & Convenience Store

This Kips Bay deli (which is now closed) was your average old-school New York City bodega—with the twist of what regulars said was a surprisingly delicious and extensive breakfast menu, right down to some of the best coffee in the area.

68 Greenwich Ave.
between W. 10th and 11th Sts.

Elephant & Castle

George Schwarz, who was once a physician at the now-defunct St. Vincent's Hospital in the West Village, opened this eatery in 1973 after becoming dissatisfied by the food options in the neighborhood. Some say the chicken schnitzel, which was the late restaurateur's favorite dish on the menu, is the best in the city.

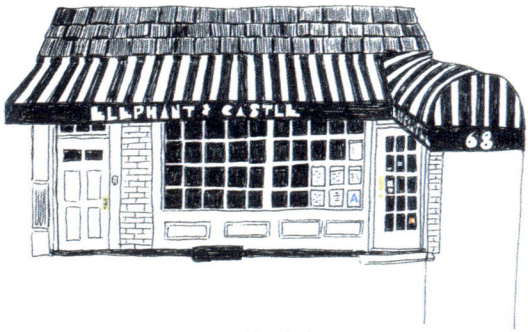

439 E. 6th St.
between 1st Ave. and Ave. A

A-1 Record Shop

Opened in 1996, this Alphabet City store is consistently named on lists of the world's best record shops because of its knowledgeable staff and extensive collection of jazz, funk, and hip-hop vinyl.

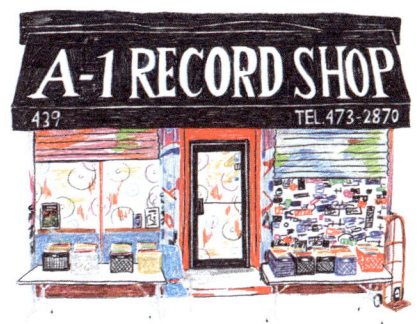

Shabu Tatsu

Located in the East Village, Shabu Tatsu is hardly the only hot-pot spot in town, but it is one of few to specialize in two distinct versions: shabu-shabu and sukiyaki. These dishes may seem similar to casual fans of Japanese cuisine, but to major foodies they are worlds apart. While both are comprised of thin slices of meat and vegetables, the shabu-shabu (which means "shake shake") is "gently swished and cooked in seconds in our housemade broth bubbling in the middle of your table," according to the restaurant's website. Sukiyaki, meanwhile, is slowly simmered in an iron pot; the pieces of meat and vegetables are then dipped in raw egg before eating. Which dish does the restaurant make better? There is a raging debate online—decide for yourself after trying both.

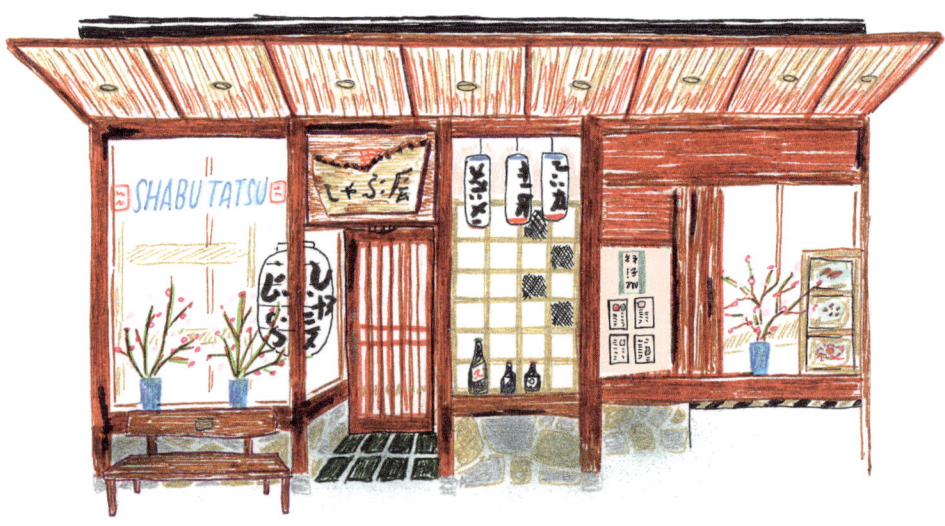

J&P Timepieces

Alex Fossner, who moved to New York City from Czechoslovakia during the 1960s, first opened this watch shop on Second Avenue in 1969—when it was known as Fossner Timepieces. Alex's son, Peter, eventually took over the business and in 1980 teamed up with Jeff Morris, renaming the store J&P Timepieces. Together, the duo continue to scour the globe purchasing what their website calls "exquisite, preowned and vintage horological pieces of art," including goods from watchmakers like Patek Philippe, Audemars Piguet, Rolex, A. Lange & Söhne, and Cartier.

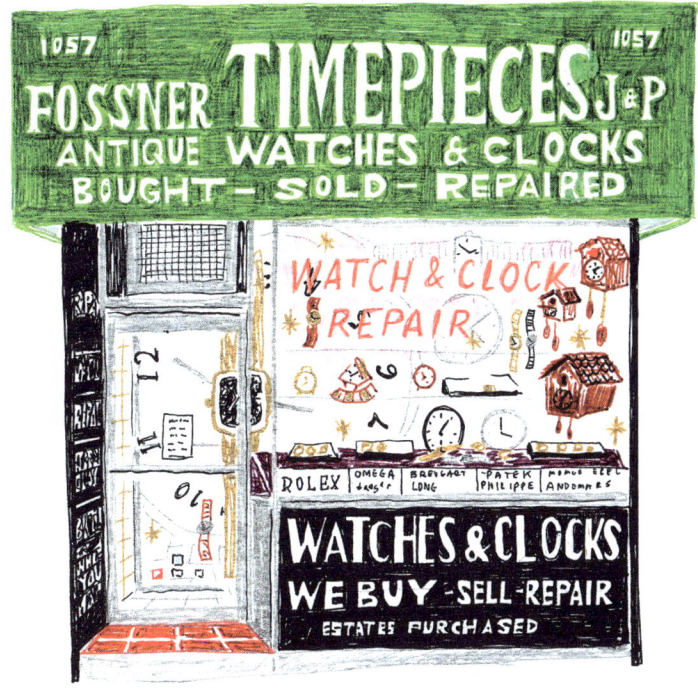

471 Columbus Ave.

between W. 82nd and 83rd Sts.

Zingone Bros.

———

Members of the Zingone clan have been selling pro-
duce in some form or another at this grocery store
on the Upper West Side for decades. The family-
run business was started in 1927 by Domenico and
Vincenzo Zingone—who emigrated from Italy's Amalfi
Coast as young men—as not much more than a fruit
stand on Columbus Avenue. In 1935 the Zingones
moved the store to its current location, which they
initially split with a shop called Quality Poultry. The
grocery remains a family operation today, so much
so that the *New York Times* once ran a profile called
"A Zingone in Every Aisle."

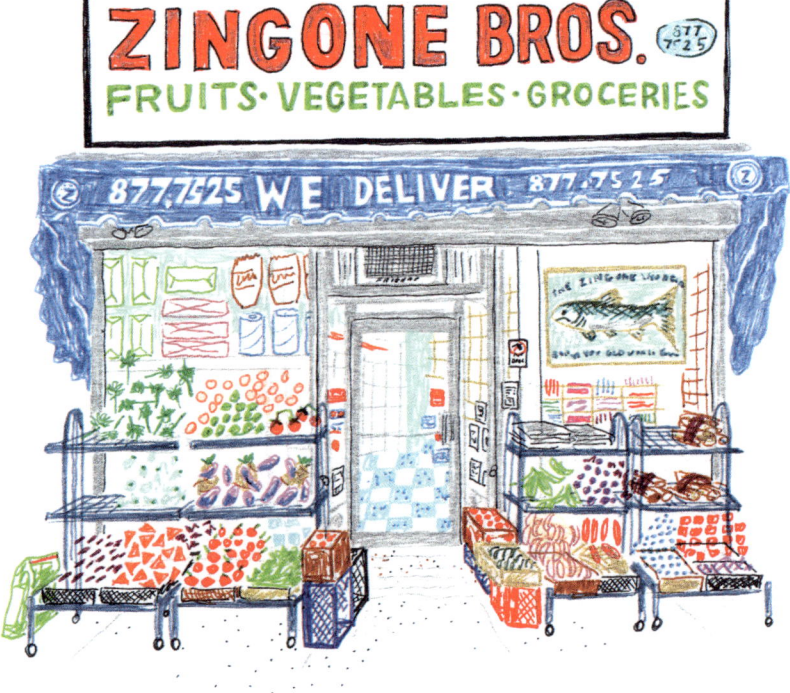

Max Fish

———

This watering hole was first opened in 1989 on Ludlow Street by local artist Ulli Rimkus, who got her start working in nightlife at Tin Pan Alley, an infamous bar in Times Square known as the inspiration for the setting for HBO's series *The Deuce*. Ulli claims Max Fish was one of the first modern bars to open on the Lower East Side. In 2014 she moved locations to Orchard Street where she had an event space on the lower level that hosted concerts and art shows. Sadly, the bar closed its doors in November 2020.

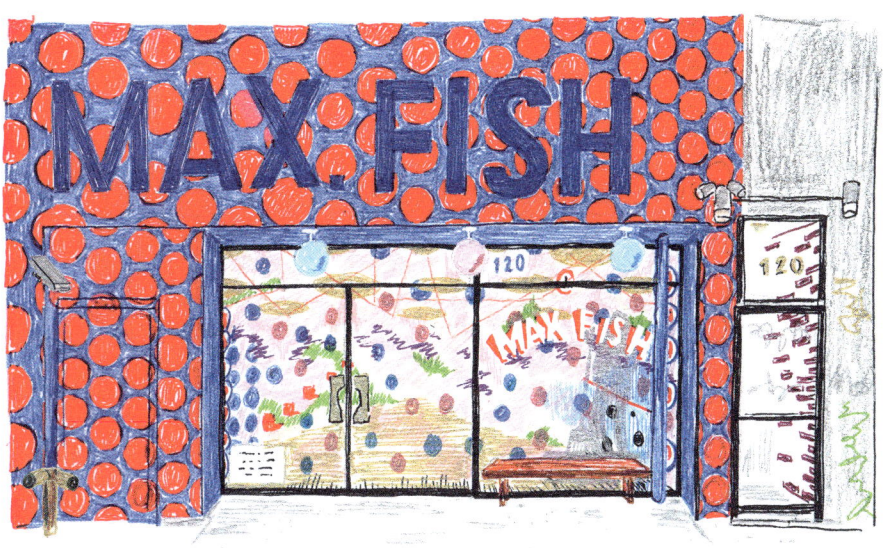

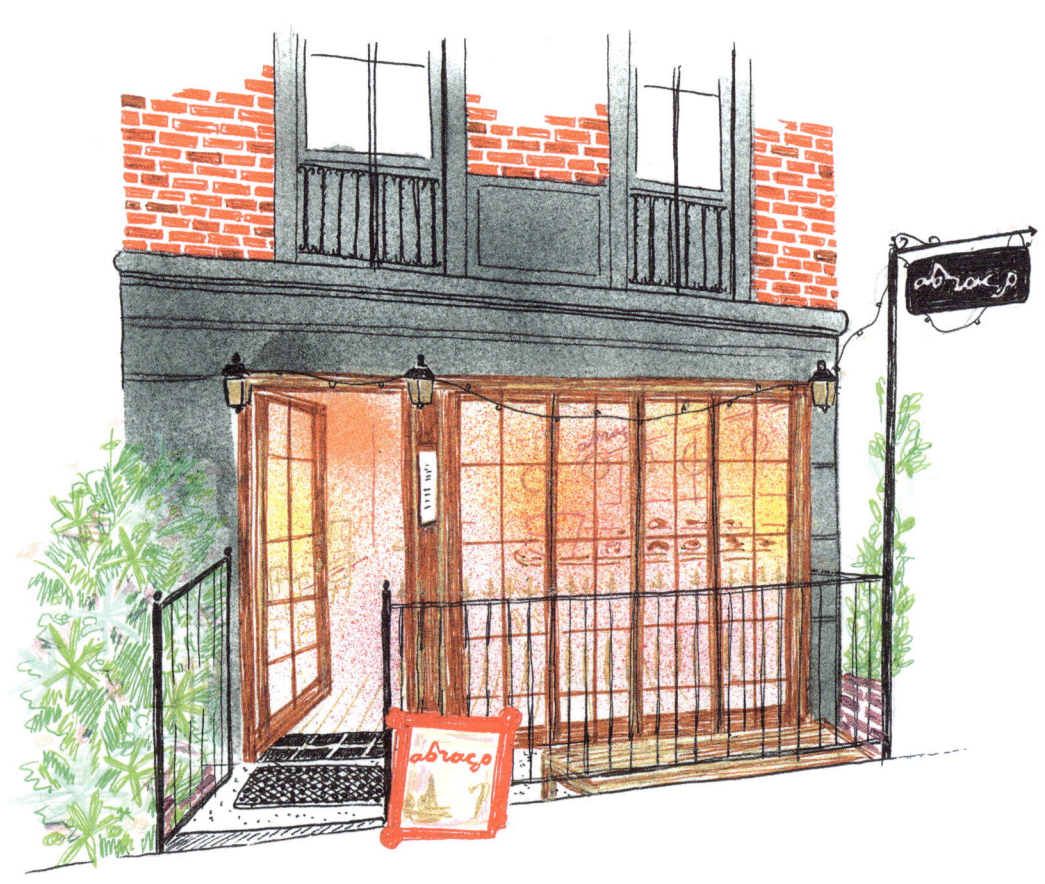

81 E. 7th St.
between 2nd and 1st Aves.

Abraço

This coffee shop—which *Bon Appétit* deemed the best place to get espresso in the city—originally opened in 2007 as a to-go storefront, without seats. But the shop's cult following eventually demanded a bigger space, which its owners secured almost directly across the street in 2016.

Liz Quijada and Jamie McCormick (who are married) named the space Abraço, which means "hug" in Portuguese, after a song by the legendary Brazilian crooner Gilberto Gil—and they take the vibe their name conveys seriously.

You won't find laptops, free Wi-Fi, or anything else to discourage you from striking up a conversation with a friendly neighbor. But if the idea of talking to strangers during daylight hours makes you want to break out in hives, stick around until evening, when the lights dim and the space transforms into a comfortable little cocktail bar.

Variety Coffee Roasters

This coffee shop, born in Williamsburg, Brooklyn, in 2008, made a jump across the East River in 2017, when it opened a branch in Chelsea. Long before entering Manhattan, Variety—which now has eight locations throughout NYC—made a name for itself within the city's intense caffeine wars by roasting its own beans, often serving single-origin java, rather than blends. Variety's Chelsea storefront, not far from the Garment District, had previously been home to Truemart Discount Fabrics for forty years (which then moved right around the corner).

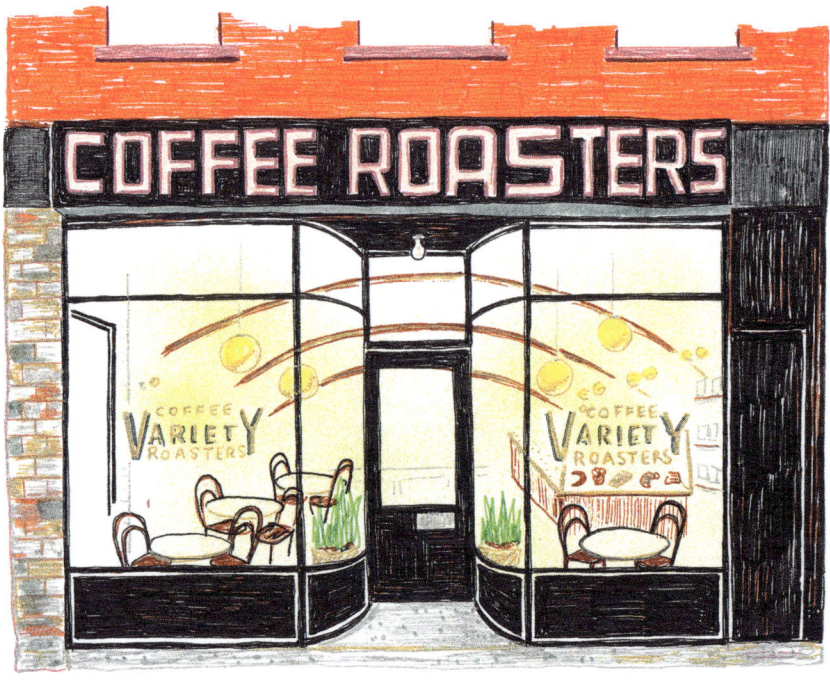

Vesuvio Bakery

Founded in 1920 by the Dapolito family, this Italian bakery operated continuously for almost a hundred years until it closed, suddenly, in 2009. A separate bakery took over the space in the interim, keeping its trademark bright-green facade intact—until 2020, when Vesuvio was ready to make its triumphant return under new ownership. The current proprietor, Adam Block, says his goal is to pay homage to the original bakery and not to reinvent the proverbial loaf. In recent years Vesuvio has expanded beyond Greenwich Village, with locations in Hell's Kitchen and inside Moynihan Train Hall at Penn Station.

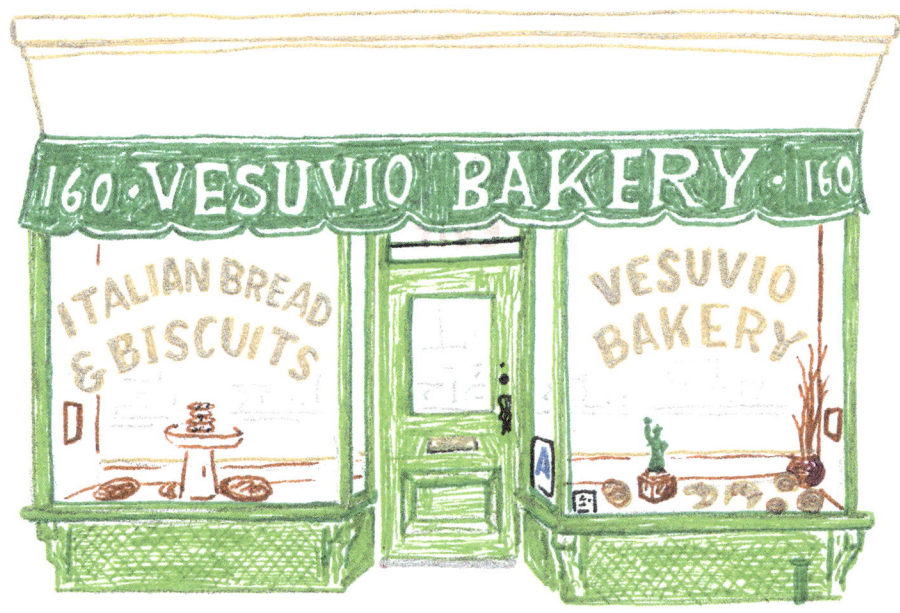

Joe's Pizza

The word "famous" is blazoned across the awnings of many a pizza shop in New York City. But most locals are actually very well acquainted with "famous" Joe's Pizza, which opened in the West Village in the early 1970s and has since established other outposts around the city. Many tourists know it, too—if only for its role in *Spider Man 2*, as the place where Peter Parker is fired from his job as a delivery boy for slacking off.

Despite its star turn, Joe's has a reputation for serving up one of the best, most reliable slices in the city. Called the "consummate New York slice parlor" by *New York* magazine, this is the place to turn if you're looking for pizza that is "exactly as excellent as the last time, and the time before that, every time."

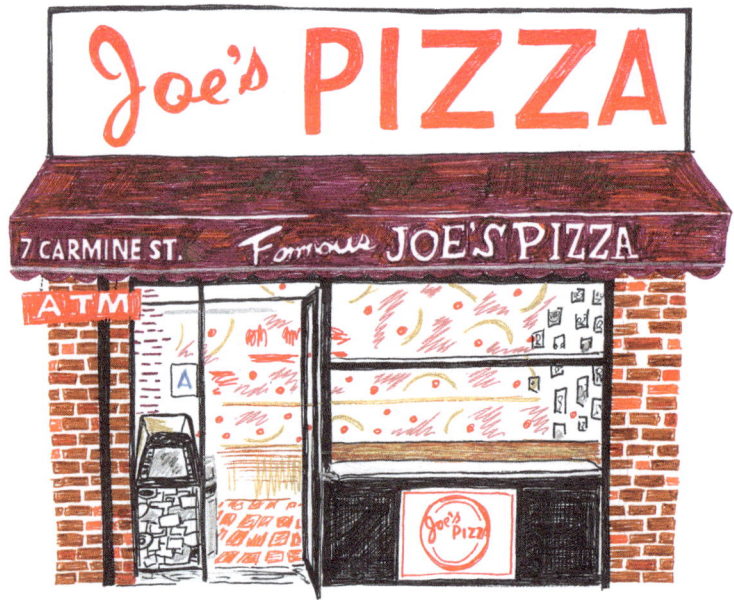

Landmark Sunshine Cinema

True to its name, this long-running movie theater really was a Lower East Side landmark—that is, until the historic structure was demolished. Built in 1844, the building had a wide variety of tenants. First it was home to a Dutch Reformed Church. In the early 1900s it became a fight club before transforming into the Houston Hippodrome, a theater hall offering moving pictures and Yiddish vaudeville shows. It became known as the Sunshine Theater in 1917. But as the silver screen gave way to television in the 1950s, it was taken over by a hardware store—until Tim Nye acquired it in 1994 and reopened it as an art-house movie theater in 2001, following a $12 million renovation. The Sunshine's lights went dim for the last time in January 2018 after a 10:15 p.m. showing of, appropriately enough, *Darkest Hour*.

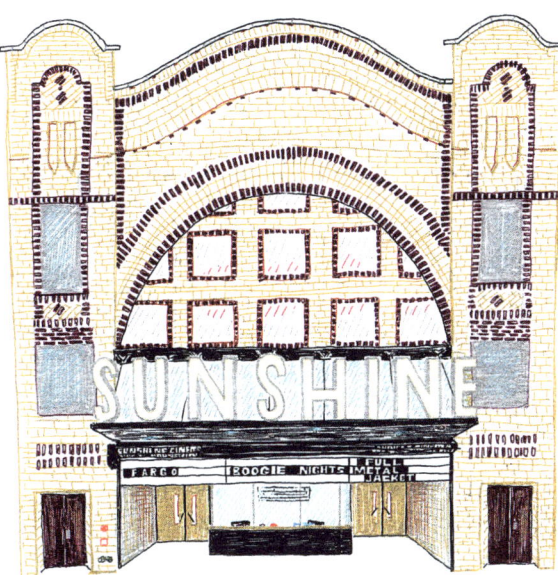

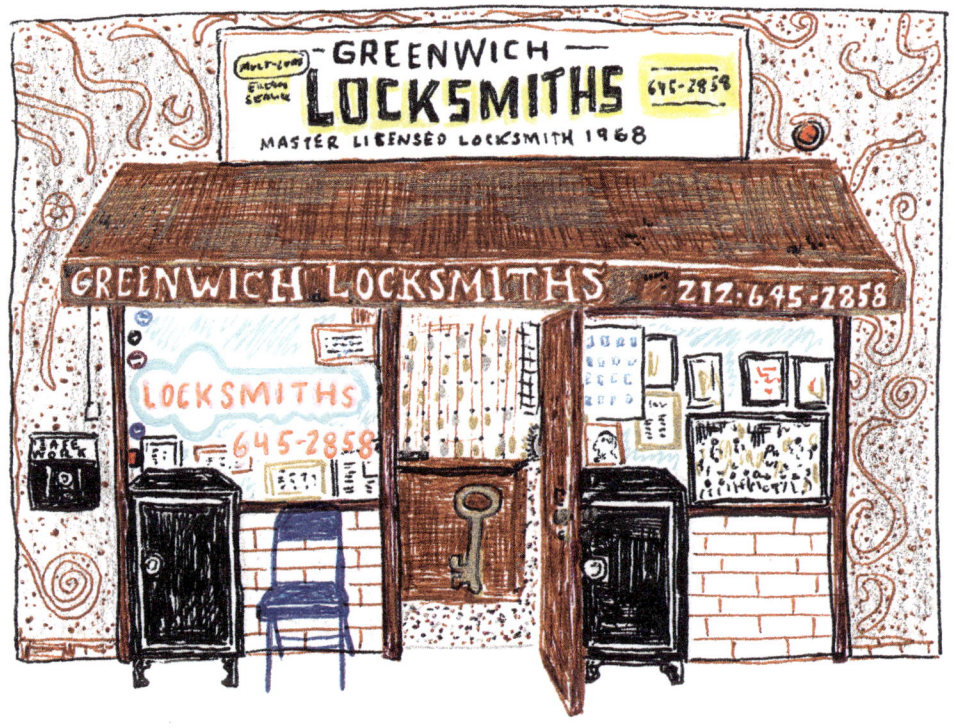

Greenwich Locksmiths

This business has been helping New Yorkers regain access to their apartments after locking themselves out since 1980. In recent years, the locksmith has also become something of an unlikely tourist attraction after the owner, Philip Mortillaro (who is also an artist), began using keys to create swirling, trippy designs and patterns on the shop's facade.

The building that houses the locksmith was already hard to miss before Philip's metal artwork appeared—because the tiny, triangular edifice is one of the only remaining single-story structures left in the West Village.

At just 125 square feet, it has also earned the distinction of being the smallest freestanding building in the entire borough of Manhattan.

To many of Philip's longtime customers, who have witnessed their neighborhood gentrify with remarkable speed over the last several decades, he is not just the best locksmith or the most creative metalworker in the area—he's also a local hero. In 2017 Chase Bank offered him $2 million to purchase the property, with the intention of turning it into an ATM (even though a Chase Bank was located right up the street). But Philip, who bought the property for just $20,000 in 1980, turned them down. "What am I gonna do with that money?" he told Suzi Siegel, author of *Tiny New York*, which documents the city's "smallest things." "I have everything I need, and that's a great way to live."

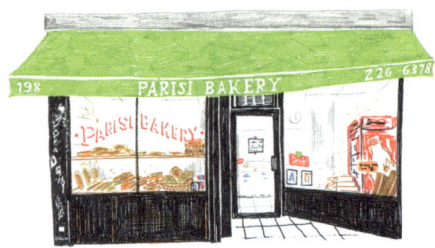

198 Mott St.
between Kenmare and Spring Sts.

Parisi Bakery

This Italian bakery, reportedly a favorite of Frank Sinatra, has been making fresh bread daily since 1903.

111 South St.
between Beekman St. and Peck Slip

Fish Market

The ginger chicken wings are a favorite at this sports bar, which also happens to serve some of the best Chinese and Malaysian food in the area.

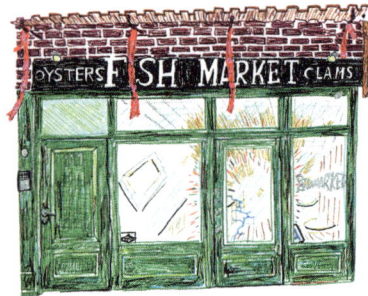

26 Mott St.
between Chatham Sq. and Pell St.

Wing On Wo & Co.

Opened in the 1890s, this shop is the oldest continually operating store in Chinatown. Currently it sells porcelain dinnerware and home goods, but the space previously served as a general store, herbalist, and temporary housing for newly arrived Chinese immigrants.

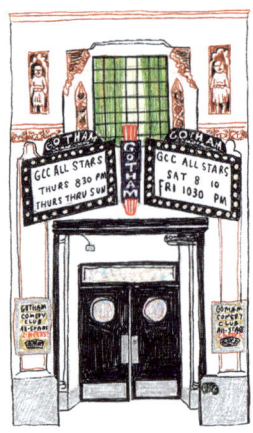

208 W. 23rd St.
between 7th and 8th Aves.

Gotham Comedy Club

Comedic legends including Trevor Noah, Jim Gaffigan, Rosie O'Donnell, and Lewis Black have all graced the stage at this Chelsea comedy club, which opened nearby in 1996 and moved to its current location in 2006.

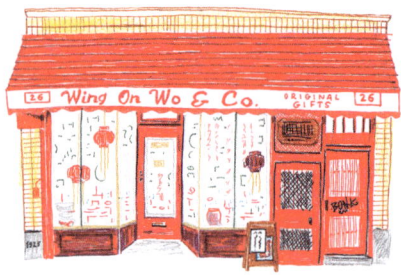

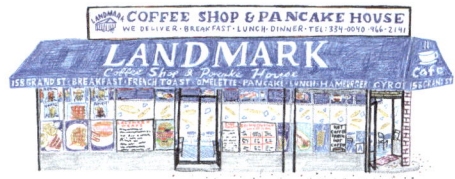

158 Grand St.
at Centre St.

Landmark Coffee Shop & Pancake House

Founded in 1962, this spot has all the trappings of a classic New York diner: endless coffee refills, blue Formica tables, and cheap, reliable food. Film buffs will also know it as the locale where Rosanna Arquette and Aidan Quinn order blueberry blintzes in the 1985 film *Desperately Seeking Susan*.

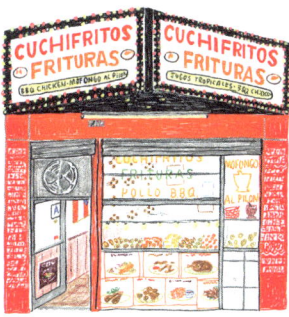

168 E. 116th St.
between Lexington and 3rd Aves.

Cuchifritos

Pig is the name of the game at this long-standing Puerto Rican institution, opened in 1961, from chicharróns (pork skin) to *morcilla* (blood sausage). If the smell of fried pig isn't enough to stop you in your tracks while walking down East 116th Street, the shop's iconic marquee-style sign will certainly do the trick.

237 E. 58th St.
between 3rd and 2nd Aves.

Just Bulbs

David Letterman made this shop the subject of a 1983 sketch by continuing to press a bemused salesperson to name other nonexistent items in their inventory. But Just Bulbs has had the last laugh: while the lights of most of its competitors have dimmed in recent years, it shines on.

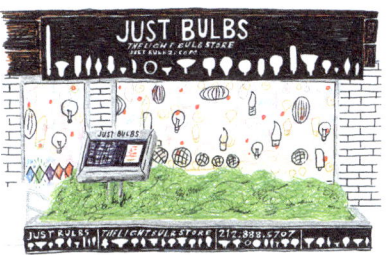

197 Bleecker St. #1
between MacDougal and Minetta Sts.

Village Revival Records

This Greenwich Village record shop—which recently changed its name (and awning)—was opened in 1992 by Jamal Jararah. Speaking with the organization Village Preservation, a regular described why he continues to visit: "I am too stupid to order online, and Bezos owns everything."

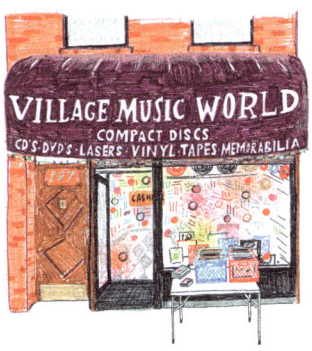

Joe Junior Restaurant

Those who have never set foot inside this Gramercy diner may still recognize its facade, which features a Dr. Seuss–like blob of a yellow head lasciviously eyeing a burger, tongue protruding and all. The real version of that cartoon beef patty, however, is thought by many—including chef Lucas Sin of Junzi Kitchen fame—to be the best in the city. Even if you don't end up agreeing that it's the *best*, Joe Junior's no-frills burger won't set you back much.

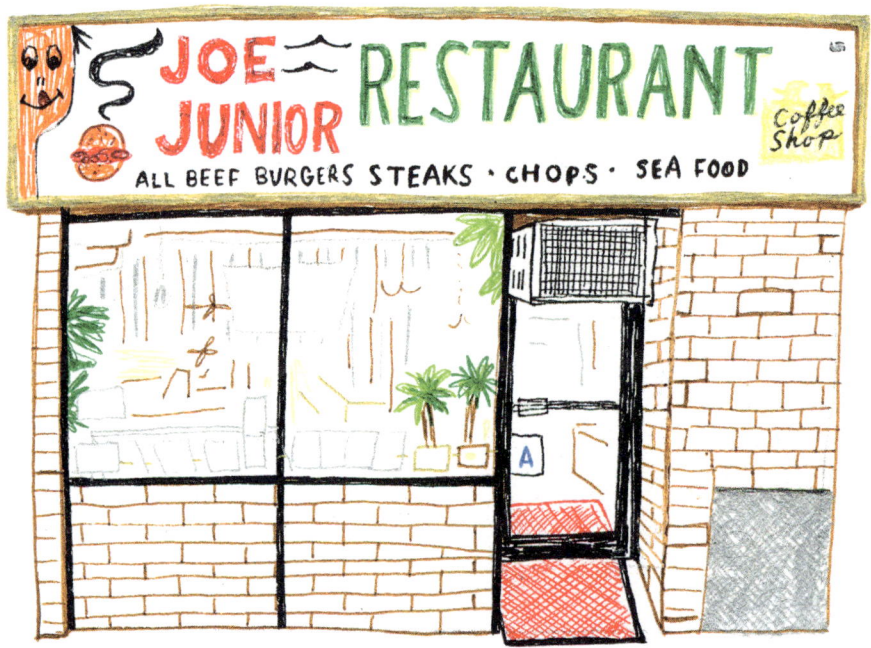

Golden Diner

———

This Chinatown diner has gained a loyal following thanks to a classic menu of comfort food, with some twists that owner Sam Yoo told a local news channel "draw from the influence of our neighborhood" and his Korean background. Avocado toast is an option here; Sam's comes with lemongrass and galangal. Many of his ingredients, down to the pickled vegetables, are sourced from over a dozen local farmers.

In 2025 Sam opened a second spot near Rockefeller Center that includes two restaurants in one. The first is Golden HOF, which pays tribute to Korea's dive-y, affordable pubs, where "anyone can come in," he told the website Grub Street. Underground in the same building is NY Kimchi, a Korean steakhouse.

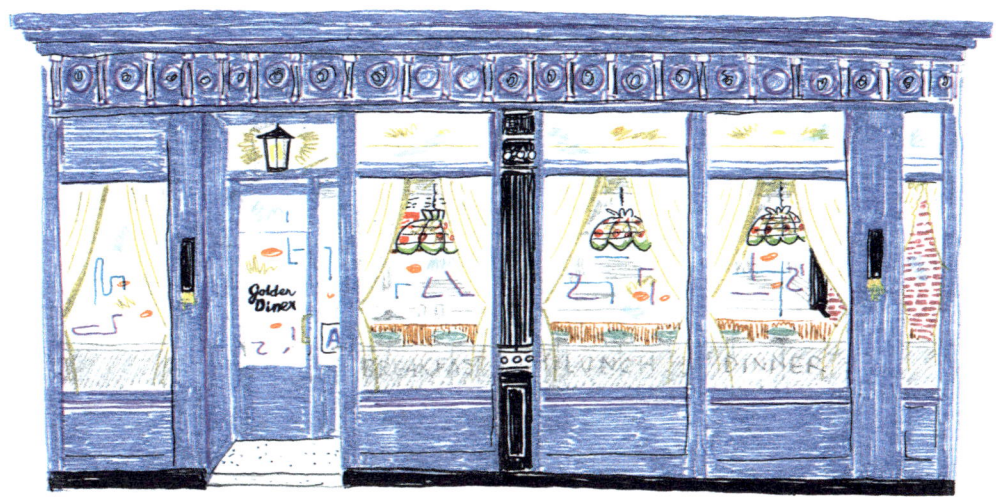

Estela

The portions at this Michelin-starred eatery, first opened in 2013 by Uruguayan-born chef Ignacio Mattos, are small, and the din of the tiny, packed dining room can make it hard to have a conversation. But as any foodie will tell you, this is one of those New York spots that lives up to the hype. You'll be hard-pressed to find a better burrata or selection of natural wines anywhere else.

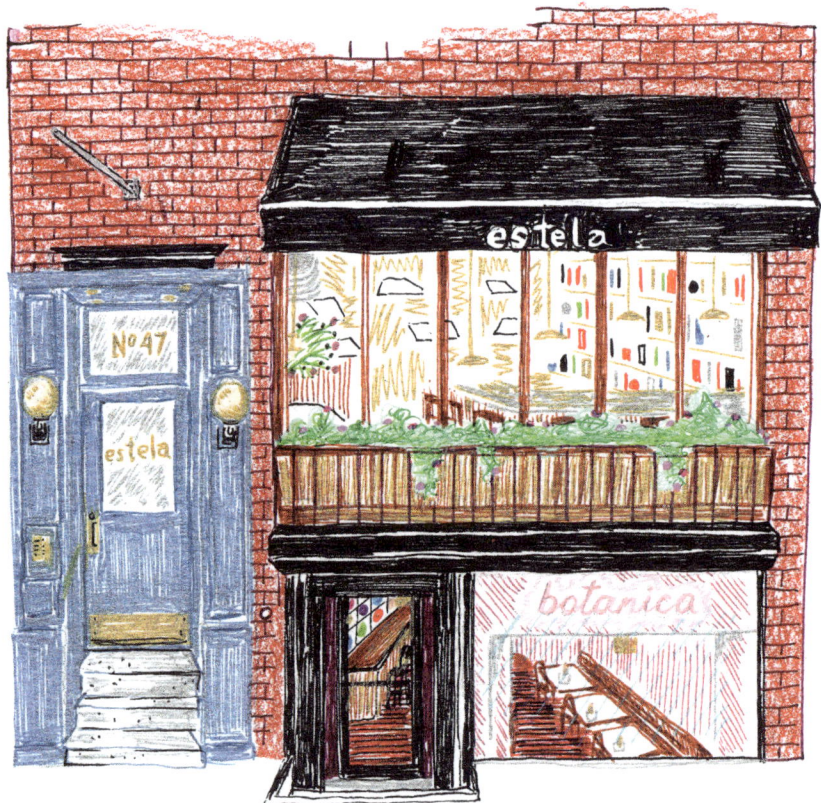

169 Bar

Established in 1916, this spot is a "not-exactly-gentrified, funky-ass, jazz oyster tavern party house," according to its current owner Charles Hanson, a New Orleans native who bought the bar in 2006. Decades ago, it was nicknamed "Bloody Bucket" thanks to the number of rough-and-tumble brawls that broke out inside.

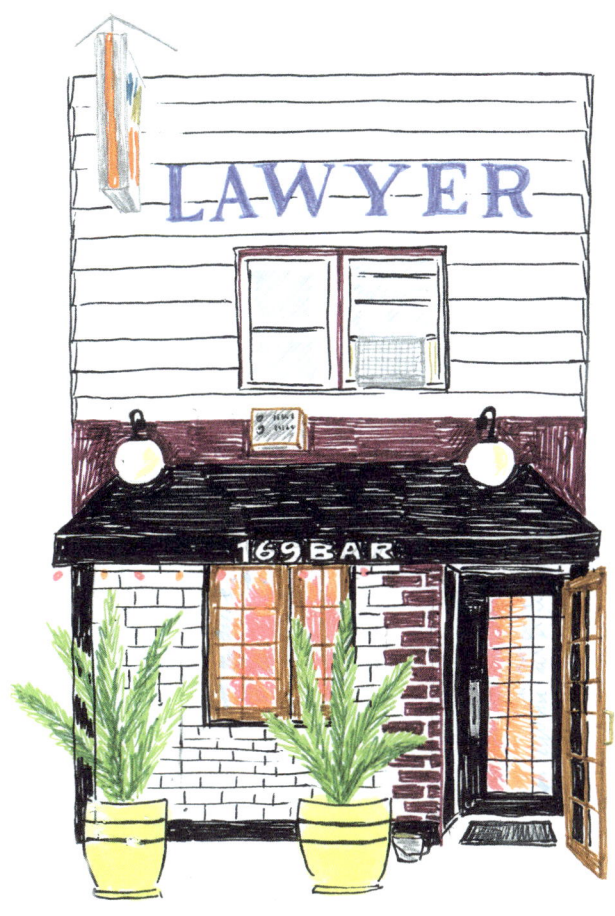

34 Carmine St.
between Bleecker and Bedford Sts.

Unoppressive Non-Imperialist Bargain Books

———

Of course, this West Village spot *did* sell books while it was in business from 1992 to 2022. But as you may gather from the name that appeared on its faded green awning, it offered a lot more than paperbacks. In 2011, owner Jim Drougas provided his space free of charge to organizers of the Occupy Wall Street protests that swept through the city. In 2016, he did the same for Bernie Sanders' presidential campaign.

For years, a psychic held court in the front window. And in early 2020, in a sign of the times, Jim even installed a no-fee Bitcoin ATM at the back of the store.

Aside from these quirks, the variety of books offered—which ranged from the latest in Eastern philosophy to a wide assortment of comics—kept customers coming back for thirty years.

Spicy Village

———

This tiny restaurant, established in 2010 on the Lower East Side, specializes in *hui mei*: wide, hand-pulled noodles. (It's also a favorite haunt of wine collectors, thanks to its generous BYOB policy.) The customer favorite is by far and away the "spicy big tray chicken," cooked in a flavorful sauce that includes anise, chili, garlic, Negra Modelo beer, and mouth-numbing Sichuan peppercorns.

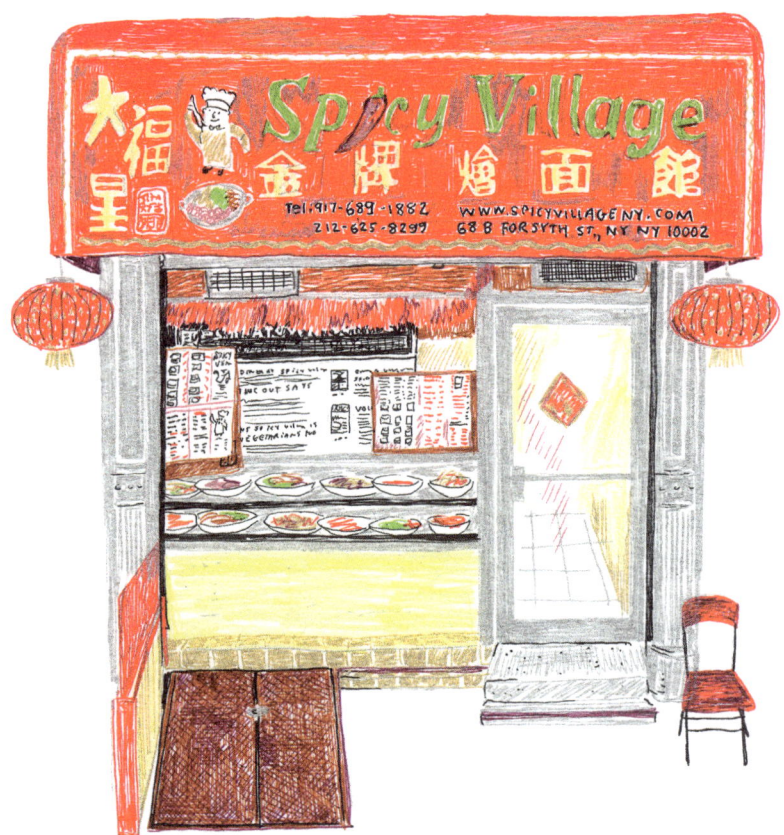

McNally Jackson

Opened in 2004, the independent bookstore McNally Jackson quickly became a SoHo mainstay, with tourists and regulars alike popping in to make a purchase, grab a beverage from the café, or simply browse the latest offerings. After nineteen years at its original location at 52 Prince (shown here), it moved down the street to 134 Prince.

The store is known for its events, which include outdoor poetry readings in the nearby Elizabeth Street Garden and book signings with authors. Rather than scraping by in the era of digital media, McNally Jackson is thriving, having expanded to four other locations around New York City.

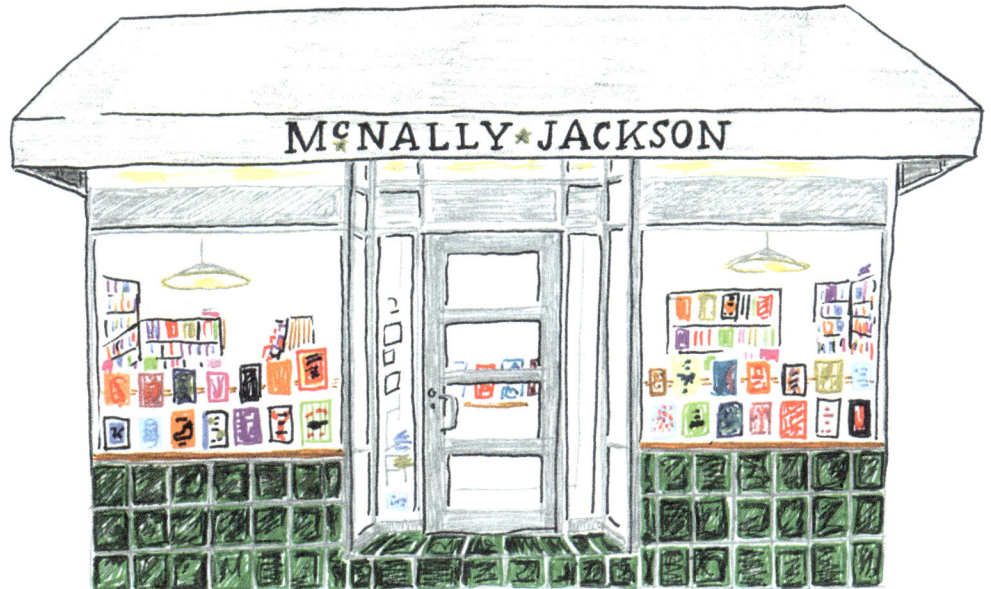

John Jovino Gun Shop

This Little Italy gun shop (yes, you read that right!), which opened in 1911, claimed to be the oldest firearms dealer in the United States before closing in 2020 amid the Covid-19 pandemic. A favorite of the NYPD and featured in Martin Scorsese's film *Mean Streets*, the store also gained notoriety because merchandise it sold was often linked to crimes committed across the city.

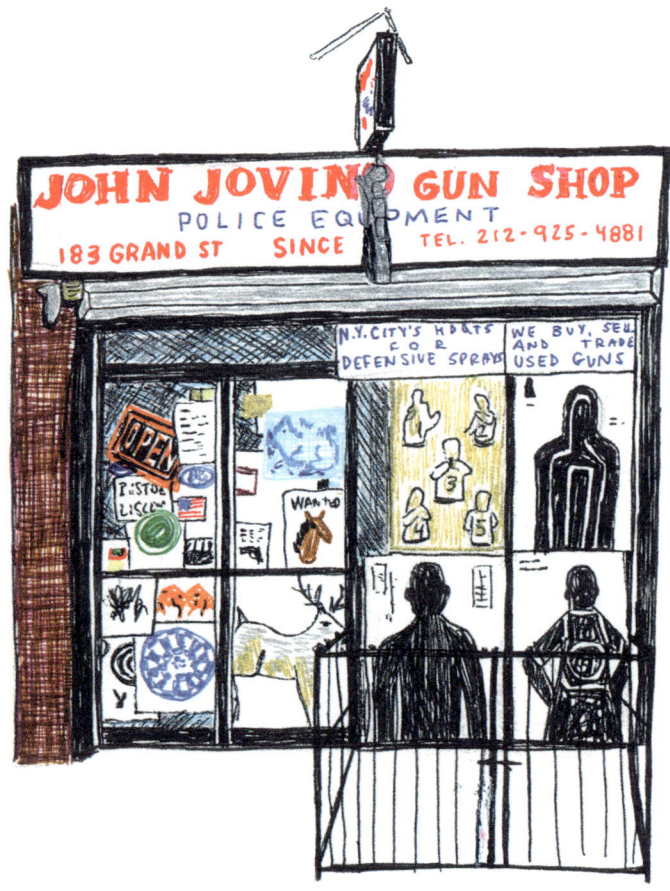

Cowboy Shoe Repair

Despite its location in the heart of posh SoHo, Cowboy Shoe Repair is known for its reasonable prices: replacing worn-out soles or getting new heels on a pair of your beloved boots won't set you back more than several dozen dollars. One online reviewer, who was a regular here for over ten years but has since moved out of New York, now packs a separate suitcase filled with boots when visiting the city—so that the owner, Byron, "can take care of them" at his "boot hospital."

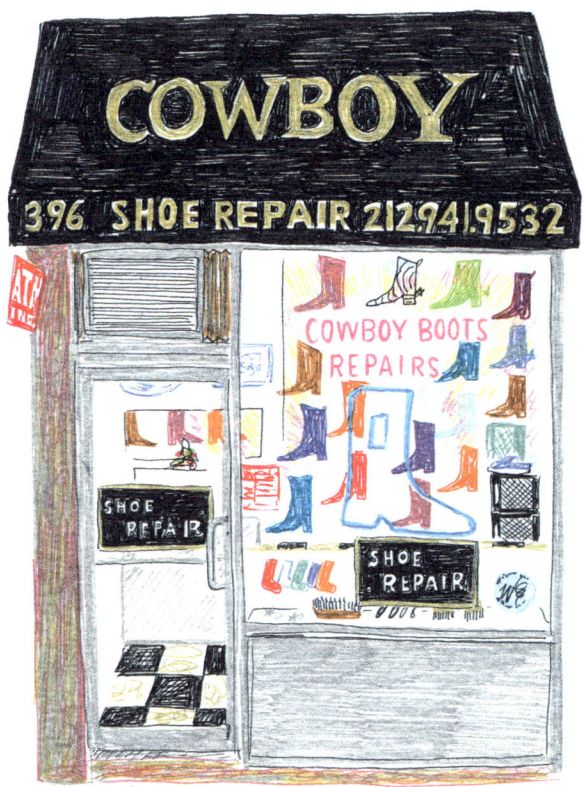

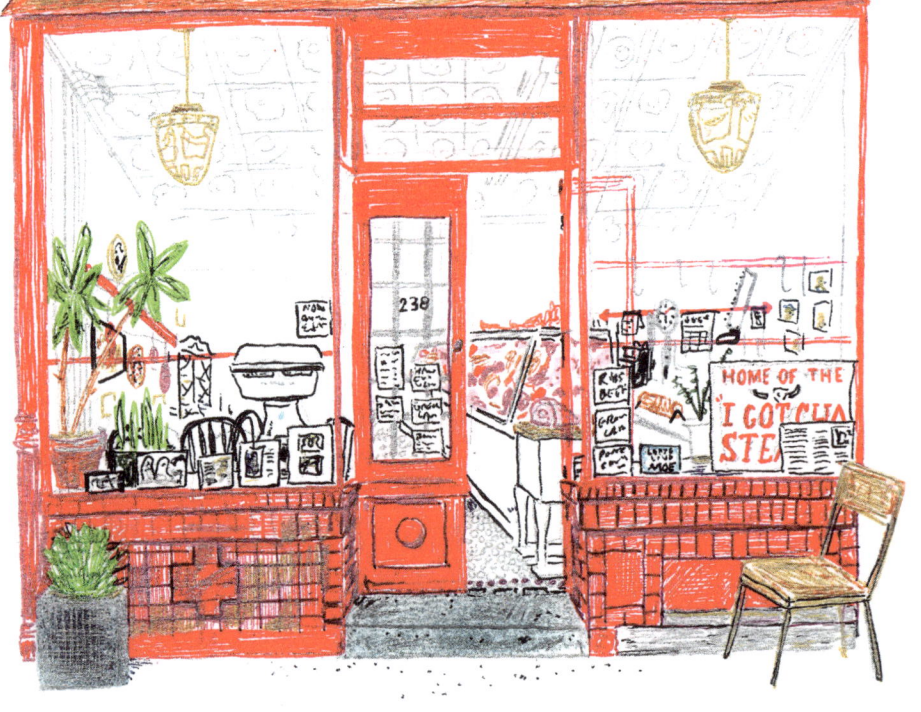

between Prince and E. Houston Sts.

Albanese Meats & Poultry

———

This butcher shop was opened in 1923 by a woman who was raised on the same block, and her husband, an immigrant from Sicily. Their son, Moe Albanese, known affectionately around the city as "Moe the Butcher," grew up helping in the store and eventually took over. Moe passed away in 2020, a week shy of his ninety-sixth birthday. But his legacy lives on in the form of his granddaughter Jennifer Prezioso, who began shadowing him a few years before his death to learn the trade.

Jennifer has been working to ensure that the butcher shop— which was once one of many in the SoHo area—stays relevant to a new generation of New Yorkers.

Albanese Meats & Poultry is beloved by locals (and Hollywood location scouts) looking for some old-world charm. But partly because of the store's rich history, Jennifer says a lot of people walk right on past it, assuming it's a relic. She's worked to entice people to pop into the store with some modern touches, like collaborating with a local artist on felt sausage sculptures that hang in the window.

Also in the window is a sign that proudly proclaims Albanese the "home of the 'I got'cha' steaks." In an interview with digital magazine The Kitchn, Jennifer explains that this name came from her grandfather's confidence in the store's meat: "His whole thing is that once you try the steak, he's gotcha as a customer."

329 W. 57th St.
between 8th and 9th Aves.

Matles Florist

———

Since 1962 this florist near Columbus Circle has been hand-delivering flowers and gift baskets to, as stated on its website, "strengthen relationships, give love and support, and celebrate life's special moments." Owner Yossi Benhamou is a friendly presence in the shop and surrounding neighborhood, and many of the florist's gushing online reviews thank him personally.

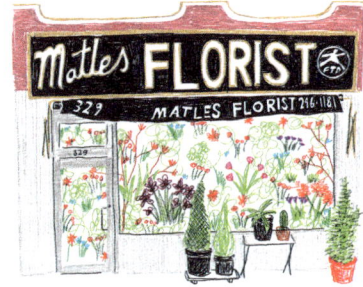

196 Elizabeth St.
between Spring and Prince Sts.

Lovely Day

———

A term often used to describe the eclectic menu at this spot in Little Italy is "comfort food," and it's not hard to see why: offerings include everything from sweet-potato fries with Worcestershire sour-cream dip to classic pad thai.

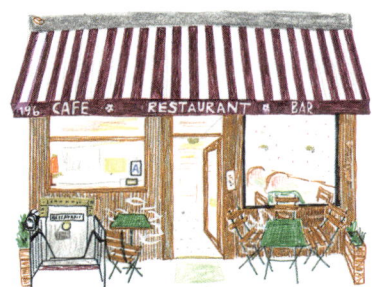

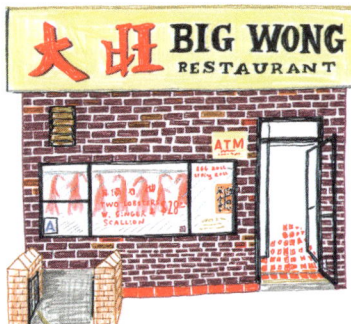

67 Mott St.
between Bayard and Canal Sts.

Big Wong

———

This Chinatown restaurant has been serving up Cantonese classics since 1984. According to several passionate online reviewers, it's best not to leave without trying one of their many congees.

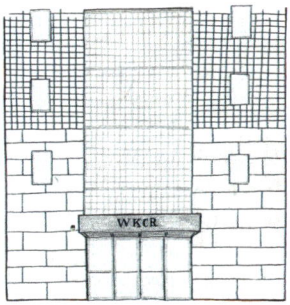

2920 Broadway #2612
at W. 114th St.

WKCR

———

The office of Columbia University's student-run radio station has been broadcasting music and journalism since it first earned its FCC license in 1941. It was home to Grammy Award winner Phil Schaap, who for more than five decades hosted jazz shows on the station before passing away in 2021.

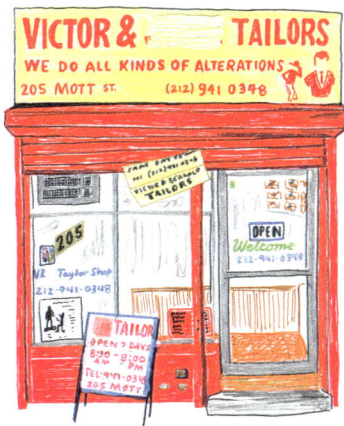

205 Mott St.
between Kenmare and Spring Sts.

Victor & Tailors

This old-school, mom-and-pop NoLita tailor will fix the hem of your jeans or dress for cheap.

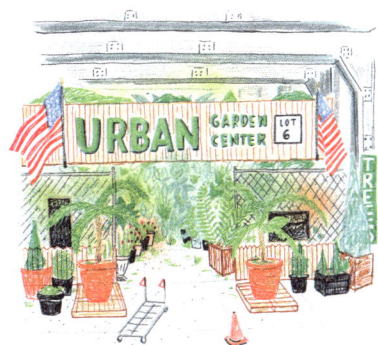

1560 Park Ave.
at E. 111th St.

Urban Garden Center

This gardening center is the city's largest, taking up 20,000 square feet of real estate under the Metro-North railway tracks in East Harlem, just south of the historic marketplace La Marqueta.

43 2nd Ave.
between E. 2nd and 3rd Sts.

Provenzano Lanza Funeral Home

Operating since 1953, this funeral home has earned a name for itself by compassionately caring for New Yorkers and their loved ones in times of grief. Its current owner, Matthew Pinto, strives to operate the business ethically and responsibly, including by working to reduce its environmental impact.

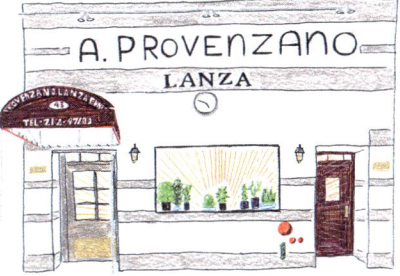

248 E. 23rd St.
between 3rd and 2nd Aves.

Lucky News

You can find everything from lotto tickets to flip-flops at this East Side newsstand.

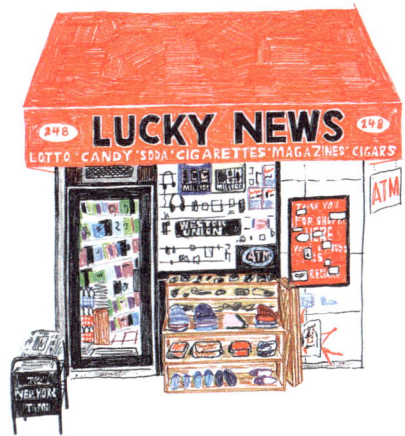

Russ & Daughters

Joel Russ opened his first store on Orchard Street in 1914 and moved it to its current location just a few years later. Inside the shop (be prepared to wait in line before your turn to enter) are family photographs of Joel and his three daughters. They look on as loyal customers purchase the same menu items that have been listed for generations—most notably the lox, which many maintain is still the best in the city. The business has since expanded, opening additional locations on 34th Street in Midtown and in the Brooklyn Navy Yard.

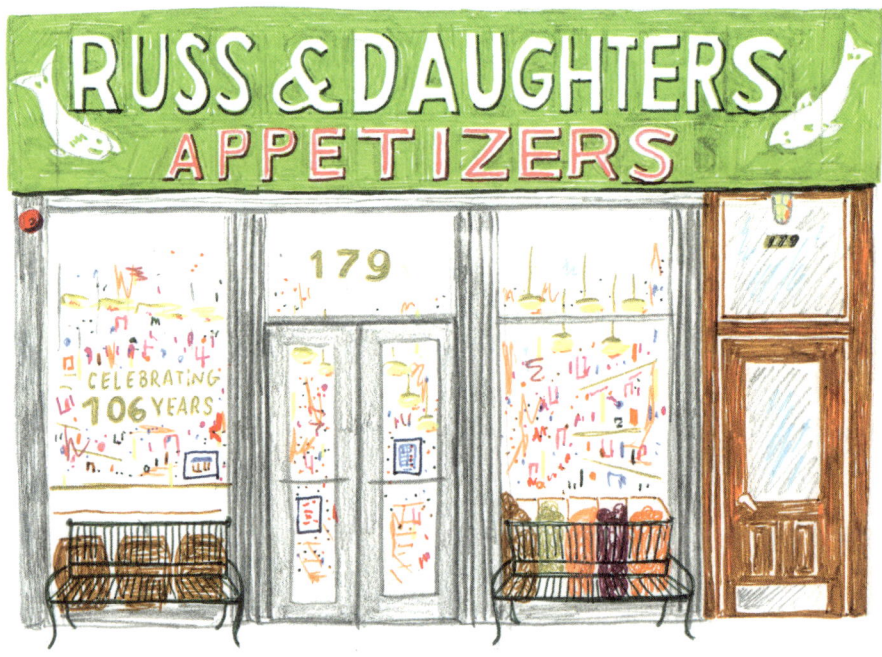

Russ & Daughters Cafe

———

Cousins Niki Russ Federman and Josh Russ Tupper are fourth-generation owners of the classic New York City institution Russ & Daughters—and in 2014 the duo decided it was time to open a separate restaurant to accompany their family's historic store. Unlike the shop on Houston Street, Russ & Daughters Cafe has places for customers to sit and enjoy their knishes or soft scramble with lox and a bagel. The offerings aren't much different from what's sold in the store, but as a *New York Times* reviewer cheekily stated, Why should that matter? After all, this is a spot that "took a century to give its customers a place to sit down."

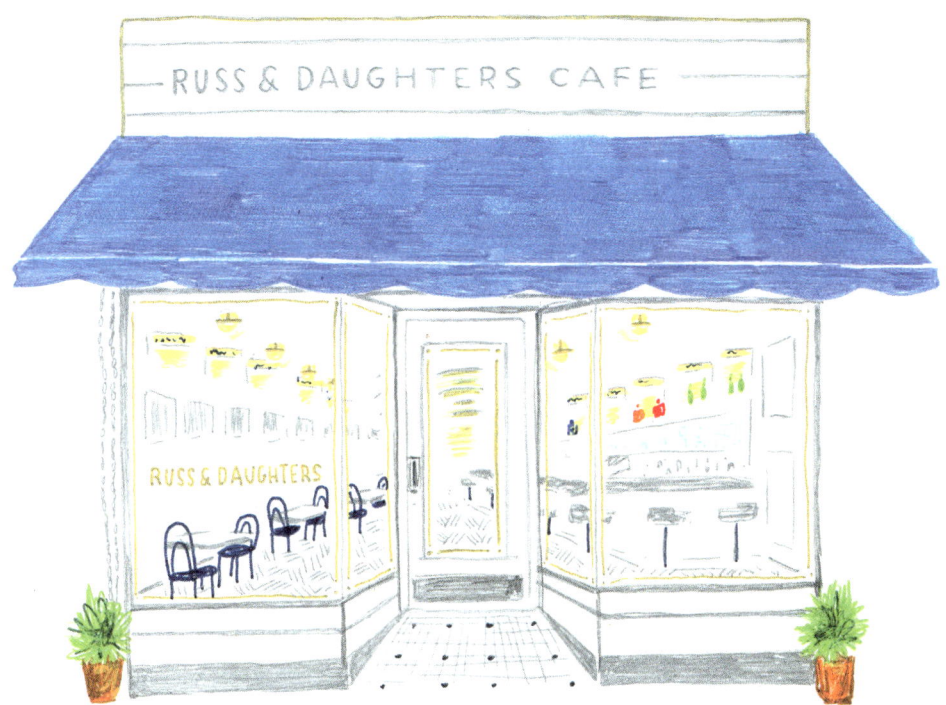

Mel

———

The mission of this bakery, which opened in 2020 in this location on the Lower East Side, can be summed up in two words: whole grains. In 2023 the owner, Nora Allen (of Roberta's Pizza fame), moved the shop upstate to Hudson, where it operates under the same name. Mel comes from *mjöl*, the Danish word for "flour." Sourdough is Allen's specialty. Over the years she has used it to make pistachio-almond croissants, focaccia with corn and blackened poblano peppers, and bialys—the less famous but equally as delicious baked cousin of the bagel.

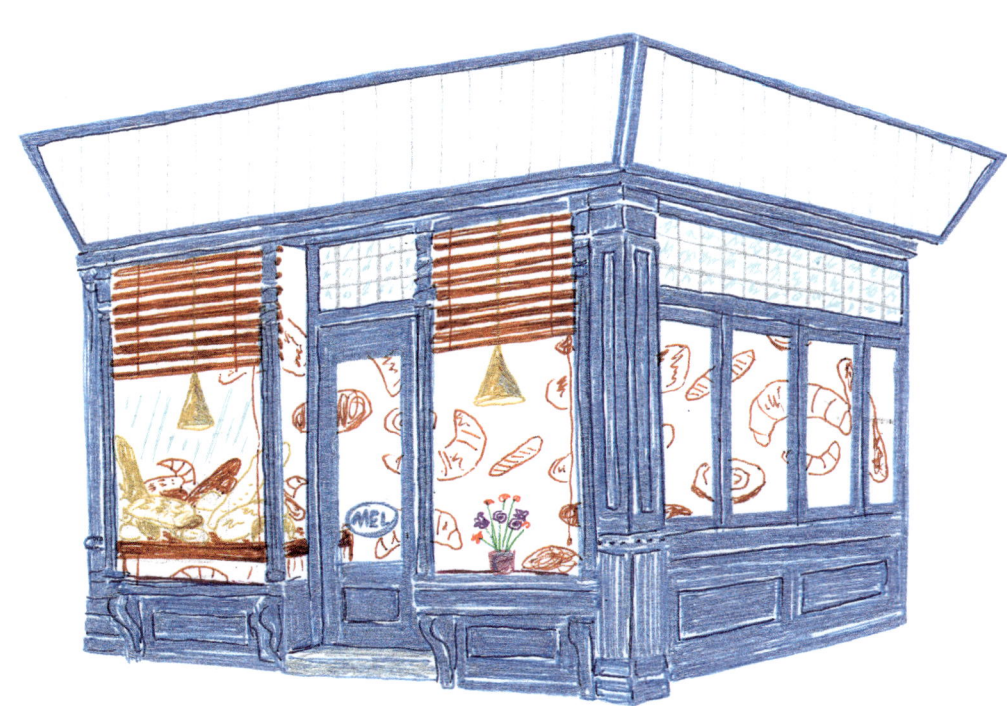

Frank Restaurant

Frank Prisinzano, the owner of Frank (and its offshoots Lil' Frankie's, Supper, and Daddies) opened his first restaurant in 1998. He doesn't keep recipes for his downtown Italian eateries and will get offended if you (or his cooks, even) ask for one: cooking, he insists, is an intensely personal journey, and one everyone must develop for themselves. But despite the bluster of the "no-recipe chef," Frank is also very much a softy. The restaurant is outfitted with furniture, utensils, and more from his late grandmother, whom he personally cared for in her later years.

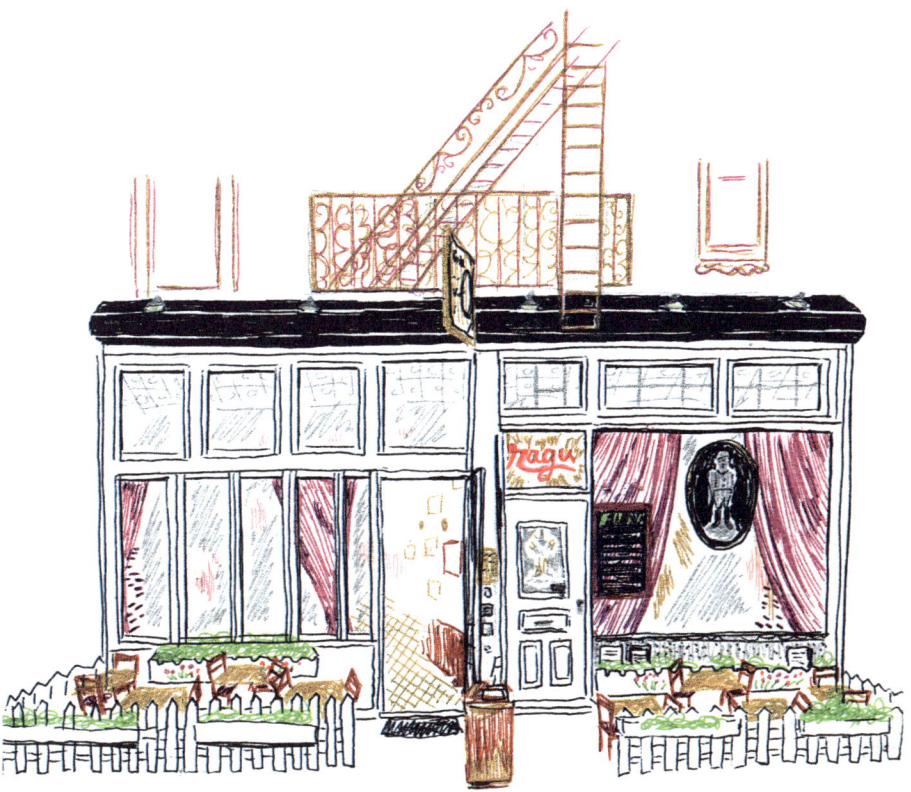

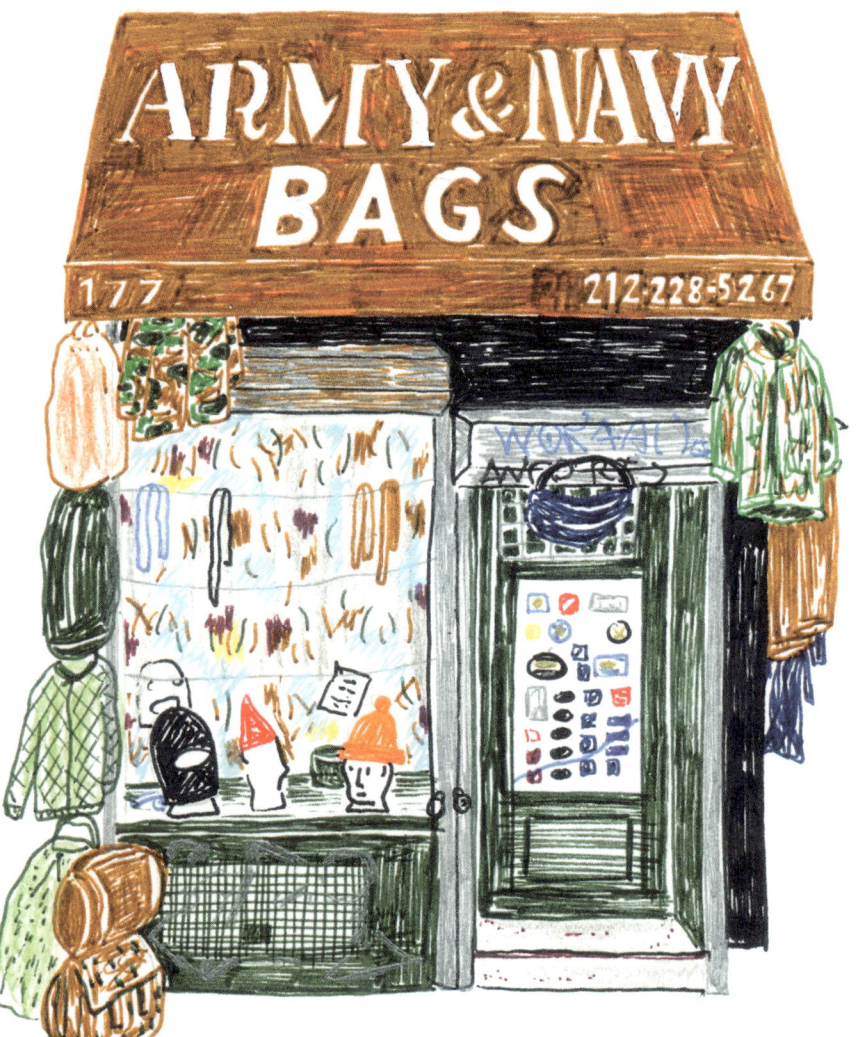

Army & Navy Bags

A Polish couple originally opened this military-surplus store in 1956, and in 2007 they gifted it to one of their longtime employees, Henry Yao. He's operated the shop by himself ever since, becoming a neighborhood fixture.

Henry has enjoyed both rewarding and challenging times, depending partly on how of-the-moment camouflage clothing seems to be for New Yorkers, he says.

In 2020 he had earned enough good will that neighbors rallied to save his small shop during the Covid-19 pandemic, when Henry was mere days away from closing for good. Regulars started an online crowdfunding page for the store when they learned it was in trouble via an Instagram post by local do-gooder and contributor to this book Nicolas Heller (aka @newyorknico). Within hours, a line had formed outside Army & Navy Bags, and the crowdsourced campaign raised over $60,000.

But Henry's fans have rallied to his defense before. In 2012, when his landlord tried to triple his monthly rent, which was then $3,800, the community expressed so much outrage that the landlord backed off. Nearly a decade later, Henry's rent has nonetheless increased by thousands of dollars a month—still less than what it would have been without the outcry. He says he's unsure how much longer he can stay in the game in the age of Amazon and rising Manhattan rents, but if his customer base has anything to do with it, the shop will likely be around for a good while.

Minetta Tavern

Established in 1937, this West Village restaurant was named after the Minetta Brook, a creek which ran through the area and out to the Hudson River before being covered over in the nineteenth century. The watering hole became a popular hangout for the likes of Joe Gould, Ernest Hemingway, E. E. Cummings, and Dylan Thomas in the 1950s and retains an old-world aesthetic today.

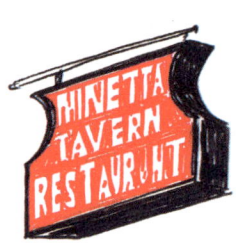

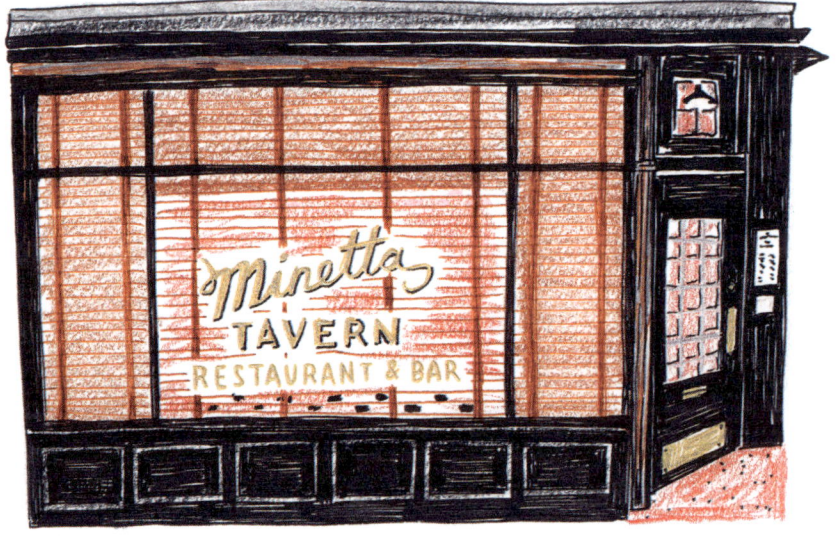

Katz's Delicatessen

Originally named Iceland Brothers when it opened in 1888 on Ludlow Street, this deli adopted its current name after the Katz family fully took ownership in 1910. In 1917 Katz's Delicatessen moved across the street to its current location. Now thousands of people shuffle into this famous eatery each week—along with its Brooklyn outpost, A Taste of Katz's—for a chance to buy world-renowned pastrami and corned beef, or to snap a quick pic of the spot where Meg Ryan famously faked an orgasm in *When Harry Met Sally*. Whatever your reason for visiting, hold on tight to your counter ticket, as losing it costs a fifty-dollar fee.

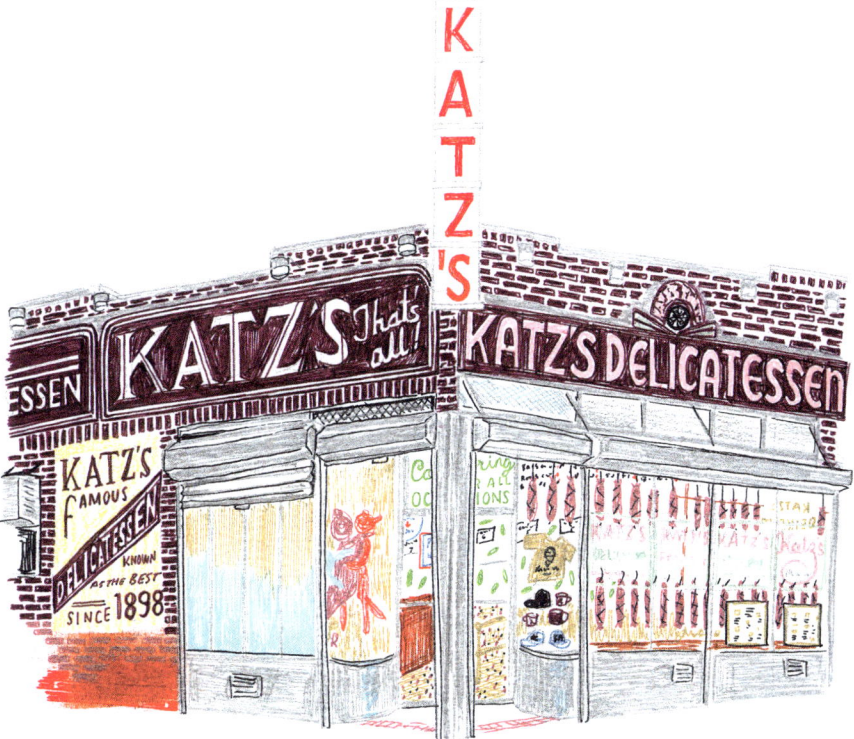

Prune

Chef Gabrielle Hamilton opened this East Village restaurant in 1999, and it quickly became one of the city's most popular brunch spots. Fans of Prune—which included food writers such as Anthony Bourdain—would often have to wait forty-five minutes or more during a weekend rush for the chance to enjoy something on the eatery's eclectic menu, such as a "Triscuits and sardines" appetizer or a massive piece of roasted veal.

In April 2020, Gabrielle closed Prune's doors during the pandemic. Soon after, she wrote an essay for the *New York Times* that explained the competing pressures facing the city's restaurateurs—like rising costs, difficulty offering living wages and benefits to employees, and pressures to continually evolve—that has since served as something of a rallying cry to reform the industry.

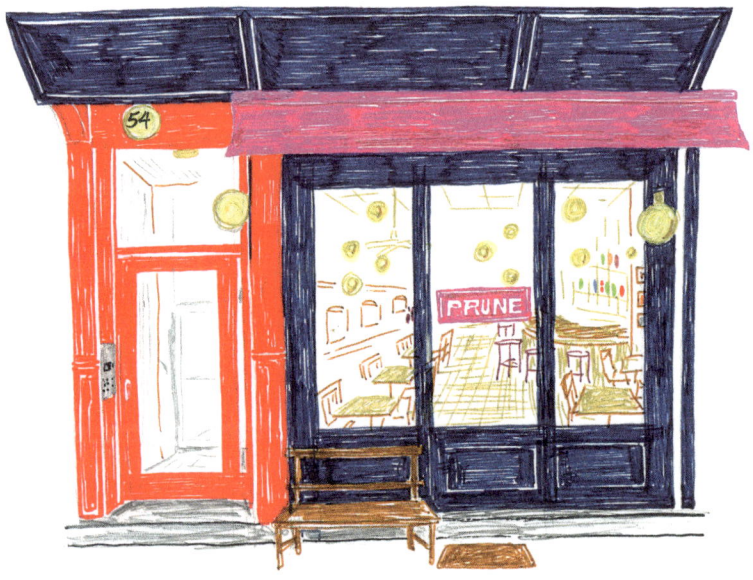

Lucy's

———————

After being forced to close for two months at the outset of the 2020 coronavirus pandemic, the owner of this beloved East Village bar welcomed patrons back with homemade deviled eggs and balloons that said, "I Love You." Regulars expected nothing less from its grandma-esque proprietor, Polish-born Ludwika "Lucy" Mickevicius, who started working there in 1981.

In early 2024 new landlords raised Lucy's rent to a whopping $25,000 a month, forcing the space to close again. The bar may live to fight another day, however, thanks to Golden Age, the hospitality group behind Manhattan institutions like Le Dive and The Nines, which has expressed interest in preserving the classic watering hole with Lucy still at the helm.

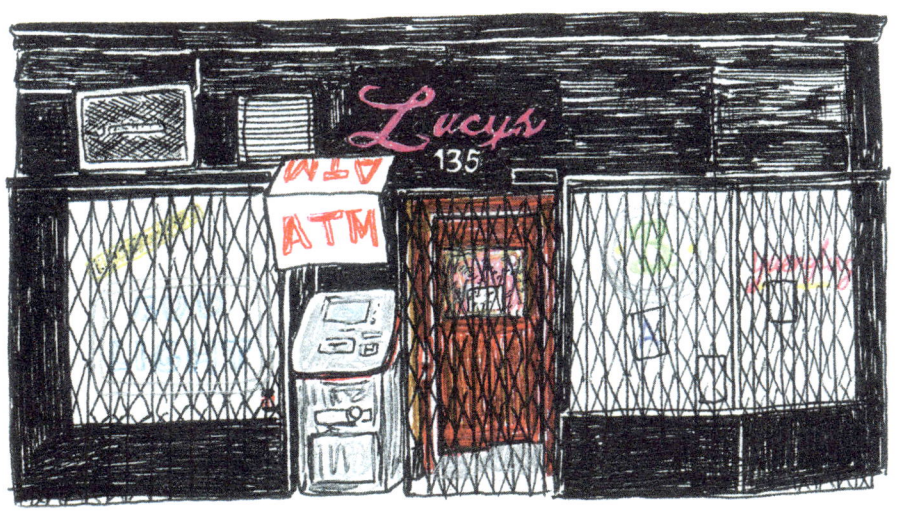

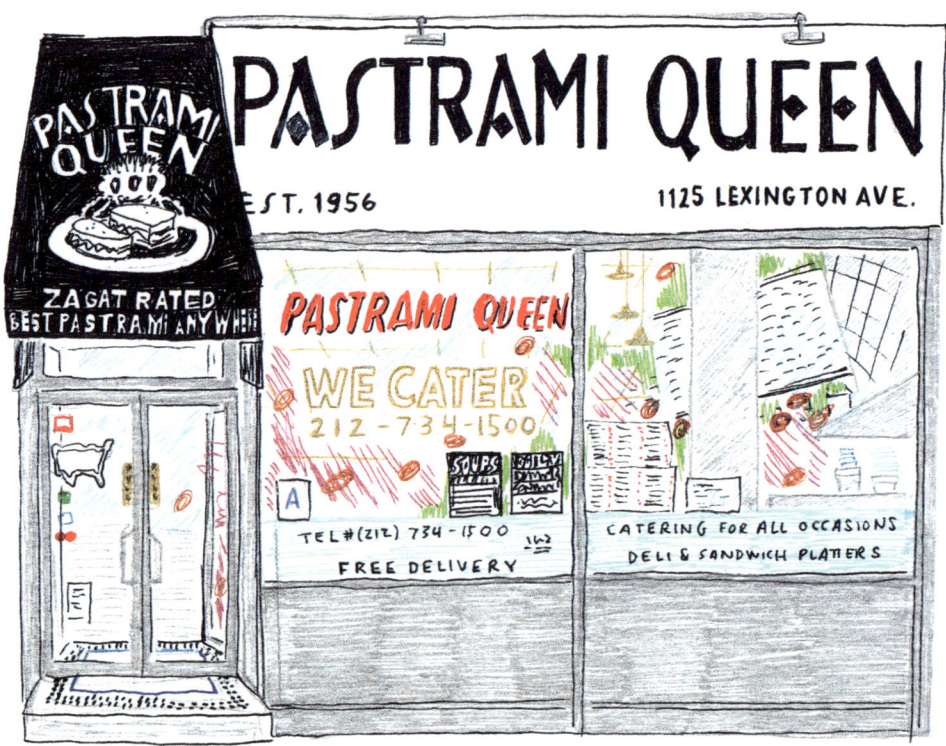

Pastrami Queen

When Anthony Bourdain was in the mood for a "quintessential New York meal," he'd order a pastrami sandwich and a cream soda from this classic kosher deli.

First opened in Williamsburg, Brooklyn, in 1956 under the name Pastrami King, it has called three different boroughs home. In 1961 it moved to Kew Gardens, Queens, and then to its current location on the Upper East Side in 1998.

During its reign in Queens, Pastrami King was located across the street from the family and civil courthouse, itself becoming something of a center of political power in the borough. When the court relocated to Jamaica, Queens, the deli said its business fell by 30 to 40 percent—prompting its move to Manhattan, to the great disillusionment of its Kew Gardens regulars. In a nod to its love of the borough it long called home, however, the owners changed the name, putting a new royal on the throne.

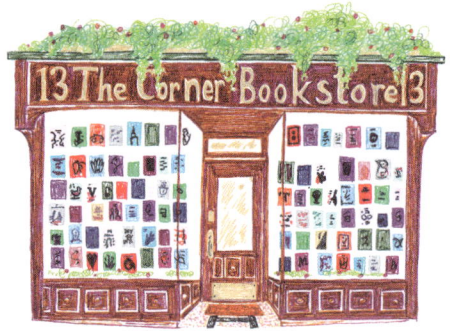

1313 Madison Ave.
at E. 93rd St.

The Corner Bookstore

Opened in 1978, this bookstore tracks orders by hand using a filing drawer instead of a computer, and they check out customers with a cash register that's over a century old.

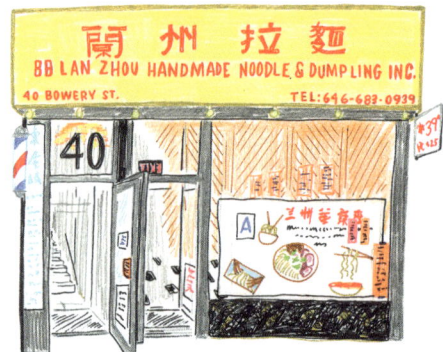

40 Bowery
between Bayard and Canal Sts.

88 Lan Zhou Handmade Noodle & Dumpling Inc.

Sadly, this shop closed in 2020 as a casualty of the Covid-19 pandemic—and its dumplings and hand-pulled noodles have been sorely missed ever since.

193 Grand St.
between Mulberry and Mott Sts.

E. Rossi & Company

This store, stocked with dishes, towels, and other souvenirs imported from Italy, has been in business since 1910—the oldest Italian American gift shop in the city.

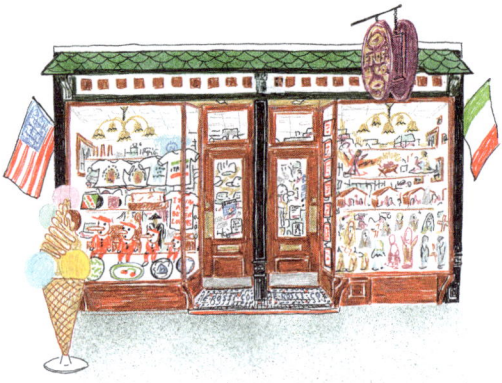

317 E. Houston St.
at Attorney St.

Parkside Lounge

This dive bar opened in 1908 and is said to have Mafia roots.. A now-boarded-up doorway in the basement, leading to the East River, was supposedly used by mobsters to reach a dumping ground. Some current patrons and staff swear they regularly see the ghosts of victims.

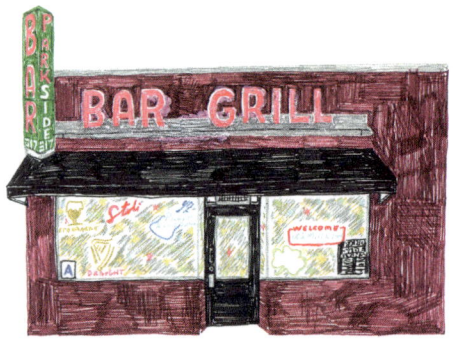

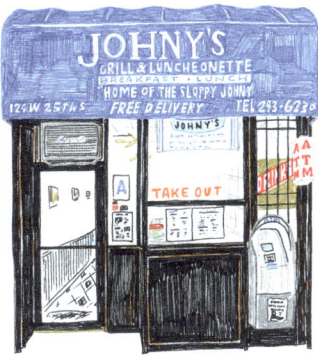

124 W. 25th St.
between 6th and 7th Aves.

Johny's Luncheonette

Founded in 1994, this greasy spoon has survived Chelsea's rapid gentrification. With its Formica countertops and blue bar stools, it hearkens back to a bygone era when lunch counters ruled the area.

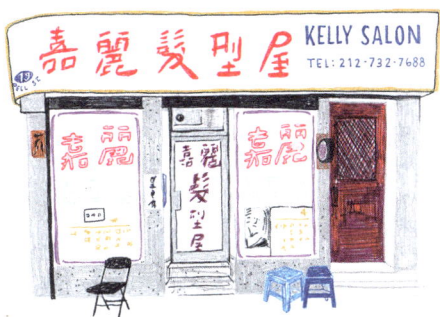

19 Pell St. A
at Doyers St.

Kelly Salon

Kwok Wing Yau, who has been cutting hair since he was a teenager growing up in Hong Kong, opened Kelly Salon (named after his daughter) in 2005. A favorite among Chinatown locals, the shop is also beloved by the Chinese community from around the tristate area.

701 8th Ave.
at W. 44th St.

Smith's Bar

This notorious Times Square bar shut down in 2014 after sixty years of serving its colorful clientele. A year later Skip Panettiere, father of the actress Hayden Panettiere, reopened it and kept the environment largely unchanged. Sadly, in 2024 it closed again, for good.

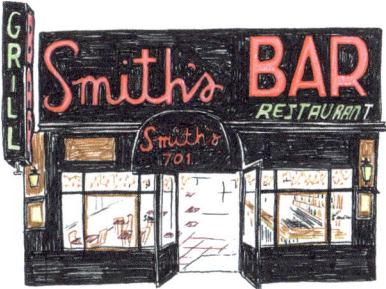

Manhattan Art & Antiques Center,
Gallery 84, E. 56th St.
between 2nd and 1st Aves.

Paul J. Bosco

If you understand phrases like "German coins in slabs," and "Bois Durci medals," then you've already heard of Paul J. Bosco, *the* place in Manhattan for rare coins and paper money—which in 2018 moved from its original location on Thirty-Second Street, depicted here, to the Upper East Side.

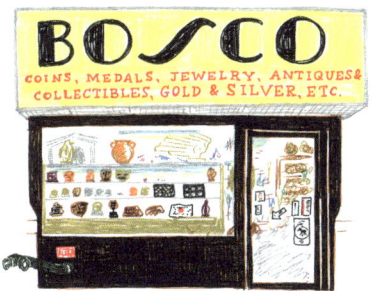

Casey Rubber Stamps

Every inch of this tiny East Village store, opened by
John Casey (who is originally from Cork, Ireland), is
filled with rubber stamps made the old-fashioned way:
with a negative, plate, and mold process. According to
a sign hanging in its window, the shop is "closed when
not open."

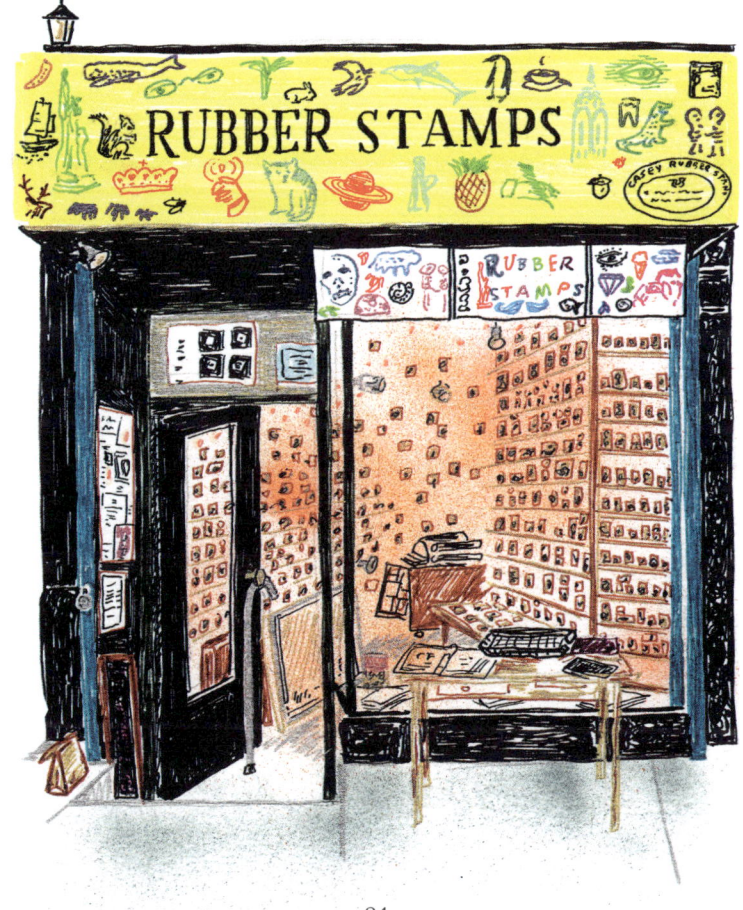

Aimé Leon Dore

Teddy Santis, a menswear designer from Queens, opened this shop in 2014. It quickly became the "coolest store" in NoLita, according to a *Vogue* headline from the time. He's earned this accolade thanks to his streetwear designs, of course, but also because of the mystique he's developed around himself. Teddy rarely gives interviews, and when he does, he refuses to be quoted directly. He has no interest in parading his designs down runways during fashion week either. He prefers his clothes—and, for that matter, his striking retail spaces—to speak for themselves. In 2023 he expanded beyond his 214 Mulberry address and opened up at 224, turning 214 into a café (and changing the exterior from white to black).

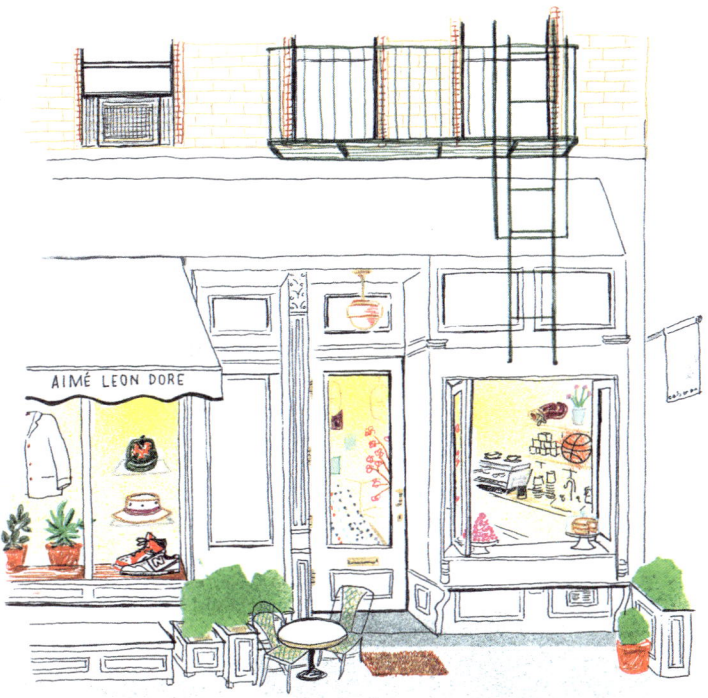

Luster Photo & Digital Lab

Luster Photo & Digital Lab, the East Village's go-to photography shop, is known for its quick turn-around, quality service, and knowledgeable staff. The internet is littered with five-star reviews from professionals insisting they'll trust no one else with their work, and from amateurs who stumble on the store after finding nowhere else in the city to develop film from a long-lost disposable camera that resurfaced decades later.

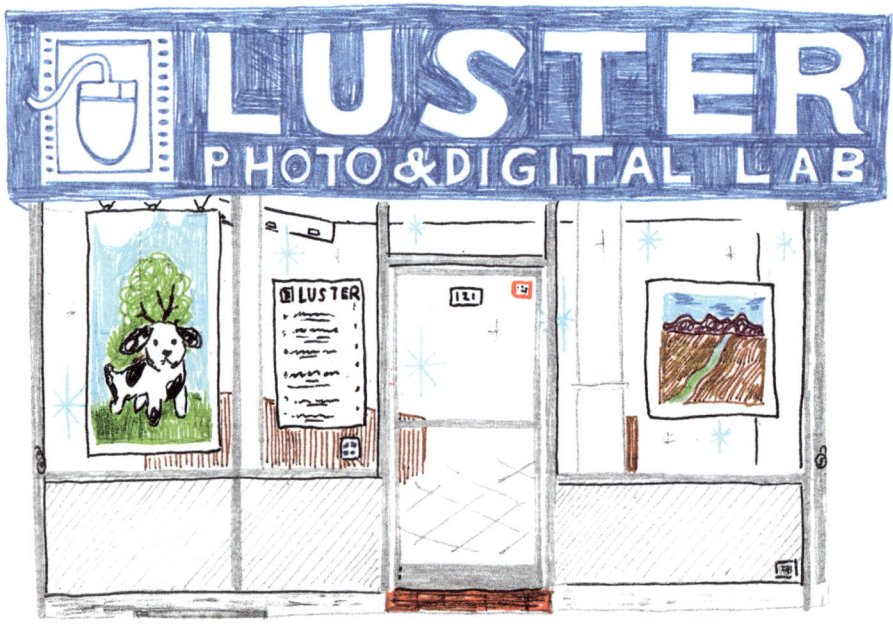

183 W. 10th St.

between 7th Ave. S. and W. 4th St.

Smalls Jazz Club

───────

Mitchell Borden, a former Navy submariner and violinist, opened this jazz club in the basement of a West Village brownstone in 1994. He invited his guests to bring their own booze (he didn't install a full-service bar until over a decade later) while enjoying the club's music for as long as they liked. In 2003 the venue went bankrupt, hurt by the city's economic slowdown following the 9/11 attacks. But Mitchell reclaimed ownership of the club in 2006 with two additional partners. In 2018 the trio formed the SmallsLIVE Foundation, a nonprofit arts organization dedicated to the "dissemination of jazz music," which counts Billy Joel among its biggest benefactors.

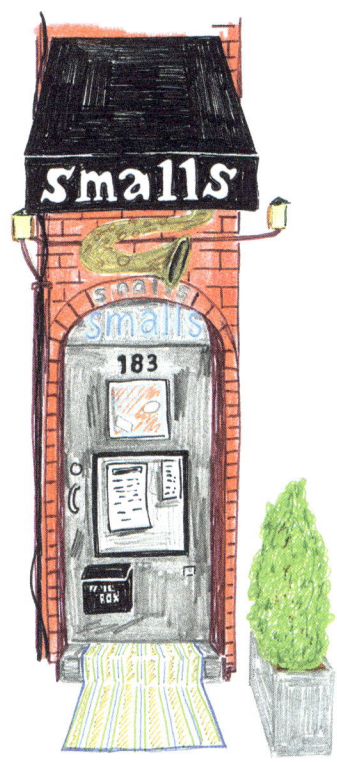

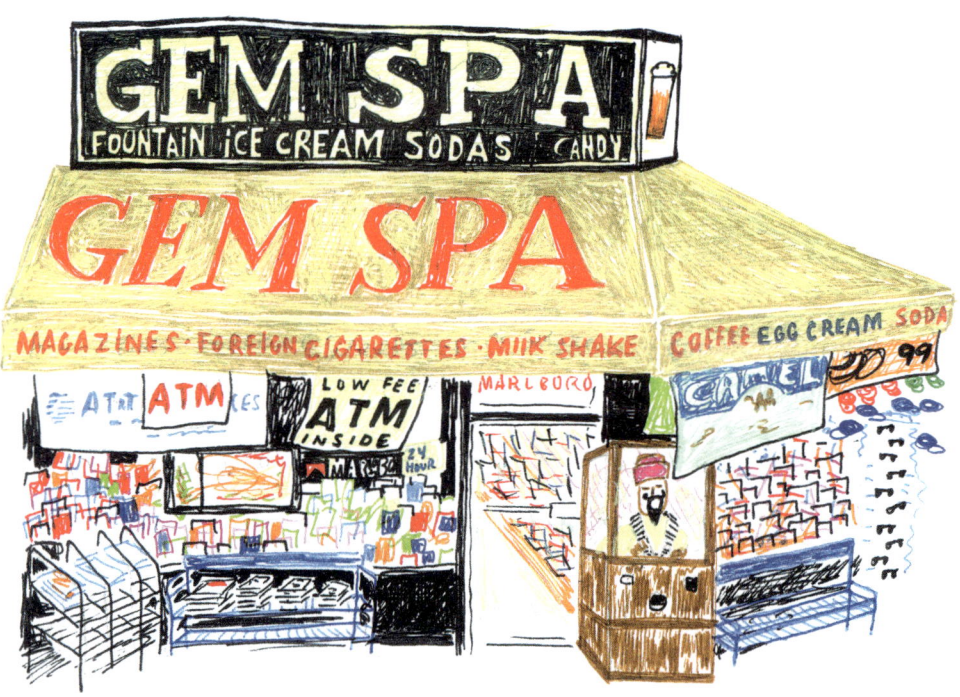

Gem Spa

This East Village corner store opened in 1920 under a different name and was considered by some to be the birthplace of the egg cream, a milky beverage that contains neither egg nor cream.

Although Gem Spa has this possible claim to fame, its iconic yellow awning humbly proclaimed that the bodega sold New York's "best" egg cream, but not its first.

Despite a passionate effort by locals to save the shop, rising rents combined with Covid-19 lockdowns forced it to shut down in May 2020. The neighborhood's reaction to the loss was perhaps best summed up by a graffiti tag that appeared days after, scrawled across the front of the store, proclaiming, "New York City is dead." Though closed, Gem Spa will live on in countless movies, artworks, poems, and other homages to the famous space: Jean-Michel Basquiat created a painting named after the store in 1982. Madonna filmed a scene of *Desperately Seeking Susan* there in 1984. Allen Ginsberg called it a "nerve center" of the city. Robert Mapplethorpe bought Patti Smith her first egg cream there.

Gem Spa's beloved sign was taken down and auctioned off. But at least one physical piece of the store is still available for public consumption. The bodega's Zoltar fortune-telling machine—which stood outside the shop since 2012 and, in recent years, was perhaps just as well-known as its egg creams—is now on display outside of OMG Pizza in Bushwick, Brooklyn.

Veniero's Pasticceria

This East Village bakery has been owned and operated by the Veniero family since it opened in 1894. Currently it even employs a fifth-generation descendent of the store's founder, Antonio Veniero, who immigrated to New York from Sorrento, Italy, at the age of fifteen. The bakery's first offerings were limited to candy, biscotti, and espresso. But today Veniero's serves up more than one hundred fifty desserts, from classic Italian offerings, such as butter cookies and cannoli, to more modern staples, including New York–style cheesecake. Get there early on weekends, as lines wrap around to First Avenue for first dibs on the fresh-baked goodies.

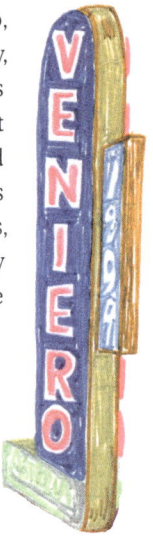

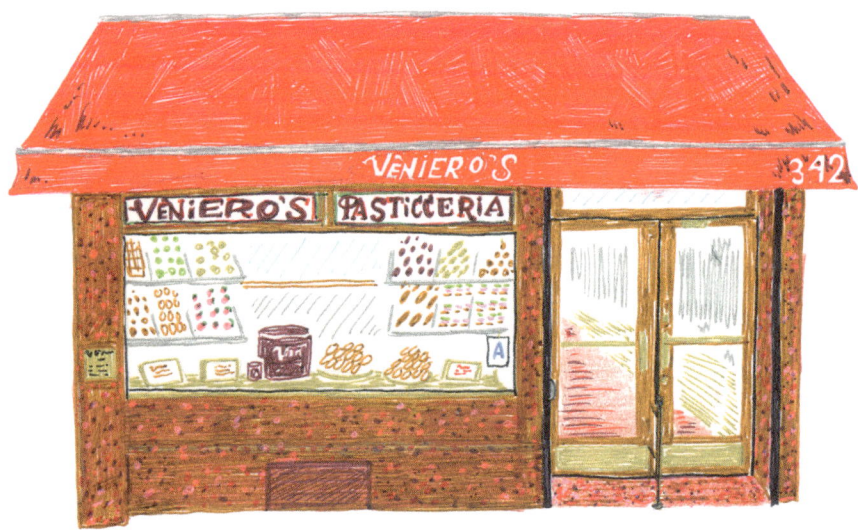

Chinatown Fair

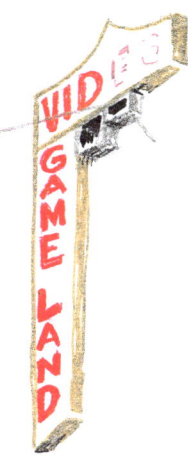

An arcade has been continually operating at this spot since 1944, save for a year starting in February 2012, when ownership of the business changed hands. Originally acknowledged for its street-fighting games, the arcade would eventually become best known for, of all things, live chickens. They weren't just any chickens, though: these birds challenged anyone who dared (and who had a couple of quarters to spare) to a rousing bout of tic-tac-toe. The arcade featured "dancing chickens," too, but they weren't as much of a draw. Though the sign outside still proclaims the space home to the "world famous" tic-tac-toe chickens, this particular novelty was retired in the early 2000s.

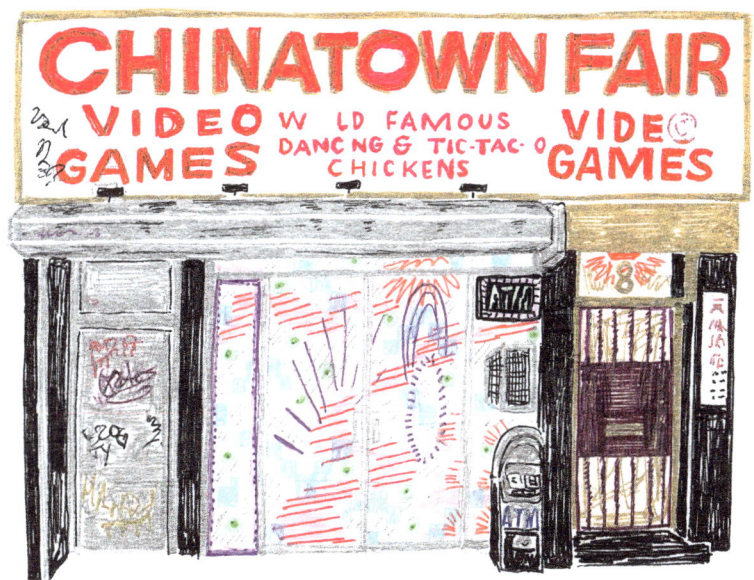

Harlem Shake

————

This Harlem restaurant first opened in 2013 on Second Avenue (illustrated here) and later moved to its current home in Central Harlem. The business works hard to reflect the neighborhood's "culture and community," according to its website. Every year patrons vote for a fellow customer to become "Mr. or Ms. Harlem Shake." The winner gets not only bragging rights but also cash and the opportunity to be the public face of the restaurant at events throughout their reign.

Two areas of the restaurant's interior are of note: first is the "Wall of Fame," covered with signed headshots from celebrities, including Maya Angelou and Janelle Monáe. But Harlem Shake may be better known for its "Wall of Fro," which showcases pictures featuring the hairstyles of its loyal regulars. In 2021 a Brooklyn location was opened, where they similarly aspire to be a neighborhood hub.

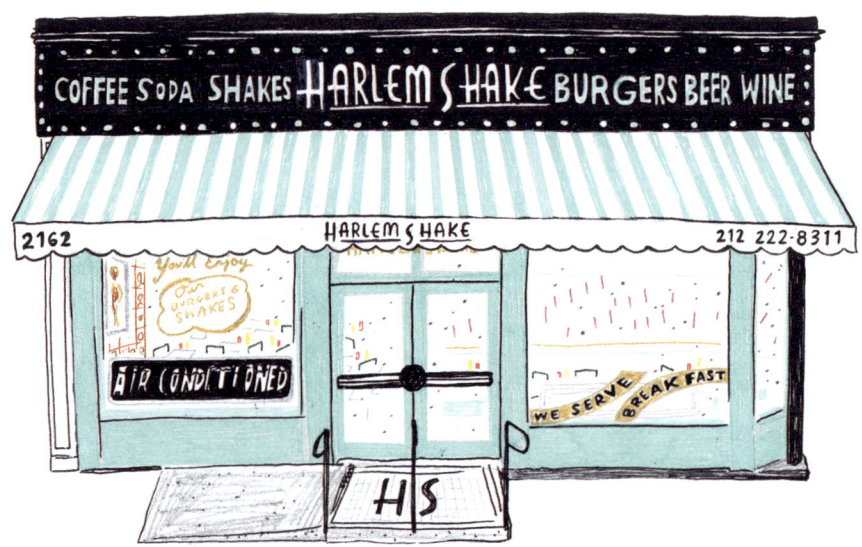

Chinatown
Ice Cream Factory

The awning outside this Chinatown ice cream spot says "since 1978"—but it was actually opened by Philip Seid and his two brothers the year before, in 1977. And although Philip's brothers have both left the business, the store is still a family-run operation: his daughter, Christina, now helps manage it, as well as two other New York City locations, on the Lower East Side and in Flushing. Chinatown Ice Cream Factory is most famous for its Asian-inspired flavors, including those made from lychee, the famously pungent durian fruit, and sweet red bean. But for those more accustomed to a Western palate, it also offers plenty of options that the owners refer to as "exotic," like rocky road, cherry vanilla, and Oreo cookie.

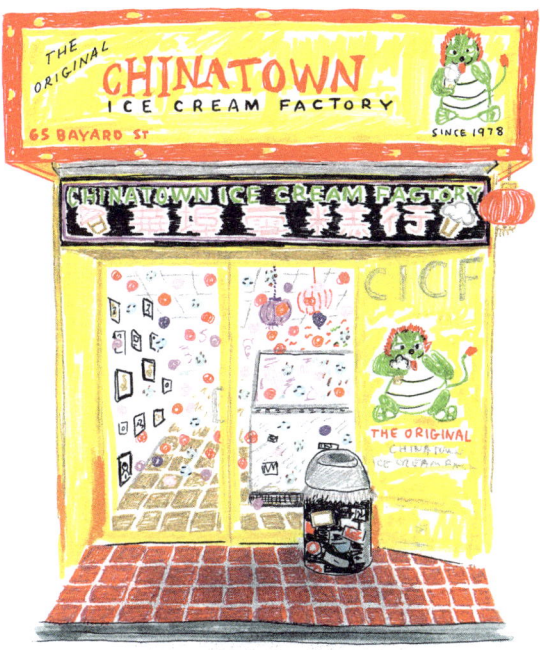

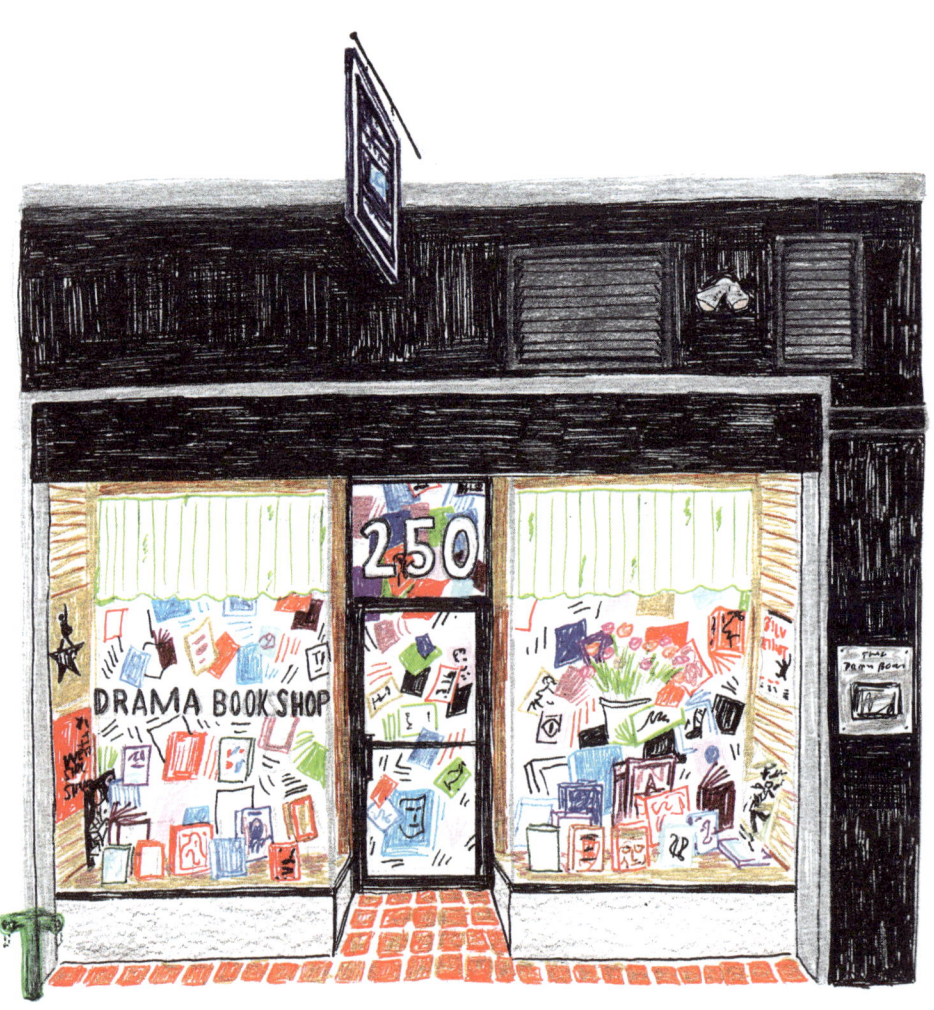

266 W. 39th St.
between 7th and 8th Aves.

Drama Book Shop

———

This beloved bookstore in the Theater District, founded in 1917, has long been the go-to place to purchase publications about acting, scripts, songbooks, and other showbiz paraphernalia. Since that time, it has managed to withstand a flood, a fire, multiple moves (including a stint on West Fortieth Street, depicted in this illustration)—and even Amazon. But in 2018, the store announced it had finally met its match, a familiar villain in the world of New York real estate: the dreaded rent increase.

However, just as the curtains were about to fall on this century-old business, there was a dramatic plot twist in the form of a new protagonist.

Broadway legend Lin-Manuel Miranda (of *Hamilton* and *In the Heights* fame) stepped in and became the store's savior, buying it with the help of three colleagues. After a brief intermission for renovations (that included an art installation involving 2,400 books that spiral and crawl throughout the space), the store reopened in summer 2021, and its story continued anew.

262 Bleecker St.

between Leroy and Morton Sts.

Trattoria Pesce Pasta

Opened in 1993, this old-fashioned Italian restaurant in the West Village is known for its friendly vibe, as well as its generous portions of traditionally made spaghetti, lasagna, and linguini.

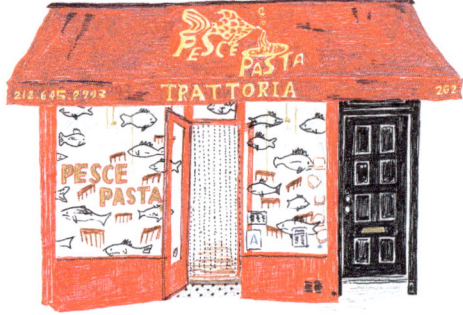

129 E. 18th St.

at Irving Pl.

Pete's Tavern

Pete's Tavern, which occupies a space that has been a watering hole since 1864, bills itself as the "oldest original bar and restaurant" in Gramercy. It even claims that it has retained its dining rooms in the "exact same condition" for the better part of two centuries.

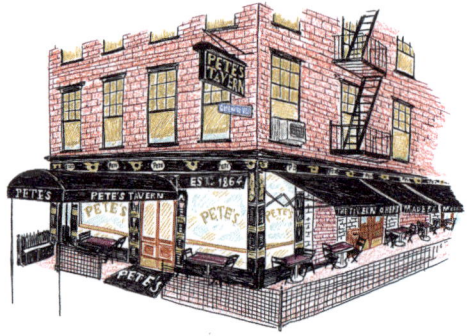

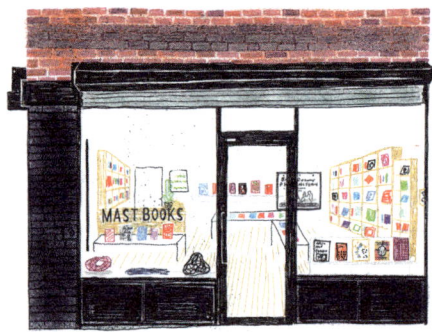

72 Ave. A

at E. 5th St.

Mast Books

Opened in 2010, Mast Books has found a niche in the New York literary and arts scene by curating rare and out-of-print titles from around the world.

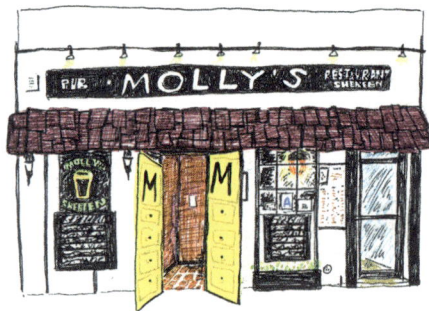

287 3rd Ave.

between E. 22nd and 23rd Sts.

Molly's Pub and Restaurant Shebeen

With its sawdust-covered floors, log-burning fireplace, and mahogany bar, this Gramercy pub—which has been slinging beers, burgers, and shepherd's pies since 1960—dubs itself the "most authentic Irish bar in New York City."

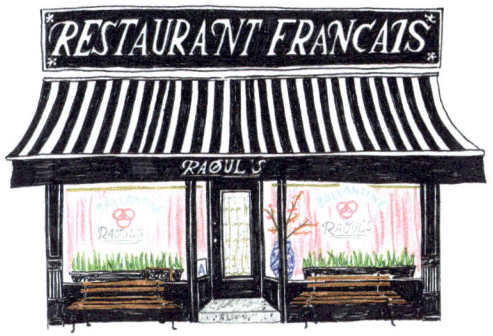

180 Prince St.
between Thompson and Sullivan Sts.

Raoul's

Open since 1975, when it was founded by two brothers from Alsace, France, this SoHo bistro served for many years as an unofficial after-hours spot for several cast members of *Saturday Night Live*, including John Belushi and Dan Aykroyd.

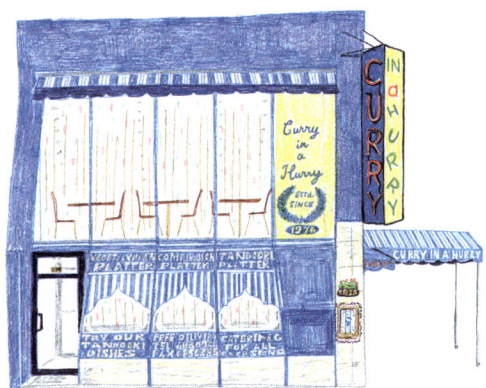

119 Lexington Ave.
at E. 28th St.

Curry in a Hurry

This Kip's Bay restaurant has been serving up "modern interpretations" of classic Indian dishes since 1976.

160 1st Ave.
between E. 9th and 10th Sts.

Gizmo

Broken sewing machine? For thirty-two years Gizmo was the place to go. It also boasted an extensive selection of "trims and notions" for sewing projects. Sadly, rising rents forced it to close in early 2024, though the couple behind the shop continue to search for a new location.

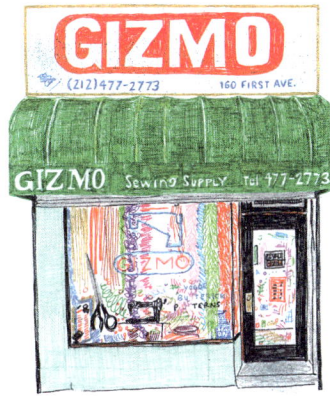

146 2nd Ave.
at E. 9th St.

Village Farm Grocery

Actor Sam Rockwell, a longtime East Village resident, told the *New York Post* in 2013 that this twenty-four-hour, family-run grocery has "everything you need," like "Yorkshire tea and all these candies from London." They also sell their own juices, including spicy carrot.

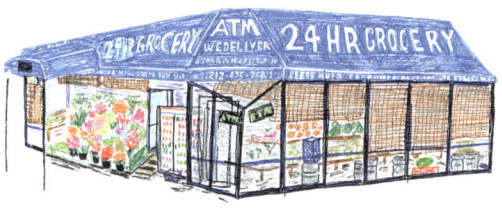

Kitchen Arts & Letters

This Upper East Side shop has over twelve thousand books on cooking, food history, and more in stock from all over the world. Opened in 1983, it has counted food legends such as James Beard, Julia Child, and Laurie Colwin among its regulars. Nach Waxman, who founded the store and was its main proprietor until his death in August 2021, worked to ensure that Kitchen Arts & Letters be known for much more than books of recipes—a reputation he earned handily. A 1995 profile in the *New York Times* referred to him as the "most sought-after expert on food history and publishing in New York."

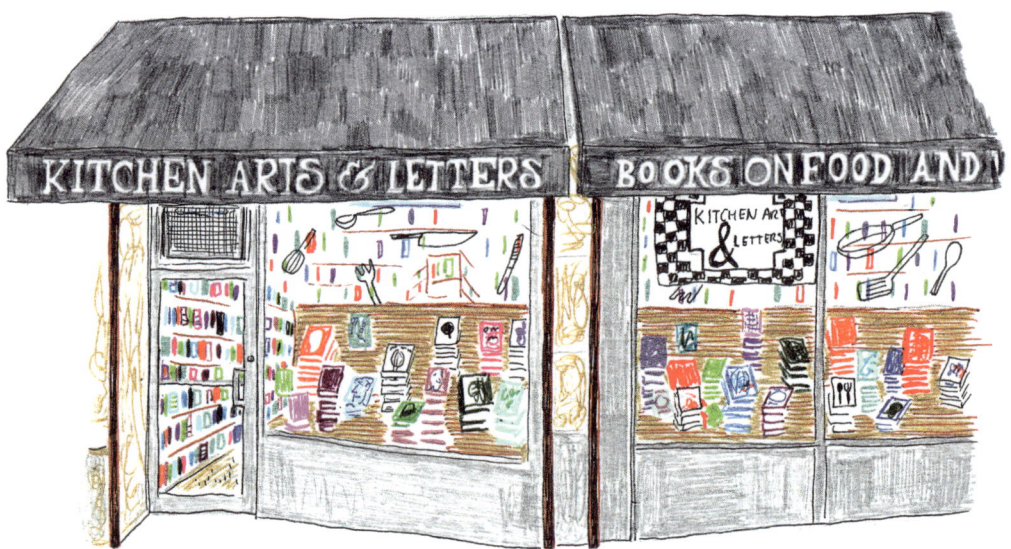

Lexington Candy Shop

As co-owner John Philis told CBS News, this historic Upper East Side spot is the "last surviving original luncheonette" in all of New York City. The restaurant retains many of its features from when it first opened in 1925, including an old-school soda fountain, vintage mixers, and padded barstools. Despite its name, Lexington Candy Shop doesn't sell much candy these days. But if you're in the mood for a chocolate milkshake, or maybe a trip through a time machine, this is the spot.

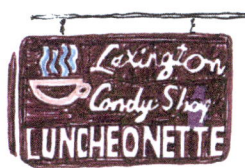

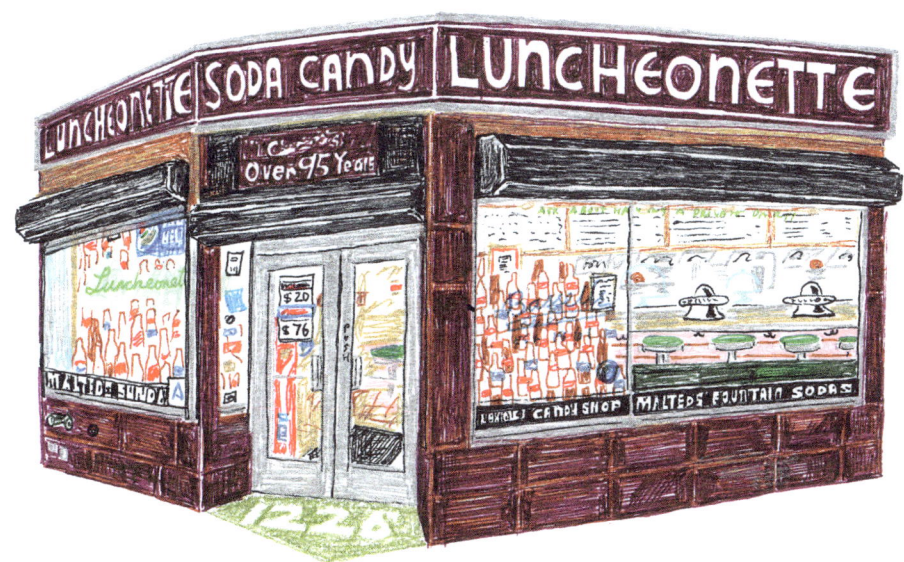

169 W. 4th St.

between 6th Ave. and Barrow St.

Music Inn

Established in 1958, this West Village music store is one of the city's oldest continually running shops of its kind, selling instruments, records, and more. In fact, it's one of the *only* places around where you can still conceivably find a balalaika, koto, zarb, or any number of other world instruments you've likely never heard of, many of which hang theatrically from the store's ceiling.

Music Inn is something of a time capsule of mid-century bohemia in the neighborhood—so much so that when the makers of *The Marvelous Mrs. Maisel* (a TV show set in New York in the late 1950s and early '60s) filmed an episode here, they didn't need to change a thing about the interior.

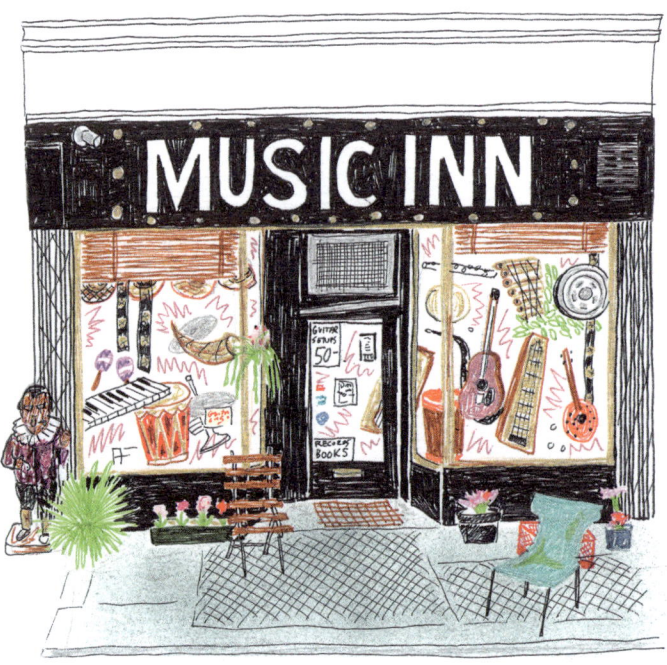

Three Lives & Company

This tiny West Village bookshop seems to have many more lives than just three. While hundreds of similar bookstores have shuttered their doors over the past several decades, Three Lives & Company has been going strong since 1978. According to its website, the independently owned shop attributes this longevity to its "living room" vibe: customers often linger for hours to discuss their last favorite read (and maybe just a bit of neighborhood gossip) with staff and fellow patrons long after their purchase has been made.

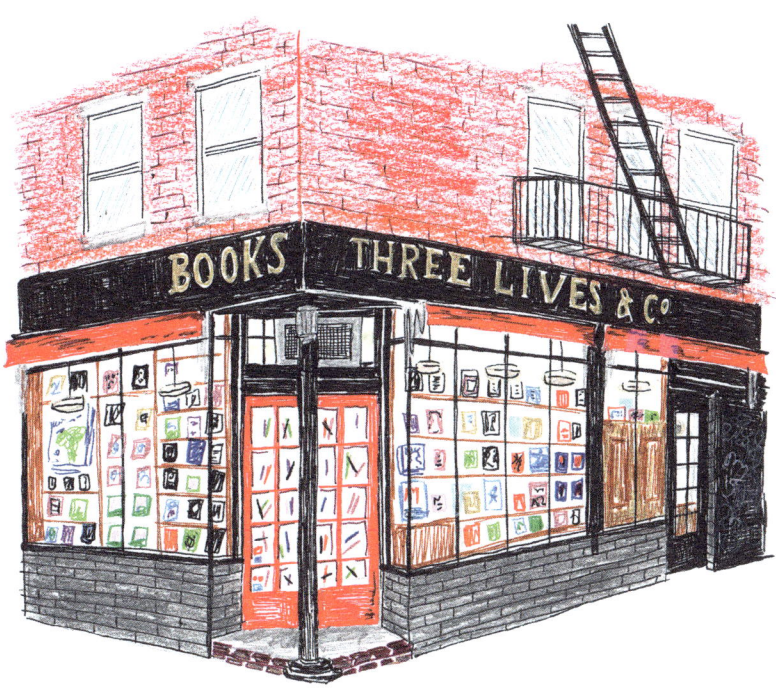

Punjabi Grocery & Deli

Kulwinder Singh, who immigrated to New York from eastern Pakistan in 1981, took over this South Asian deli in 1994 (it had opened a year earlier). Before managing the store, Kulwinder worked as a taxi driver. Understanding how challenging the job can be, he decided to make the space welcoming for others earning their living behind the wheel.

He offered his deli— and importantly, he says, his bathroom—for drivers to relax for a bit between rides or shifts, at any hour of the day or night.

Punjabi Grocery & Deli has become an East Village icon but has suffered some close calls in its recent past. Most notably, in 2010 a long-term development project in the area caused business to suffer to the point where Kulwinder began to struggle to pay the rent. Two neighborhood regulars, Ali Najmi and Himanshu Suri (of alt-rap group Das Racist) lobbied the city to install a "taxi relief stand" nearby, where drivers could park and easily access the store. The successful effort was the subject of a TriBeCa Film Festival short, *#SavePunjabiDeli*.

Many longtime customers are unaware of the deli's star turn on the big screen, knowing it instead as the place to get some of the best (and cheapest) South Asian food around. The samosas, in particular, tend to be a crowd-pleaser.

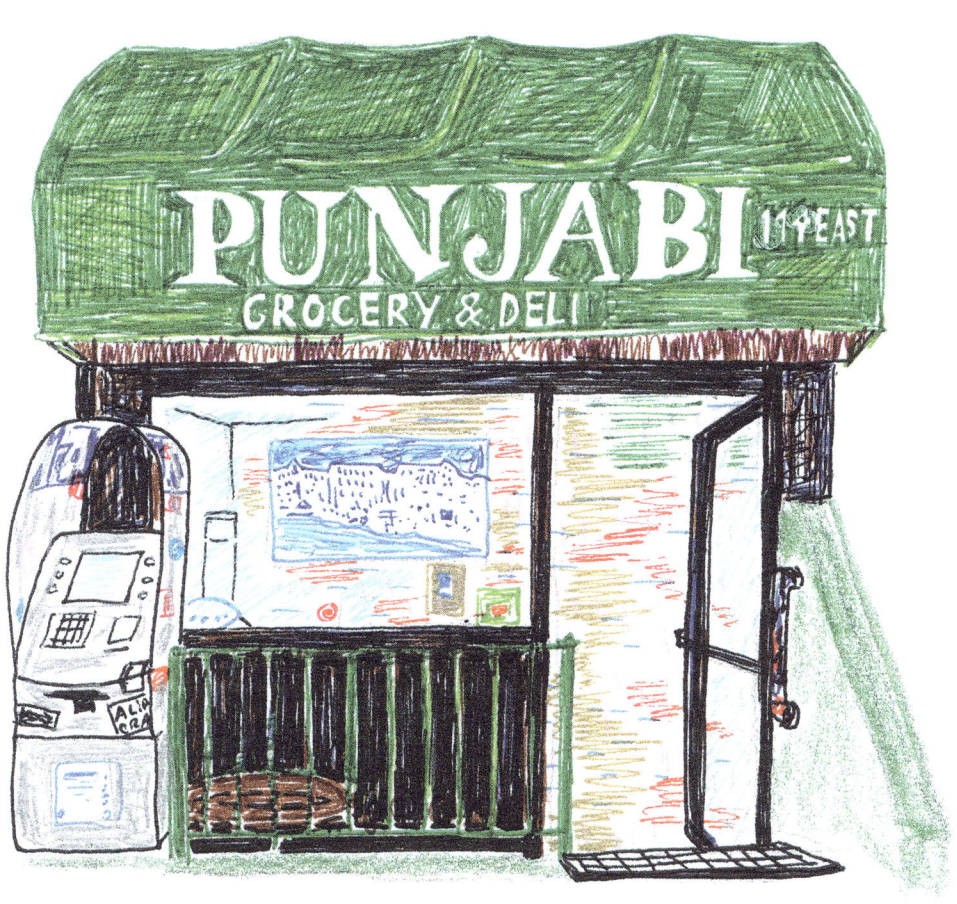

World Hats

———

Opened in 2003, this tiny shop sells an impressive variety of men's hats, with styles (as you might have guessed from the name) from all around the world, including straw hats, fedoras, and newsboy caps. Don't have any idea how to pick one out? The staff will be happy to help you select the perfect piece to cover your noggin—that is, as long as it isn't filled to the brim with customers looking to do the same.

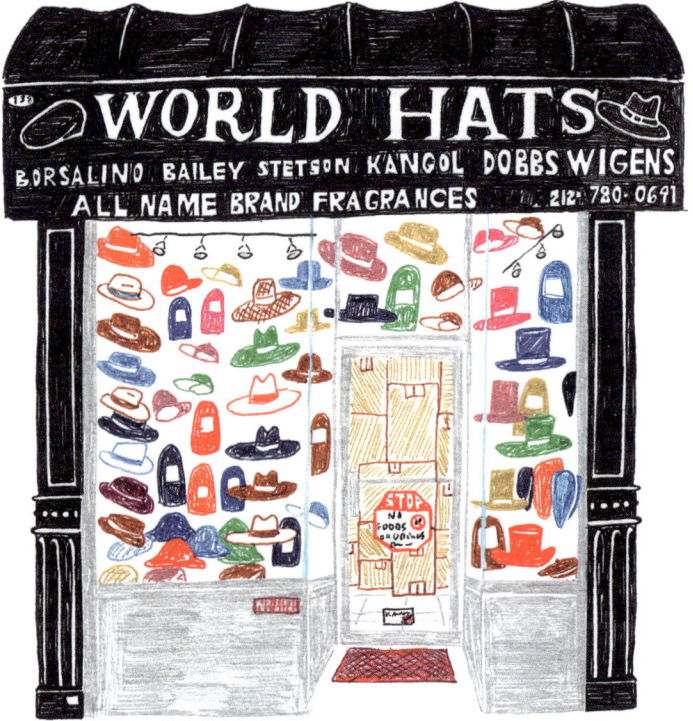

Bill's Place

Saxophonist Bill Saxton and his wife, Theda Palmer Saxton, have owned and operated this iconic Harlem jazz club since 2006. Bill, known as Harlem's Jazz King, learned to play the saxophone during an eighteen-month stay in Auburn State Prison. As he told the *New York Times* in 2014, by the time he got out, "Any song I heard, I could play." The building that houses Bill's Place has a storied past in the jazz world. It opened during Prohibition as a speakeasy. (In fact, the club's website maintains that it's the "only authentic" speakeasy still operating in Harlem.) Over the decades, jazz and blues legends like Fats Waller, Duke Ellington, and Gladys Bentley all graced its stage. And it was here that producer John Hammond first heard a seventeen-year-old Billie Holiday sing.

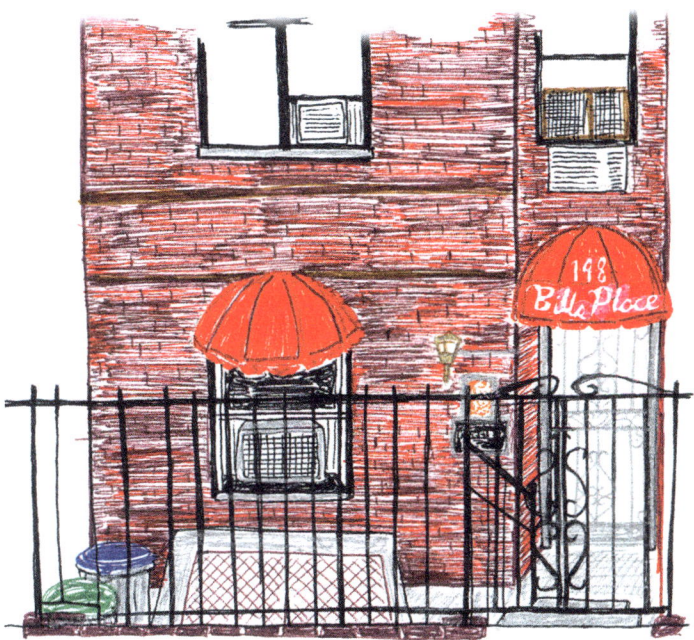

Veselka

Veselka, which means "rainbow" in Ukrainian, opened its doors in 1954. Founded by Wolodymyr and Olha Darmochwal, refugees of World War II, the space originally operated as a newsstand. Several years later, the business expanded into the restaurant next door, where it began to sell many of the Slavic specialties it's known for today, like borsch, kielbasa, and pierogi.

Now boasting a location in Williamsburg and an outpost in Grand Central, Veselka has endured thanks to its quality food and loyal customers—but the owners also admit they've had their fair share of luck over the years. In 1967, following the launch of the New York State Lottery, Veselka became one of the first places in the city to sell scratch-off tickets. People traveled from far and wide for their chance to get rich quick (and maybe have a pierogi or two). The eatery also enjoys below-market rent thanks to its landlord, the Plast Foundation, a nonprofit committed to preserving the neighborhood's Eastern European roots.

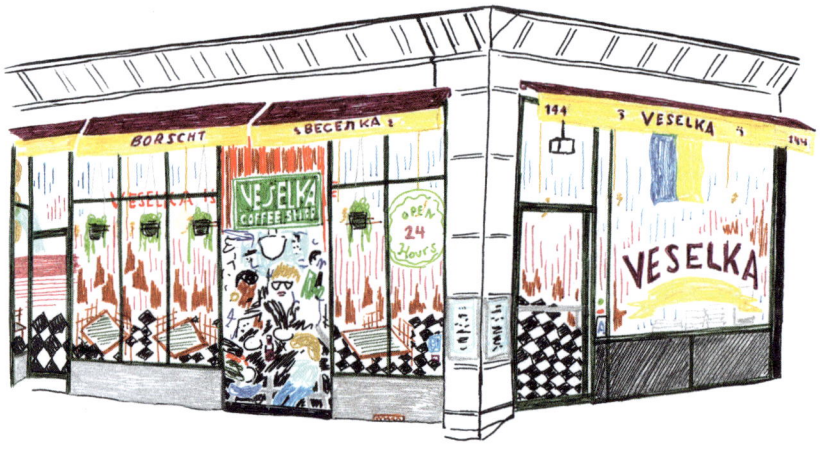

206 W. 118th St.
between Adam Clayton Powell Jr. Blvd.
and St. Nicholas Ave.

Minton's Playhouse

Known as the "birthplace of bebop," Minton's Playhouse has featured Charlie Parker, Dizzy Gillespie, and many other jazz greats who helped pioneer the genre. In 1938 saxophonist Henry Minton founded the club on the first floor of Harlem's Cecil Hotel. A 1974 fire, however, prompted a three-decade hiatus, and the venue wouldn't reopen until 2006.

Unlike many other legendary jazz spots in the city, this one is also well known for its grub. This is partly thanks to Henry's offer of free soul food for hungry musicians—the catch being that they needed to keep up with the experimental sounds of the house band, anchored by none other than Thelonious Monk and Kenny Clarke.

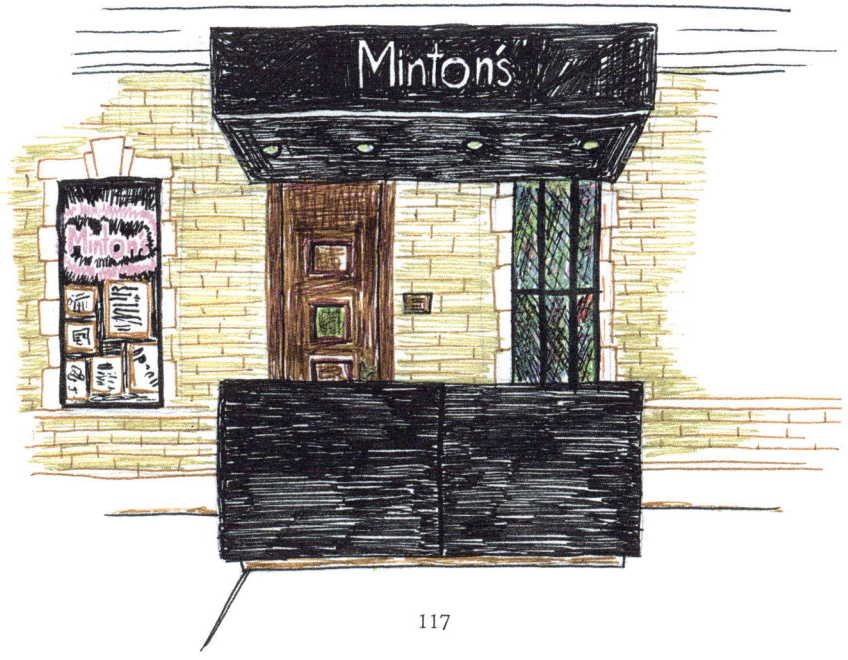

181 Grand St.
between Baxter and Mulberry Sts.

Baz Bagel

———

Mel Ottenberg, who was named *Interview* magazine's editor in chief in August 2021, told the *New York Times* that he was equally as proud of that professional accomplishment as he was of having a bagel named after him at this SoHo bakery. But Mel's namesake, a turkey Reuben on a pumpernickel everything bagel, may be among the more traditional items on the menu. The shop, which opened in 2015, is perhaps best known for its "tie-dye" bagels, with custom colors of your choosing: serve up some white-and-blue striped bagels at your next Hanukkah celebration, or rainbow swirls for Pride.

Baz offers more than just colorful gimmicks, though: it's among a dwindling number of bakeries in the city to roll its bagels by hand, an art form increasingly replaced by machines.

Aficionados say there's no substitute for the hand-rolled technique, which is why the shop continues to sit at the top of many "best of" lists. That they can make bagels in the colors of your favorite sports team probably doesn't hurt either.

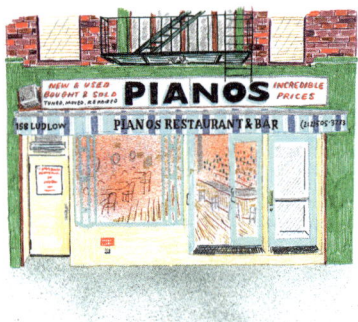

158 Ludlow St.
between Rivington and Stanton Sts.

Pianos

———

Despite what the sign outside may say, this space hasn't been in the piano-peddling business for decades. But in homage to the Lower East Side of yore, the beloved bar and performance venue, which opened in 2002, kept the name and sign of its previous owners.

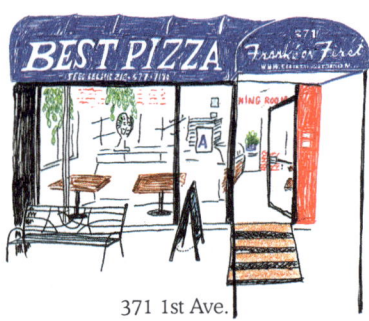

371 1st Ave.
between E. 21st and 22nd Sts.

Frank's Trattoria

———

With a semisecret red-and-white table-cloth spot in the back, this pizza parlor, open since 1980, is a go-to place in Gramercy for a quick slice or a sit-down meal from its full-blown Italian menu (featuring everything from eggplant parmigiana to baked ziti), topped off with a bottle of wine.

28 Bowery
at Bayard St.

Great N.Y. Noodletown

———

This Chinatown spot is a popular choice among the after-hours crowd. But its bare-bones dining room is often packed at all hours of the day with locals slurping wonton soup or chomping on roasted or barbecued meats, the shop's specialty.

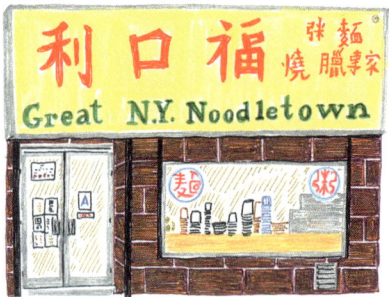

194 Bleecker St. #1
between MacDougal St. and 6th Ave.

Artful Posters

———

This family-run store has been selling vintage prints, collectible postcards, and original movie posters since 1987. They'll also custom-frame any treasure you happen to find.

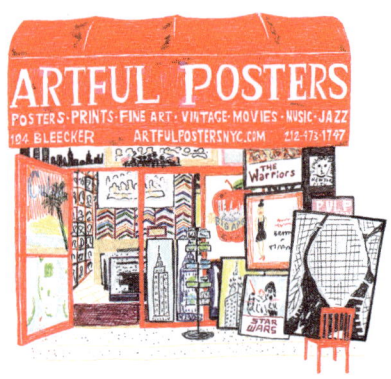

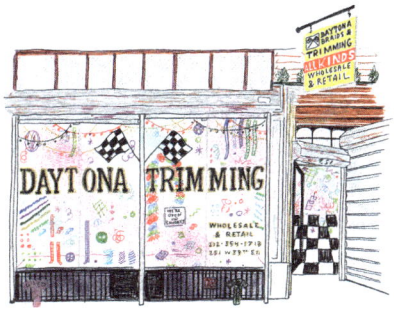

251 W. 39th St.
between 7th and 8th Aves.

Daytona Trimmings

This family-owned sewing-supply store may be small, but it's bursting at the seams with braids, buttons, threads, and anything else that could conceivably be considered "trimmings." For years, the owner's friendly orange tabby cats, Ric and Rac, served as mascots, following customers around and helpfully batting at ribbons or lace to consider.

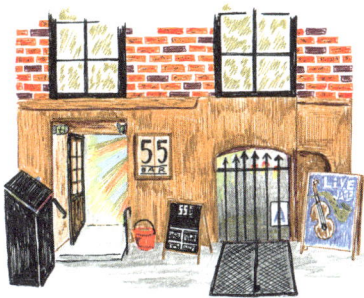

55 Christopher St.
between Waverly Pl. and 7th Ave. S.

55 Bar

Over the years this space hosted jazz and blues ingenues and legends alike. In May 2022 it closed permanently, but not before one final jam session attended by over a hundred local musicians who came to pay their respects—and play the bar's last tunes.

30 Irving Pl.
between E. 15th and 16th Sts.

John's Shoe Repair

Devotees of this shoe-repair shop trust John and his employees with mending beloved pairs of boots, bags, and everything in between. "Beautiful work," gushed one online reviewer, "on my precious Prada stilettos."

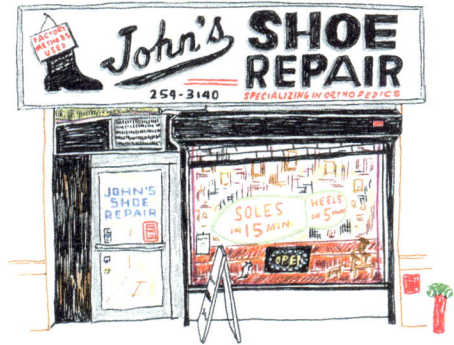

59 2nd Ave.
between E. 3rd and 4th Sts.

Allied Hardware

Located in the East Village, this family-run hardware store went out of business in 2015—but its rainbow-hued sign lives on somewhere in the world, sold to an admirer for a hundred dollars.

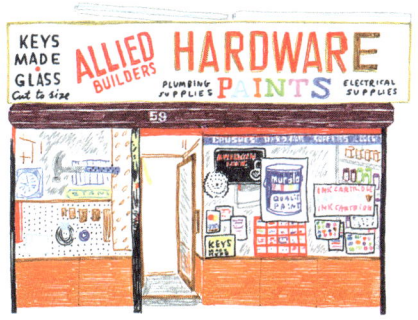

JJ Hat Center

———

The early twentieth century's version of today's "keys, wallet, phone" refrain when leaving the house would have definitely included this indispensable item: a hat. So ubiquitous were they in New York that, when JJ Hat Center first opened its doors in 1911 (then called Young's), it was one of forty-eight such stores in the city. Today it's the only one from the time still standing.

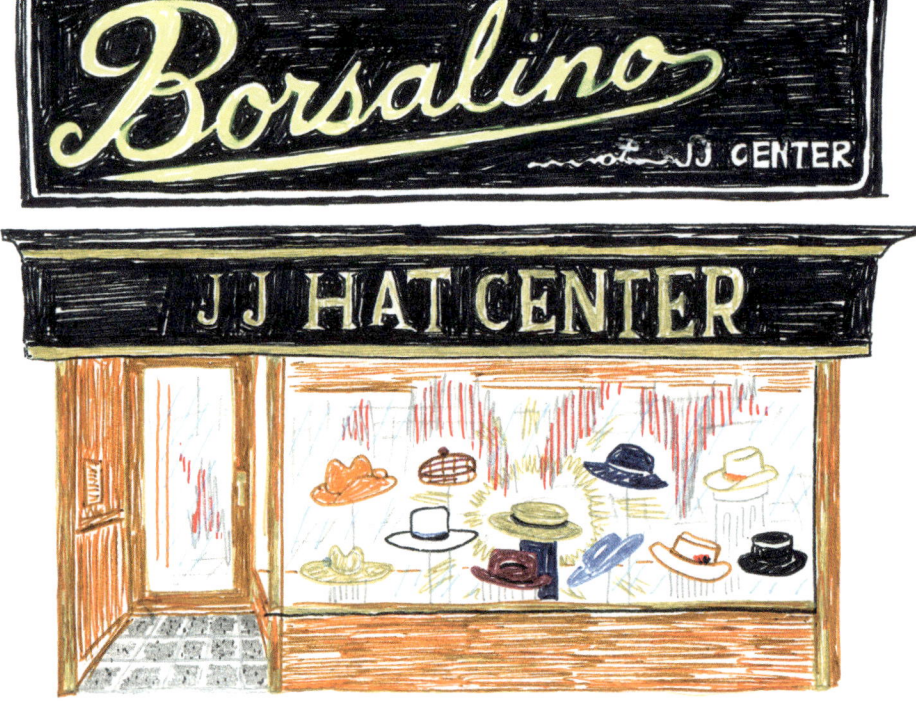

Economy Candy

When Economy Candy first opened in 1937, it was nothing more than a pushcart outside of a shoe and hat repair shop. Today the candy store stands out for its extensive menu of over two thousand items. Some are the same products you can get at a corner bodega, but you very likely haven't seen a lot of the sweets on the shelf here since you were a kid, like Bazooka bubble gum, wax lips, and butterscotch hard candy. Even if you lack a sweet tooth, a visit is worth it alone for the trip down memory lane. In 2023 a second location opened at Chelsea Market.

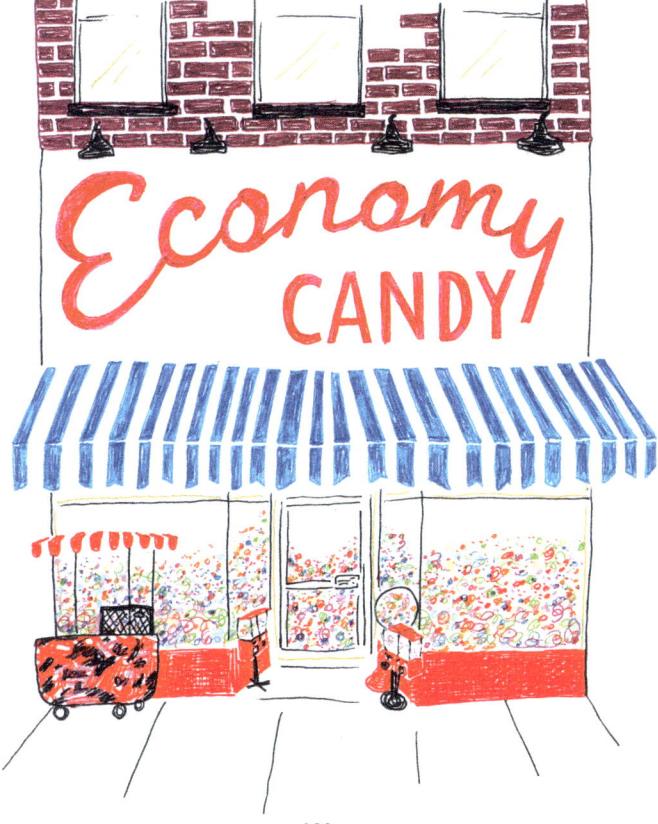

40 Hester St.
between Essex and Ludlow Sts.

Joy's Flower Pot

Thanks to the scent of roses, orchids, and other exotic plants wafting from Joy's Flower Pot, you may smell this Chinatown flower shop well before you see it. Even after many predicted its demise after the trendy L.A.-based Cactus Store opened a branch nearby on Essex Street in 2017 (which has since closed), Joy's still thrives, thanks in part to an impressive selection of succulents and exotic plants that keep green-thumbed enthusiasts loyal.

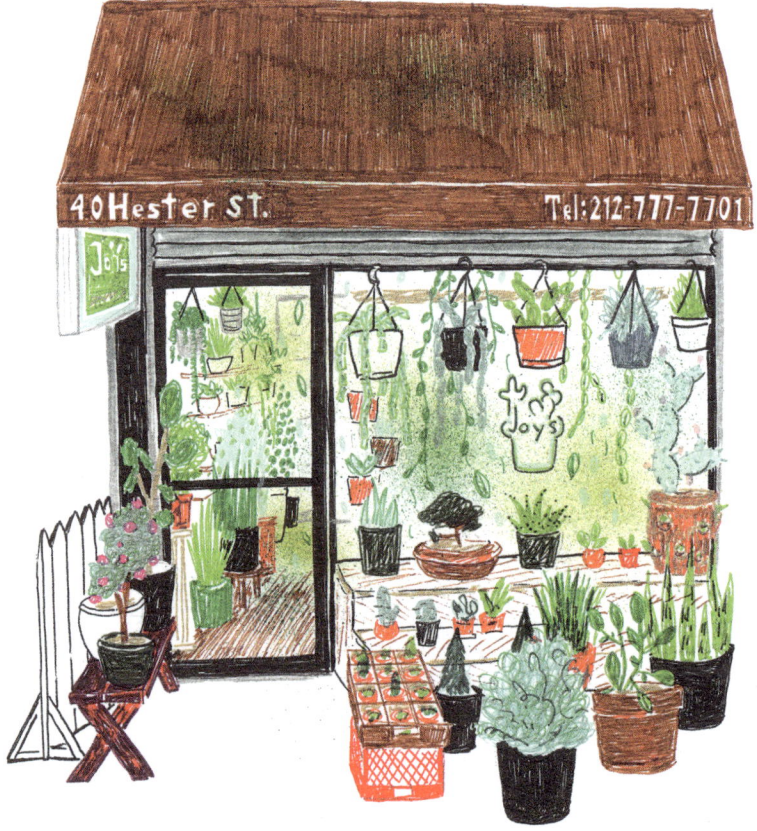

215 Ave. A
between E. 13th and 14th Sts.

Zaragoza

This tiny, unassuming East Village deli, opened in 2000,
is widely considered to cook up some of the best
Pueblan-style Mexican food in the entire city. It's
also one of the only places in the area where you can
get a Mexican Coke, the good stuff that comes in a
bottle and uses sugarcane as its sweetener instead
of high-fructose corn syrup. For those in the know,
Zaragoza also makes for a welcome late-night-snack
alternative to the neighborhood's many pizza joints.

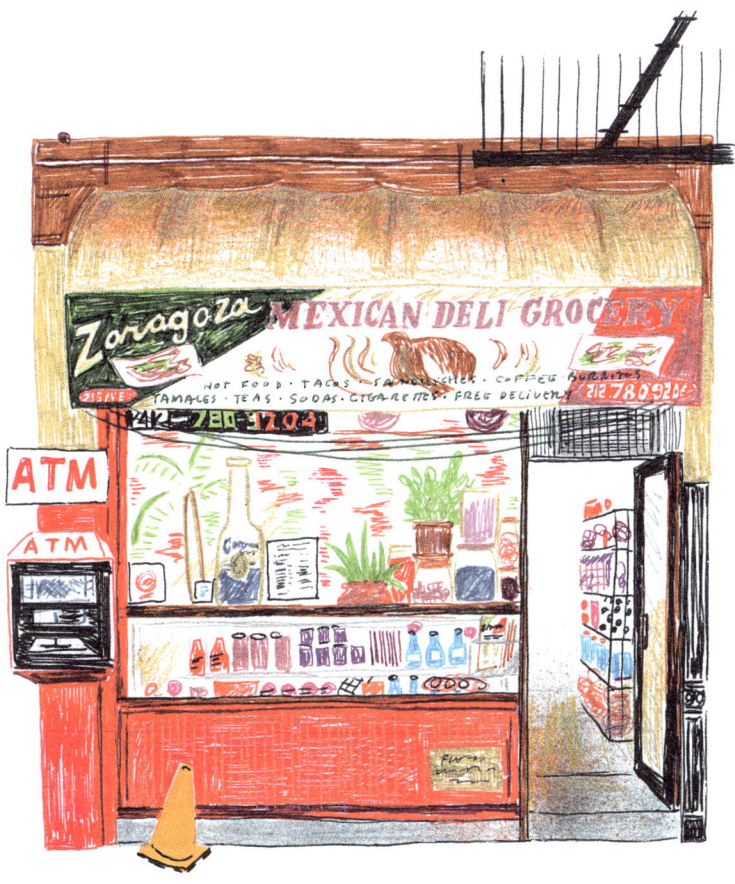

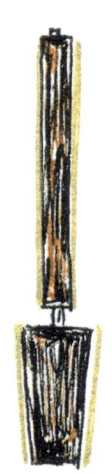
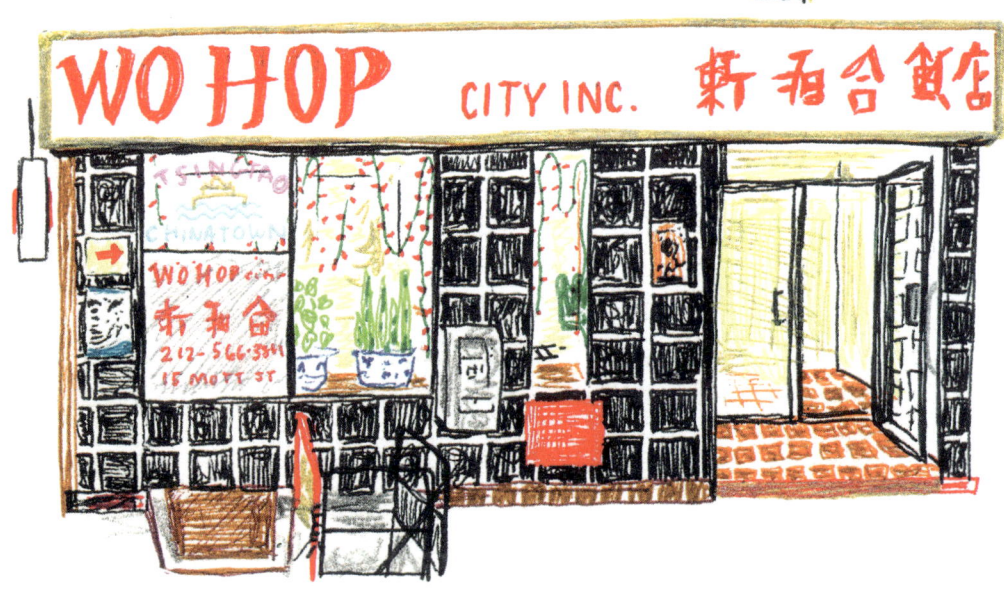

15–17 Mott St.
between Worth and Mosco Sts.

Wo Hop

––––––

Opened in 1938, this Mott Street institution is the second-oldest still-operating restaurant in Chinatown (the oldest being Nom Wah Tea Parlor [see page 13], which opened in 1920). Its Cantonese menu has been unapologetically influenced by the American palate over the years.

In Chinatown there is an ongoing debate as to where you'll find better food: upstairs or downstairs—but they're actually separate restaurants.

"Upstairs," located at 15 Mott and illustrated here, opened decades after the restaurant at 17 Mott and officially called itself Wo Hop City before its owners changed the name to Wo Hop Next Door. In the "downstairs" space (17 Mott), you'll find an older-school Chinatown scene, with dim lights, low ceilings, and blue-jacketed waiters. Devotees of downstairs claim "upstairs," which is actually on street level, is for tourists—but fans of 15 Mott say it has a lighter, livelier vibe.

231 E. 14th St.
between 3rd and 2nd Aves.

Beauty Bar

———

Part bar, part performance venue, Beauty Bar has been open in the East Village since 1995. As its name implies—and the decoration makes clear—this spot pays homage to the beauty parlors of yore, including the one that used to operate in this same space for many years. Owner Deb Parker kept many of the remnants from the former business intact, from the black-and-white checkered floors to the antique bonnet dryers. But the decor isn't just all for show: you can get a legit manicure here, with a cocktail thrown in for good measure.

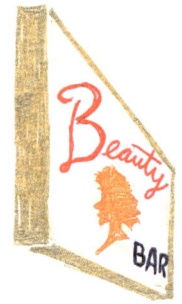

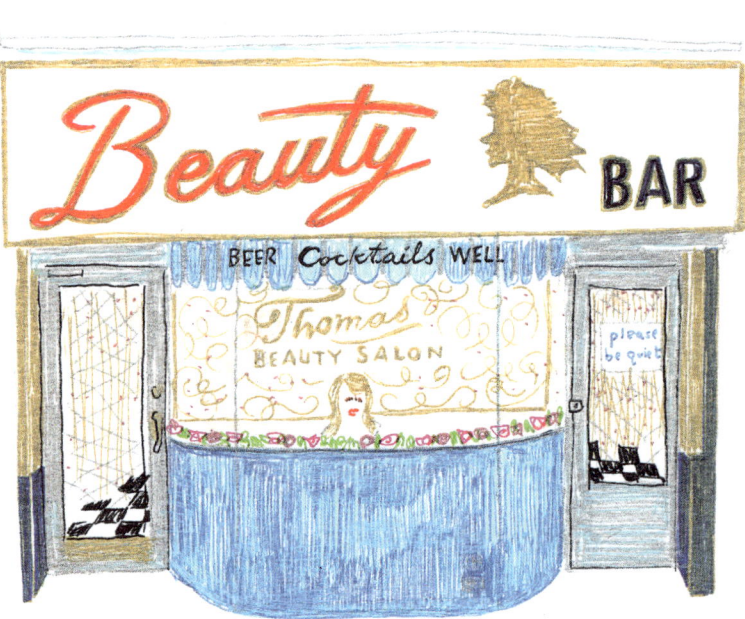

Hop Kee

———

This popular Chinatown spot has been serving up Cantonese food since 1968 in the same basement location. Peter Lee, who immigrated to New York from Hong Kong with his family at the age of two, took over ownership of the restaurant from his father but has left the menu more or less the same. The biggest change he's made is adding a few new items that he says cater to a younger crowd, like Peking pork chops and pan-fried noodles. "People are not as into the old-style chow mein anymore," he told the food blogger Hangry Alice.

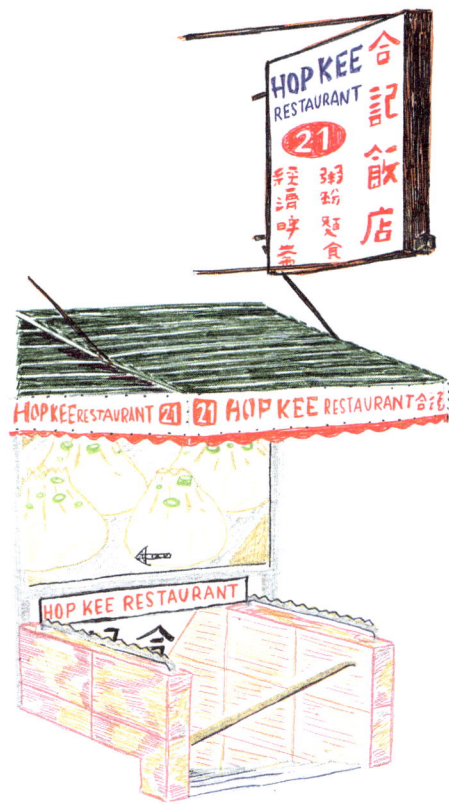

48 Spring St.
at Mulberry St.

Spring Lounge

———

This SoHo spot has been around since the 1920s, when it operated (illegally) as a place to grab a bucket of beer on the go. In the 1960s the bar changed its name to Wilson's 10:30, after the starting time of the (also illegal) evening craps games that operated in the basement. Spring Lounge took on its current name in the 1970s, but it is known informally by the many regulars of this classic, beloved beer pub as the Shark Bar—not for anything illegal (that we know of), but for the number of stuffed sharks displayed throughout the space.

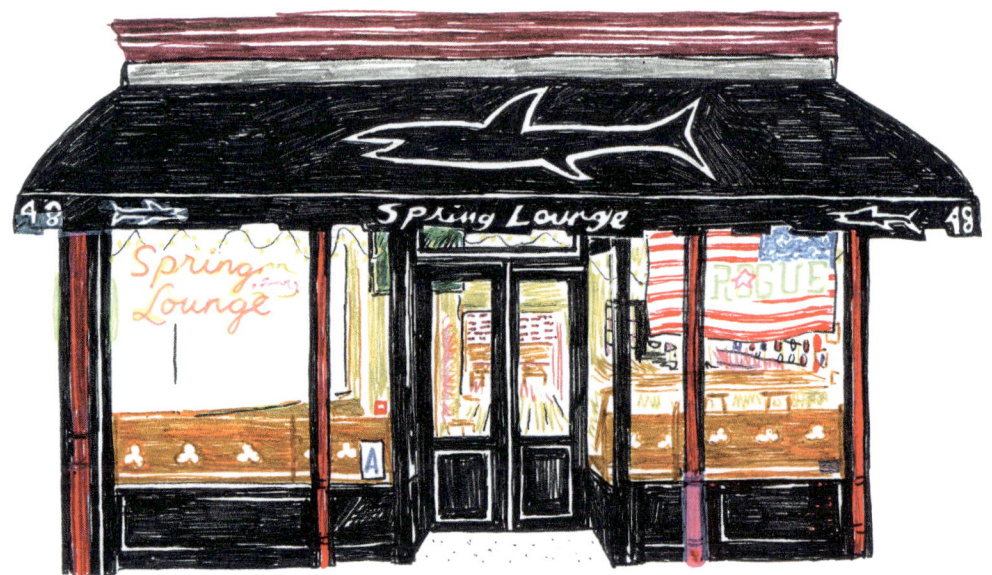

Stonewall Inn

The original Stonewall Inn, established in 1930 around the corner from its current location, operated as a speakeasy during Prohibition, and (in a premonition of things to come, perhaps) was routinely raided by the police. The bar moved to 53 Christopher Street in 1934, where it also served food, until it was destroyed by a fire in 1964. A couple years later, in 1966, members of the Mafia bought the space and began running it as a gay bar; a side hustle involved blackmailing regulars and demanding payment for "protection." Though plenty of examples of queer activism predate the 1969 riots that took place here— spurred on by regular police raids—the Stonewall Inn is now synonymous with the modern movement for LGBTQ equality and liberation, not just in the United States but across the globe.

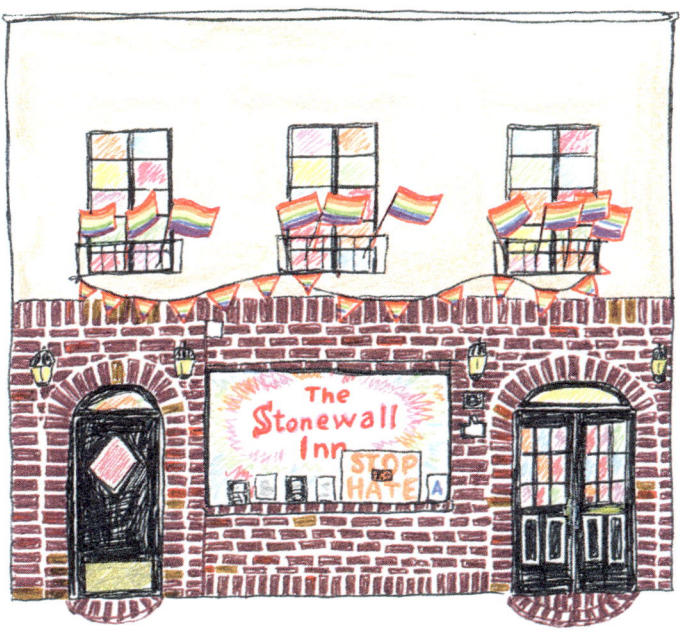

K. K. Discount Store

Affectionately known by locals as the "mom-and-pop Target," this kitchen-supply store has over one thousand items for sale.

Whatever it is you're looking for, you'll find it here (along with plenty of things you didn't even know you needed, like a handwoven bamboo strainer or a cast-iron Japanese teapot).

Owners Mr. and Mrs. Li first immigrated to the United States in 1978 with just a few dollars in their pockets and a dream to open their own store. For years, the couple worked twelve- to fifteen-hour days to save up enough money, managing to start the business in 1990. "As cliché as it may sound, we truly wanted to do what we can to give our children the education and opportunities we did not have ourselves," Mrs. Li told Welcome to Chinatown, a local community organization.

To stay afloat and compete with the likes of giant digital retailers, K. K. Discount Store has an extensive online operation of its own, selling everything you can expect to see in the store along with some of its more obscure goodies—from an "Espaceler Ironwood Chopsticks Pack" to a "Fortune Lucky Cat Maneki Neko Children Utensil Set."

Thanks to their earnings, the Lis were able to put both of their children through college. Nowadays, their rambunctious young granddaughter often sits in the store with them and has become such a staple that she has her own Instagram account, @littlemisschinatown. "I help my grandparents sell soap,"the bio long read.

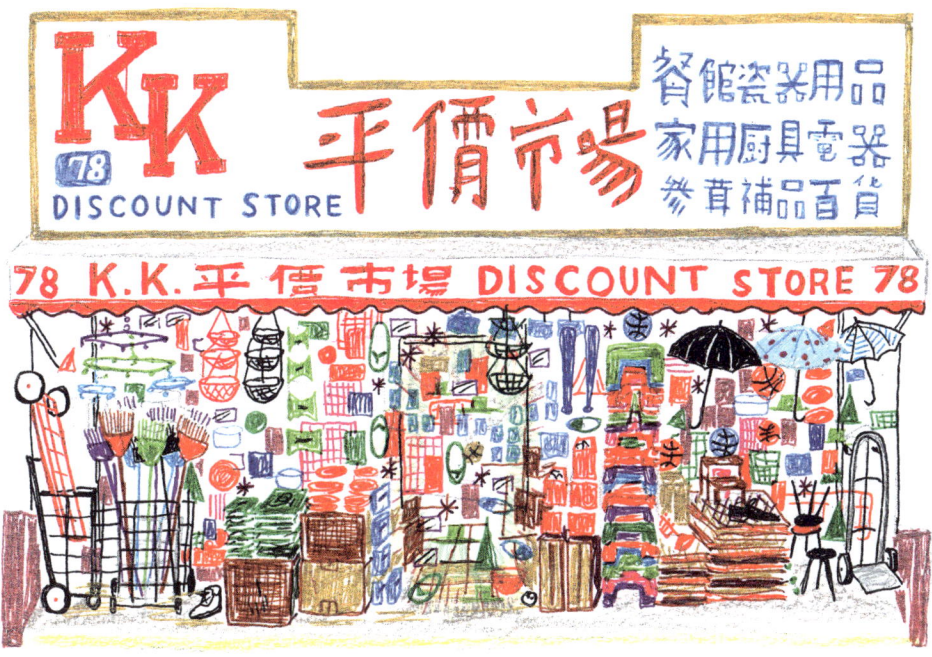

106 Mosco St.
between Mulberry and Mott Sts.

Fried Dumpling

Spend just a few dollars at this spot, offering both frozen and cooked dumplings to-go, and you can turn your own kitchen into a mini pot-sticker factory.

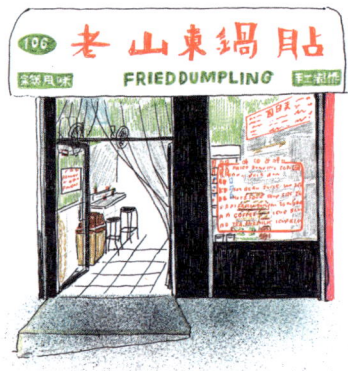

385 6th Ave.
at Waverly Pl.

Waverly Diner

A trademark green-and-red neon sign welcomes this old-school West Village diner's patrons—which have included many actors over the years, as evidenced by the dozens of headshots inside.

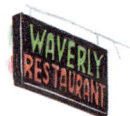

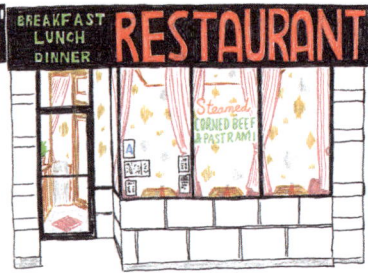

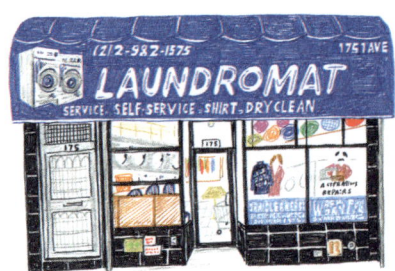

175 1st Ave.
between E. 10th and 11th Sts.

Quick Coin Laundromat

Its name may reference its coin-operated machines, but locals that favor wash-and-fold service can call ahead to have their laundry picked up too.

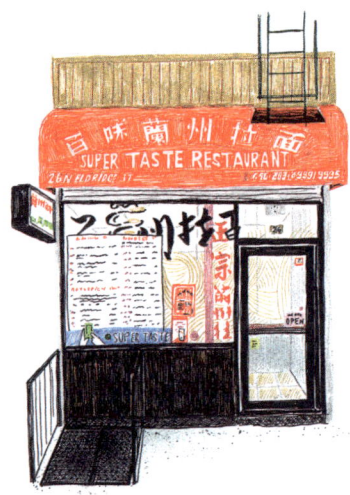

26 Eldridge St.
between Division and Canal Sts.

Super Taste

Hand-pulled, Lanzhou-style noodle shop Super Taste may be tiny, but it offers some of the most popular bowls of noodle soup in Chinatown, for a price that's hard to beat. The beef in hot-and-spicy soup, in particular, is a hit.

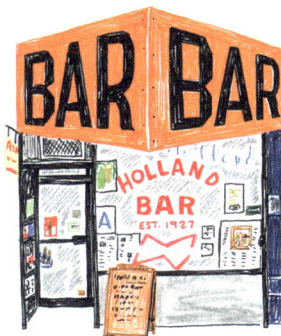

532 9th Ave.
between W. 39th and 40th Sts.

Holland Bar

From 1987 to 2022 this dive bar doled out drinks to Hell's Kitchen revelers. (A sign painted on the window proclaimed it was established in 1927, but even its last owner, Gary Kelly, didn't believe it had been around that long.)

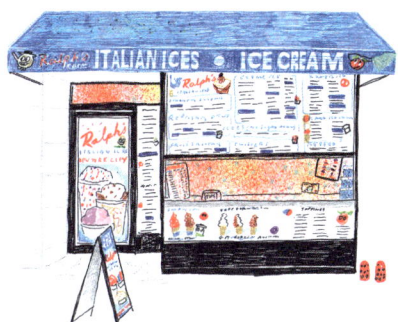

370 2nd Ave.
between E. 21st and 22nd Sts.

Ralph's Famous Italian Ices

This ice cream franchise got its start in Staten Island in 1928. Now it offers its more than one hundred flavors at over eighty locations throughout the New York City area, including this spot in Gramercy.

57 Grove St.
between Bleecker St. and 7th Ave. S.

Arthur's Tavern

This West Village institution opened its doors in 1937. It earned the nickname "Home of the Bird" because saxophonist Charlie Parker regularly performed here. Trumpeter Roy Hargrove was known to play a hard bop at Arthur's too.

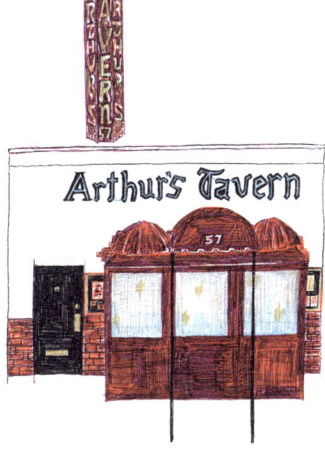

79 Baxter St. A
between Bayard and Walker Sts.

Whiskey Tavern

Whiskey isn't top of mind when most people think about Chinatown, except for fans of this tavern, which offers forty different types of the spirit (along with a shot of pickle juice, if that's your thing).

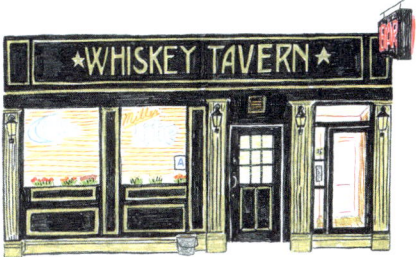

Sammy's Roumanian

In 1975 the steakhouse Sammy's Roumanian first opened its doors in a basement-level space on Chrystie Street. Though the original location—illustrated here—closed in January 2021, owner David Zimmerman was determined to keep the party going. He reopened in 2024 on Stanton Street, where he continues to offer crowds garlicky cuts of meat and a boisterous atmosphere. The lively mood at Sammy's may well be aided in large part by the spot's famous drink, "vodka in ice": literally a bottle of vodka served to customers encased in a block of ice. The restaurant has been described by food writers as everything from a "vodka-fueled party spot" to a "Jewish disco."

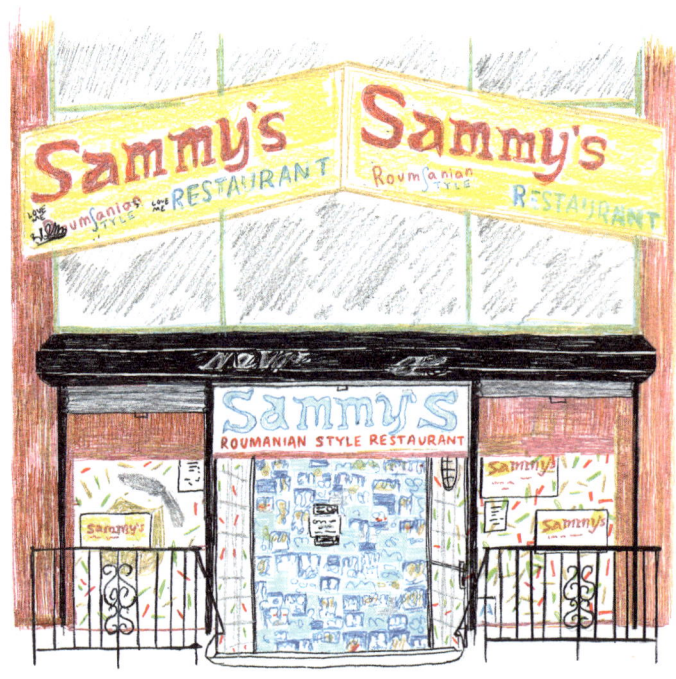

Manero's Pizza

———

The owners of Regina's Grocery (see page 15) waded into the competitive world of Little Italy pizzerias by opening this small shop in 2019. Manero's advantage, however, as proudly proclaimed on its website, is that it is the only spot on Mulberry Street to grab a single slice, made in what owner Roman Grandinetti calls a "hybrid" of Neapolitan and New York styles. Though Manhattan's pizza aficionados are often merciless to newcomers, Manero's has managed to make a quick name for itself, so much so that it expanded its operations from a to-go spot to a full-blown restaurant in spring 2022.

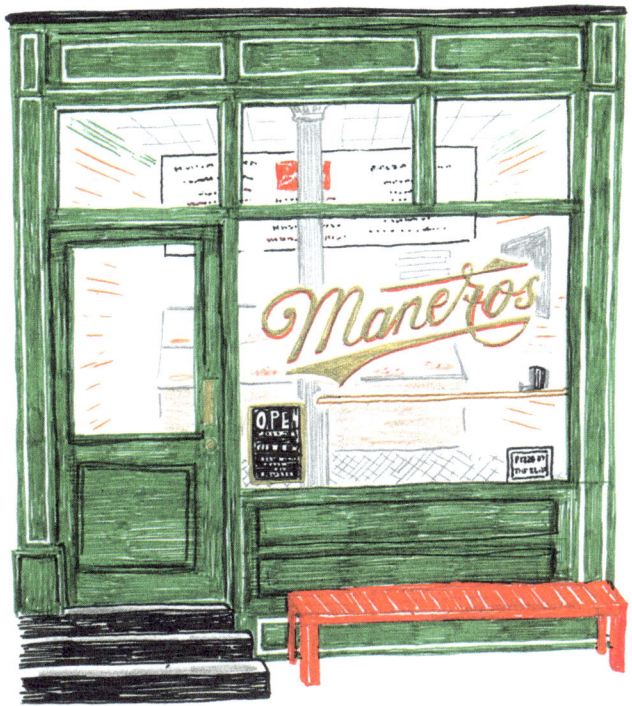

Bedford Cheese Shop

Looking to impress with a charcuterie board chockablock with wheels of hard-to-find cheeses whose names are just as hard to pronounce? The Bedford Cheese Shop, operating since 2012, will be happy to oblige. (The original, in Williamsburg, Brooklyn, opened almost a decade earlier but has since closed.) Not only will you find over one hundred fifty different types of cheese from over twenty countries here, but you can also enroll in cheese school and learn all about them from the shop's knowledgeable cheesemongers.

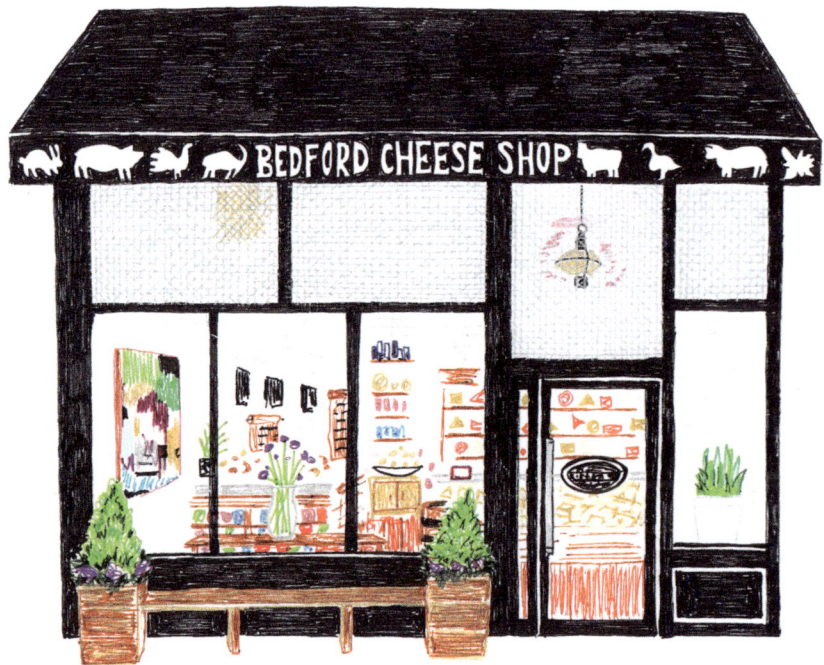

Porto Rico Importing Co.

————

Simply walking by this coffee shop on St. Marks Place (one of three operated by the Porto Rico Importing Co.) may be enough to get a decent caffeine buzz going: you'll be able to smell the aroma wafting from massive bags filled with high-quality coffee and espresso beans from halfway down the street.

Despite its name, the store sells coffee sourced from all over the world: one hundred thirty different varieties, in fact, from twenty-eight countries. (They sell tea leaves, too, if you're into that sort of thing.) The odd spelling is something of a mystery, but current owner Peter Longo suspects it was because Puerto Rican coffee was all the rage back in the early 1900s. And the shop's founder, an Italian immigrant named Patsy Albanese, used the name of the island in his native tongue.

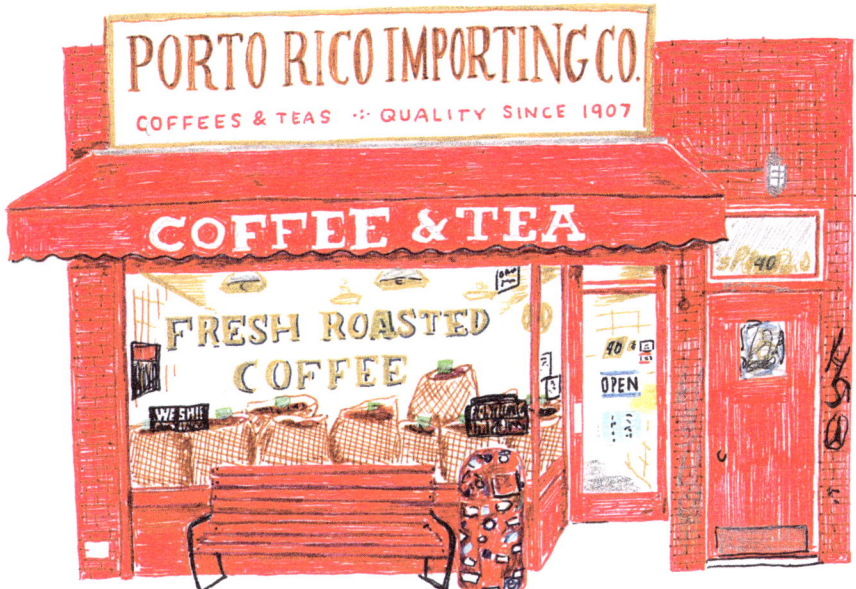

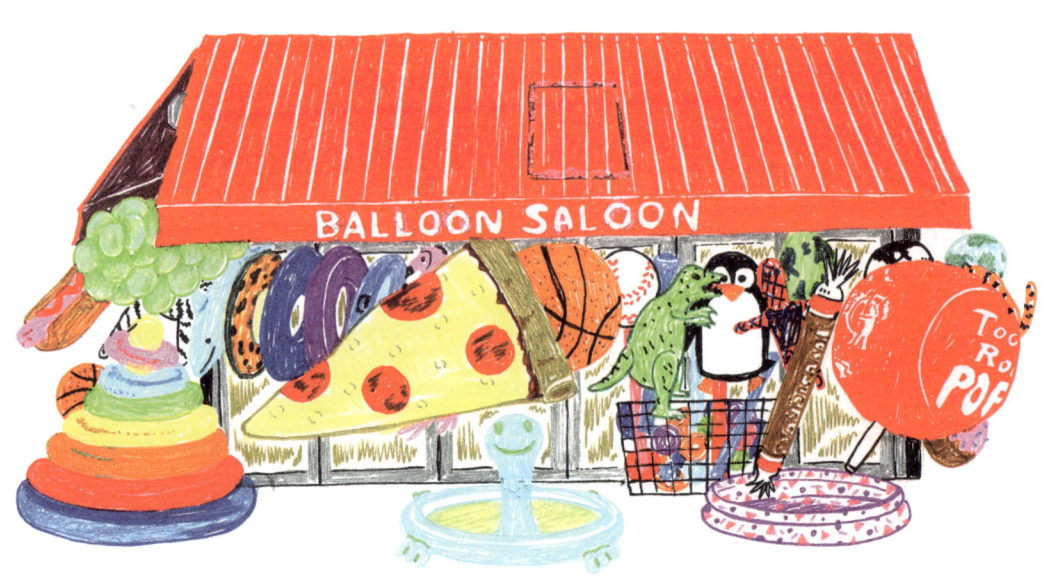

133 W. Broadway
at Duane St.

Balloon Saloon

Just try to walk by the giant inflatable lollipops and penguins outside this TriBeCa shop without cracking a smile.

Opening the store with her late husband in 1980, Sharon Hershkowitz now runs Balloon Saloon with her daughter and son—and has a lot of fun doing it. "Sometimes when I'm at the Armory or a ballroom installing balloons, I stop and look around at what we've created and I think, I'm getting paid for this!" she told the *Tribeca Citizen*.

Originally, the Saloon was better known for selling novelty sex items (wind-up penises and whatnot), and not so much for the Dora the Explorer balloons seen outside the store today. But as the area gentrified over the years into a neighborhood filled more with baby strollers than dive bars, the shop changed along with it. Still, Sharon admits that balloons are not the most popular item for sale: that distinction goes to fake plastic poop.

Tompkins Square Bagels

Get here at the crack of dawn on Saturday or Sunday, or be prepared to wait in a line that extends well down Avenue A by midmorning. Devotees of this beloved East Village spot—which also has two other Manhattan locations—say its bagels, even in a city with no shortage of options, are well worth the wait. The owners take bagel-making seriously—always hand rolled, boiled, and baked fresh throughout the day—but let their hairnets down (figuratively speaking, of course) when it comes to their smears. Flavors change constantly and feature some innovative options you won't see anywhere else, including chocolate-chip cookie dough, espresso, and wasabi.

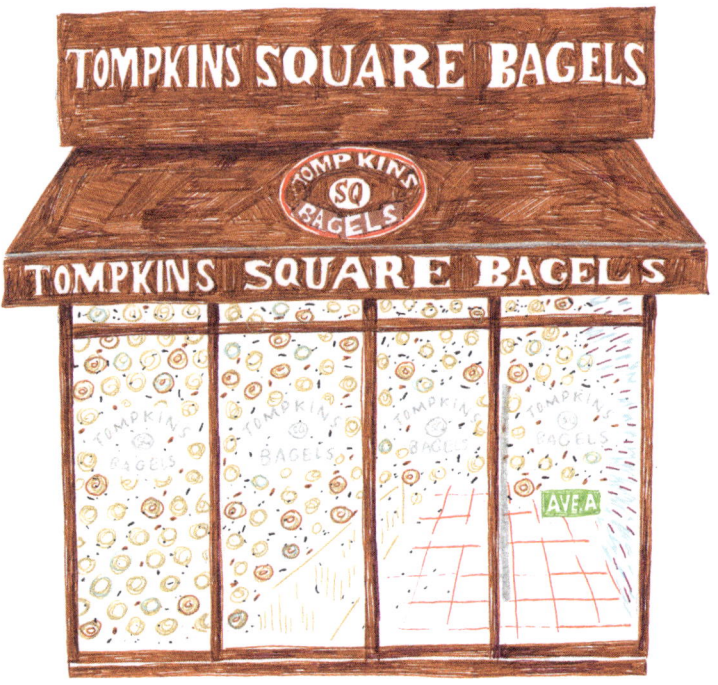

Hector's Cafe & Diner

This quirky spot in the Meatpacking District opened, according to current owner Danny Manesis, in 1949—though he is unaware of who "Hector" is, if the place is indeed named after one. The midcentury diner stands out from its flashy neighbors like the Standard Hotel, straddling the High Line, and the new home of the Whitney Museum. And it's survived where so many other area institutions have failed thanks to a deal brokered by the city. In exchange for giving part of its space to the Whitney, Hector's (and the area's seven last remaining meatpacking factories) were offered rents well below market value until 2032. You can be sure that devotees of this dive will be fighting to keep it around for much longer than that.

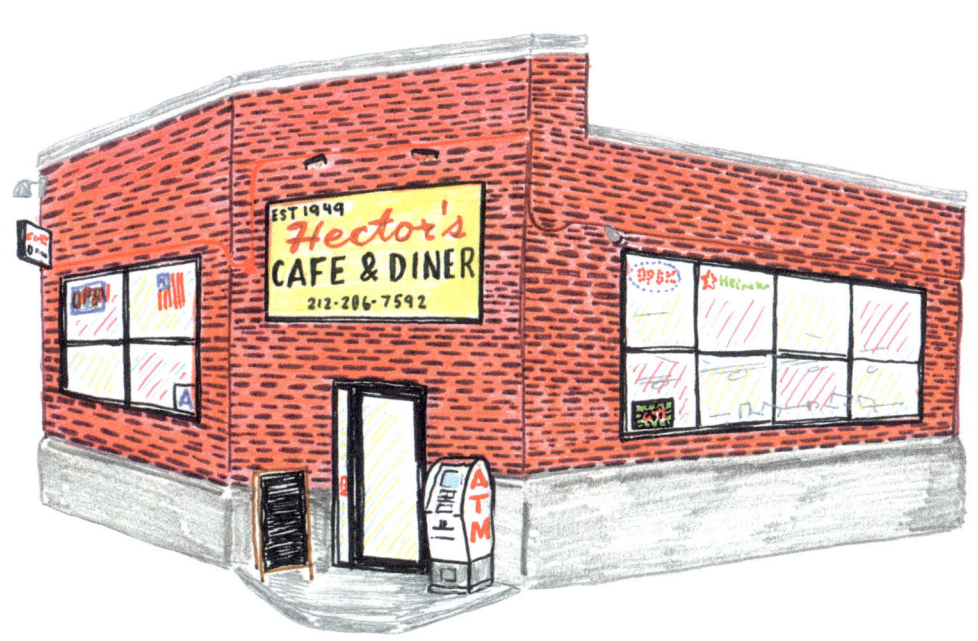

Hi-Tech Electronic Service Center

Spilled coffee on your laptop? This "full-service, repair and maintenance" shop has got you covered. Hi-Tech Electronic Service Center has been operating in Chinatown since 1983 and is known by regulars as the place to turn to in the event of an electronic mishap. It's gained a loyal following among fans of vintage electronics, since its staff will happily repair your malfunctioning reel-to-reel, turntable, or tube radio. Or if you're in the market for an analog device, pop on in to see what they have for sale in their impressive inventory.

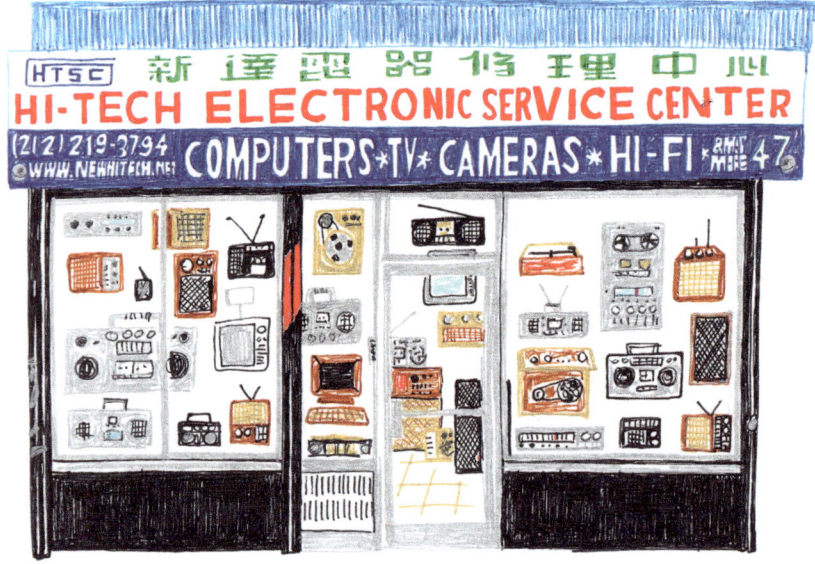

The Famous Cozy Soup 'n' Burger

————

The Stratidis family has owned and operated this twenty-four-hour diner, famous for its nine-ounce burgers and split pea soup, since 1972. According to the autographed headshots adorning its walls, Sylvester Stallone, Lynda Carter, and even TV's ALF have all dropped in over the years. Adam Sandler is a devoted customer, as well, and prominently featured the Greenwich Village favorite in his movie *Big Daddy*. Stop by at night for a chance to snap a photo of the diner's iconic neon sign, long a staple of the Broadway streetscape.

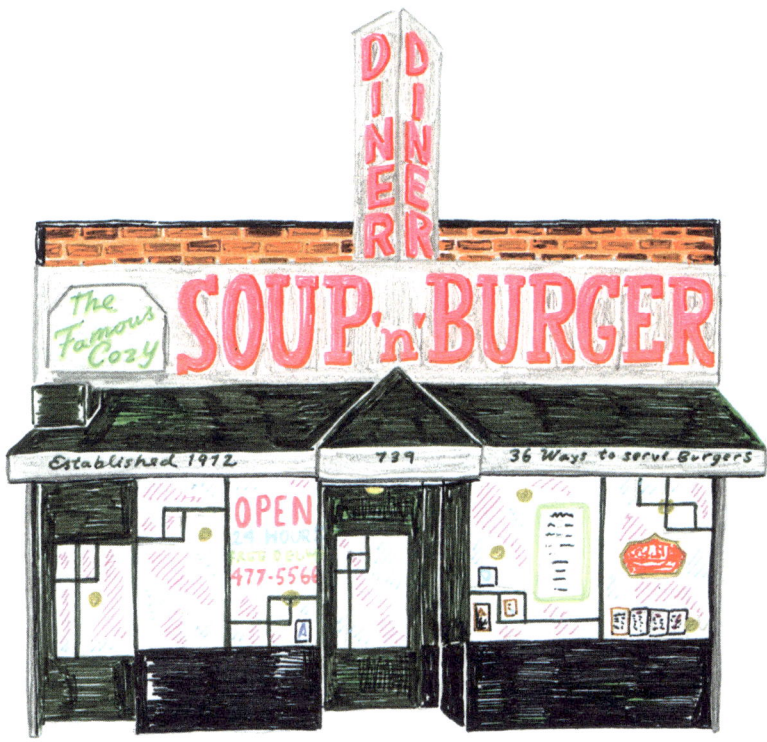

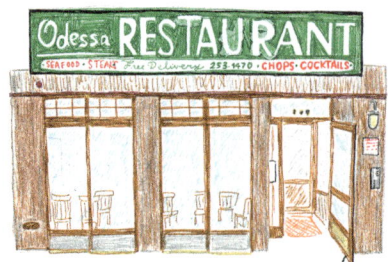

119 Ave. A
between E. 7th St. and St. Marks Pl.

Odessa Restaurant

Originally opened in the mid-1990s as an extension of the Odessa Café and Bar next door, Odessa Restaurant, a twenty-four-hour Ukrainian eatery in the East Village, closed its doors in 2020 due to financial constraints caused by Covid-19. In 2022 another neighborhood favorite, Superiority Burger, opened its doors in the iconic space.

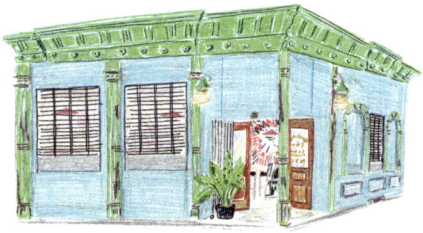

40 Market St.
at Madison St.

Mr. Fong's

The owners of this Chinatown bar—a favorite of downtown artists, models, and fashionistas—named their unassuming spot after a local real-estate broker who showed them the space. Don't leave without peeping the painting by Brooklyn-based artist Paul Wackers.

309 E. 9th St.
between 2nd and 1st Aves.

Davey's Ice Cream

Davey's Ice Cream has "been chill" since 2013, according to its website. This original location closed in spring 2022 but moved nearby to Ninth Street. Its owners have also opened storefronts in Brooklyn and Queens, plus an outpost at Penn Station's Moynihan Train Hall.

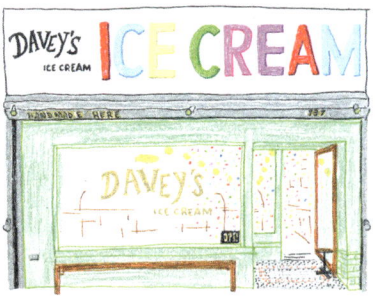

961 Lexington Ave.
at E. 70th St.

Neil's Coffee Shop

Despite the name spelled out on its neon sign outside, this Upper East Side spot, which is now closed, wasn't a coffee shop—it was a classic New York diner, Formica countertops and all.

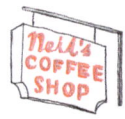

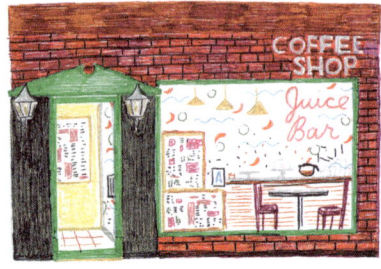

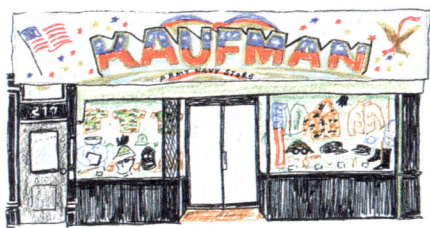

319 W. 42nd St.
between 8th and 9th Aves.

Kaufman Army Navy Store

The *New York Times* once referred to this Times Square army surplus store as a "musty, chaotic spot for camouflage and boots." It has been serving up its wares since 1938.

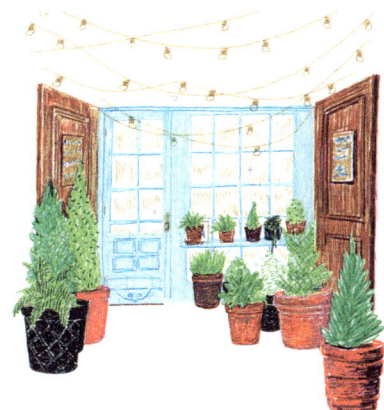

Freeman Alley, off Rivington St.
between Bowery and Chrystie St.

Freemans

Upscale American bistro Freemans, opened in 2004, is one of the most popular restaurants on the Lower East Side. But a visit to this romantic spot, located in one of the few alleyways that exist in Manhattan, feels like discovering a neighborhood secret.

203 W. 14th St.
between 7th and 8th Aves.

The Donut Pub

Dessert trends come and go in the city, from cupcakes to fro-yo and back again, but this pastry spot has been steadily serving up classic New York donuts to downtown residents since 1964.

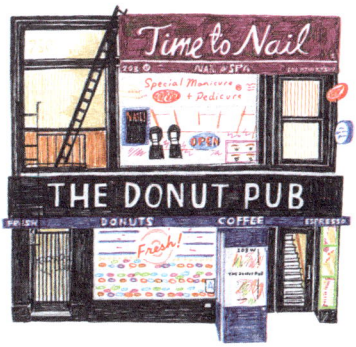

47 Ave. A
between E. 3rd and 4th Sts.

Essex Card Shop

Essex Card Shop, which for years stood a block south of its current location, at 39 Avenue A (depicted here), moved to its new home in June 2020. In January 2022 a two-alarm fire broke out in the space, destroying it—but the owners managed to remodel and reopen by September of the same year.

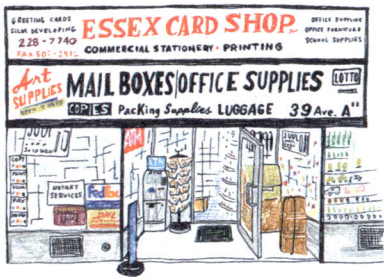

Pommes Frites

This late-night favorite has been shelling out Belgium's most popular street food to the downtown masses since 1997. And these are not your average French fries: they come thick cut, double fried, over-flowing from a paper cone, and with a choice of thirty indulgent sauces. After a tragic explosion occurred here in 2015, the owners of Pommes Frites had to move from their original storefront on Second Avenue (which is the location shown in this illustration). But they were fortunate to secure their current MacDougal spot a year later.

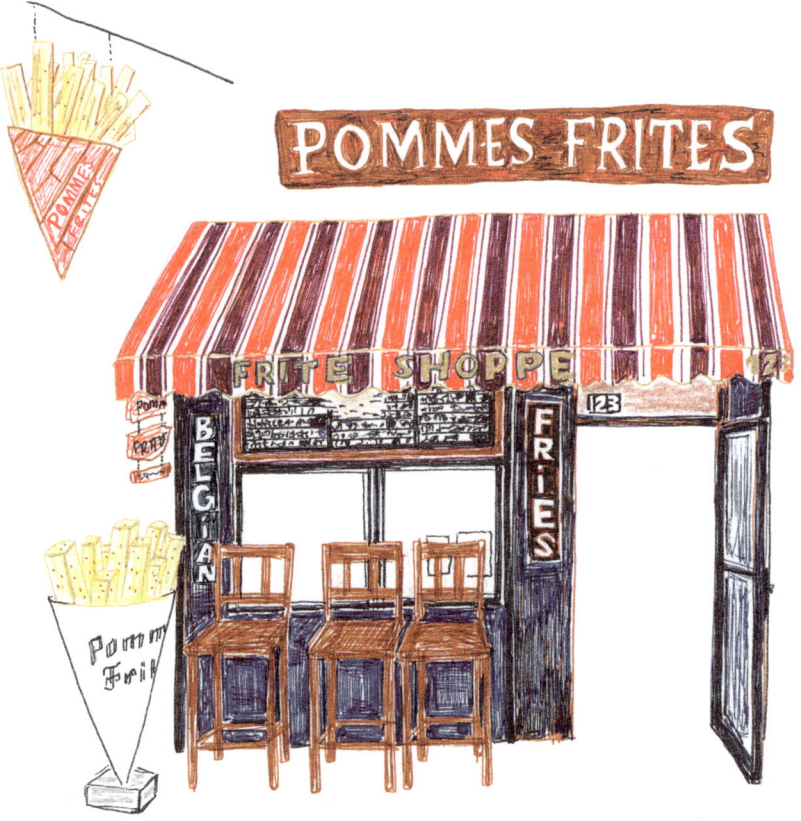

Gramercy Typewriter Co.

———

One of the last typewriter stores in the country, this gem was founded by Abraham Schweitzer in 1932. Originally located in Manhattan's Gramercy neighborhood (hence its name), the shop enjoyed a stint in the Flatiron Building before its current owners, Abraham's son Paul and grandson Jay, moved to its present-day location in Chelsea. As computers began to make typewriters collectible items rather than office necessities, the store adapted by offering printer repairs to stay relevant. But for fans of fully reconditioned vintage typewriters (a group that includes Tom Hanks), Gramercy Typewriter Co. is the place to go.

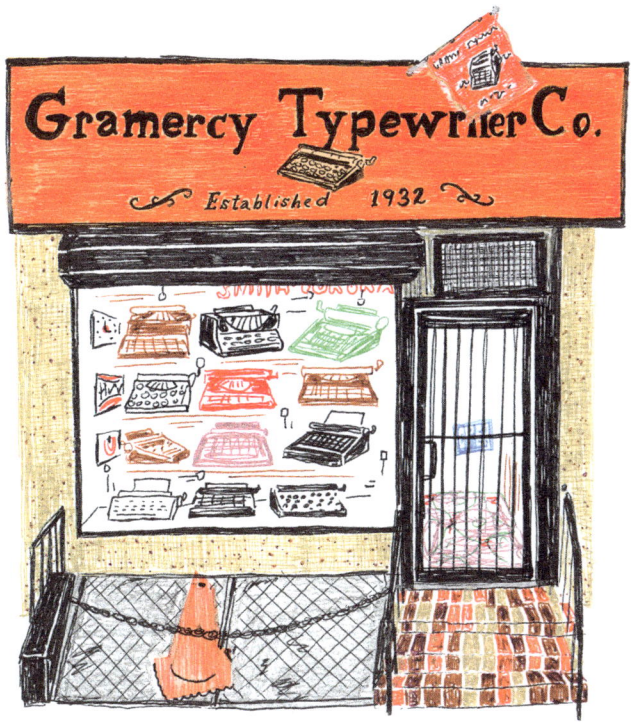

Yokkoyama Hat Market

———

For a decade, milliner Hirohisa Yokkoyama made high-end hats for luxury Japanese stores before opening his own shop in 2015. You can find run-of-the-mill fedoras here, if that's what you're looking for. But regulars gush about one-of-a-kind finds like, say, a black cap fringed with red-and-yellow flames. Yokkoyama Hat Market is also known for its colorful sweatshirts, emblazoned with the store's name.

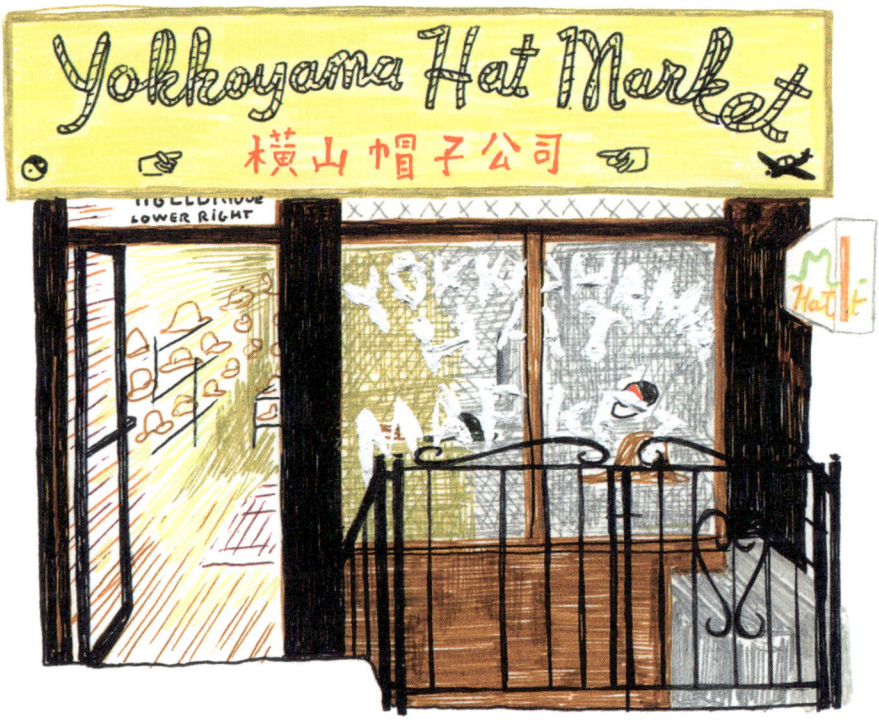

Niagara

In 2009 Japanese artist Yoshitomo Nara casually did some doodles of rocker chicks playing instruments on the walls of this East Village dive bar, which opened in 1997. The owners preserved the work, which at least one art appraiser estimates to now be worth $5 million (and this is likely why they threw out a Gothamist reporter in 2015 for taking a picture of it). But the NYPD, apparently, was less impressed with Yoshitomo's artistic endeavors that night, arresting him some hours later as he was drawing smiley faces on the wall of an L-train subway stop.

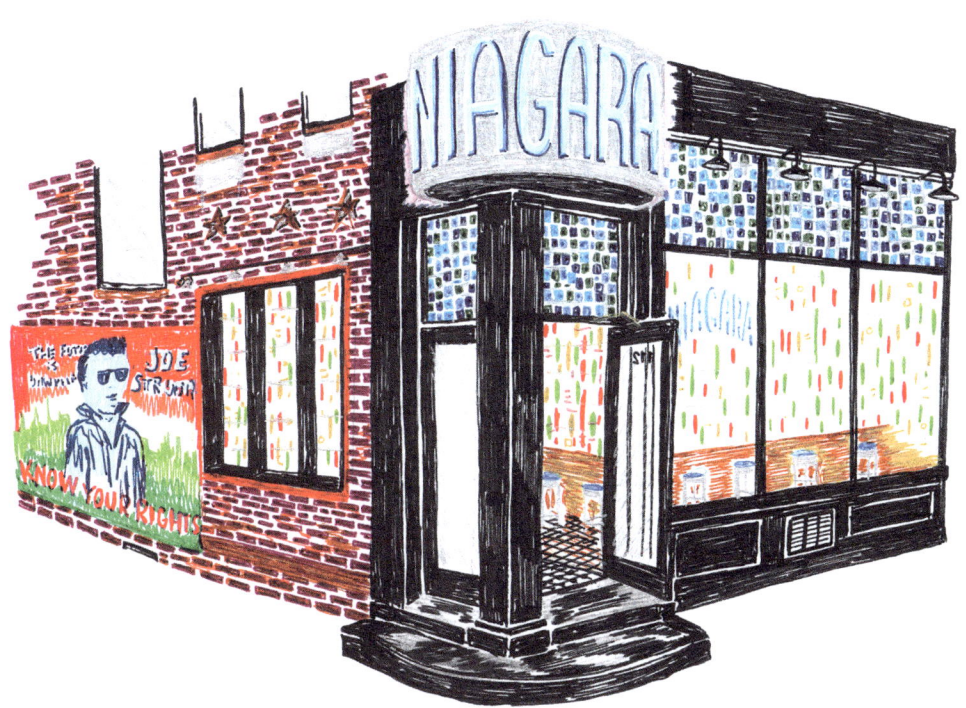

Strand Bookstore

Lithuanian immigrant Benjamin Bass opened New York's most famous independent bookstore, the Strand, at its original location on Fourth Avenue between East Tenth and Eleventh Streets in 1927. At the time, the Greenwich Village icon was part of "Book Row," which stretched over six city blocks and included at least forty-eight bookstores. In 1958 Benjamin's son Fred moved the Strand a couple blocks north to its current home on Broadway. And today it's the last of the Book Row shops still standing—a distinction its owners seem determined to make up for by offering over 2.5 million titles for sale (which, if their signature red logo is to be believed, translates into "18 miles of books").

The Strand is known just as much for the variety of its books on offer as the quantity.

A gander through the "dollar carts" on the sidewalk might turn up titles like *So You're Going to Have Brain Surgery* and *I Didn't Know I Could Do That on CompuServe!*

Meanwhile, in the rare-book room, you'll be surrounded by collectibles, some of which are worth tens of thousands of dollars. It's also available to rent for private events, meaning you could celebrate your birthday or, say, your wedding vows in the same room that houses a $45,000 limited edition of *Ulysses*, illustrated by Henri Matisse.

The store's staff is intimidatingly well-read, which is not by accident: since 1970 applicants for jobs there must complete a "literary matching quiz," pairing authors to books' titles. (Quick! Who wrote *Waiting for Godot*?)

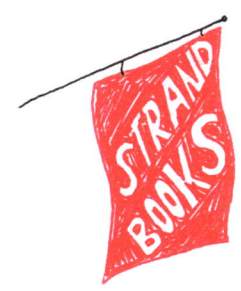
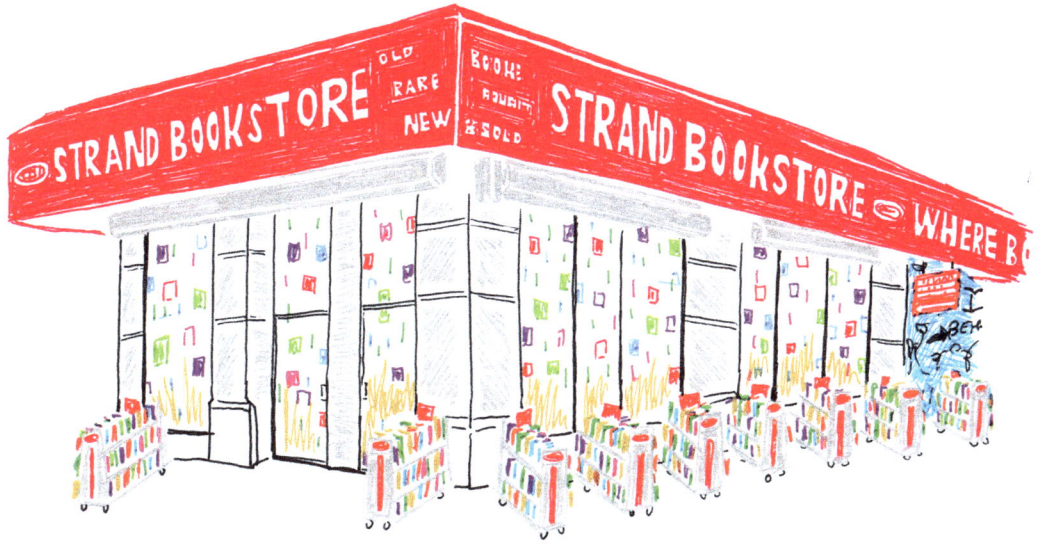

Nha Trang One

One of several Vietnamese eateries on Baxter Street, Nha Trang One is best known for its pho. According to restaurant recommendation website the Infatuation, it's also the best place in the area for a "thoroughly satisfying lunch" whenever you're on jury duty at one of the nearby courthouses. It has some distinctive French offerings as well, such as frog-leg salad.

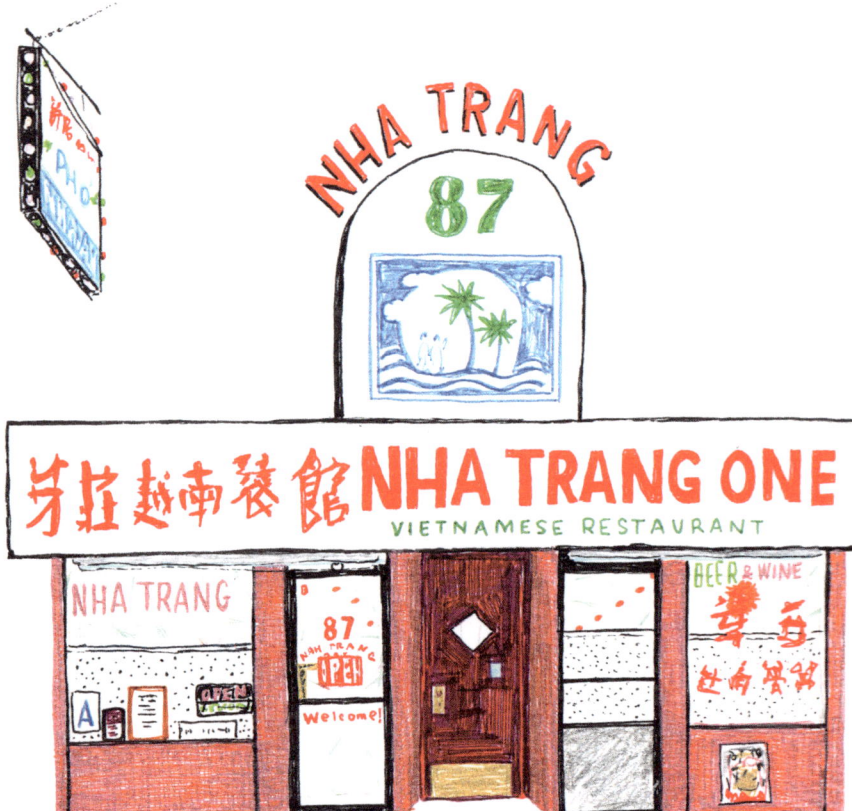

C. O. Bigelow Pharmacy

This apothecary, the oldest in the United States, has been operating continually since 1838 in Greenwich Village. It's sold lotions, potions, and—for a good chunk of the twentieth century—food and soda at a popular lunch counter. The Ginsberg family, who have owned the business since 1939, have turned it into something of a museum, as well, collecting notable prescriptions, recipes, photographs, and packaging from its nearly two-century history. The shop's clientele has included everyone from Eleanor Roosevelt to Mark Twain.

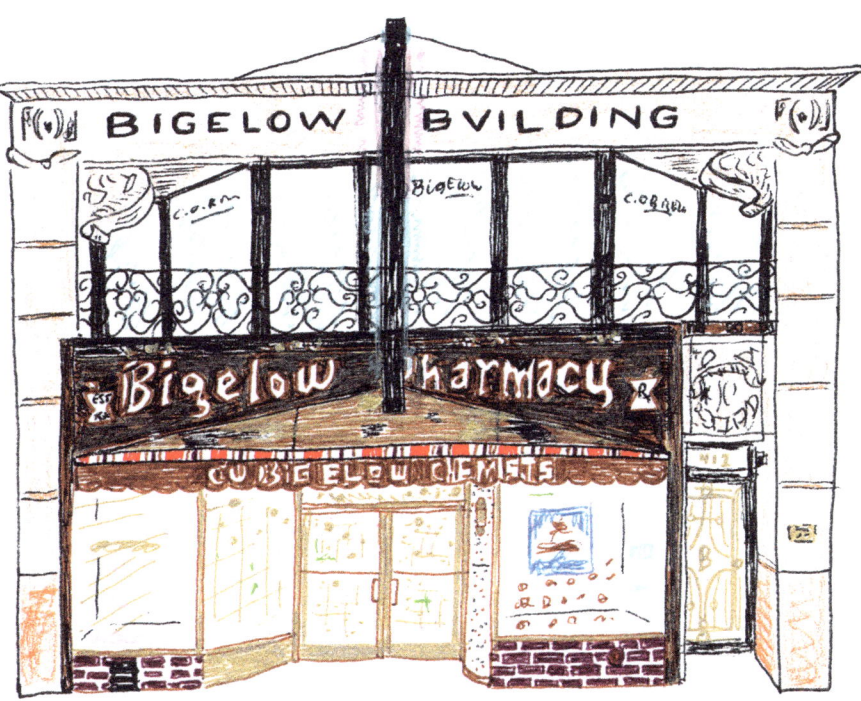

Oliver Coffee

Oliver Coffee's website was bare-bones (describing itself as simply "a coffee shop," along with its location and hours), however, the store's social media presence was anything but. Its Instagram grid was filled with pictures of regulars, drinks in hand, posing in front of the trademark yellow door and windows. Until it closed in 2022, the shop was also known for presenting a diverse collection of magazines, zines, and art installations—each of which was photographed in front of the facade and shared online.

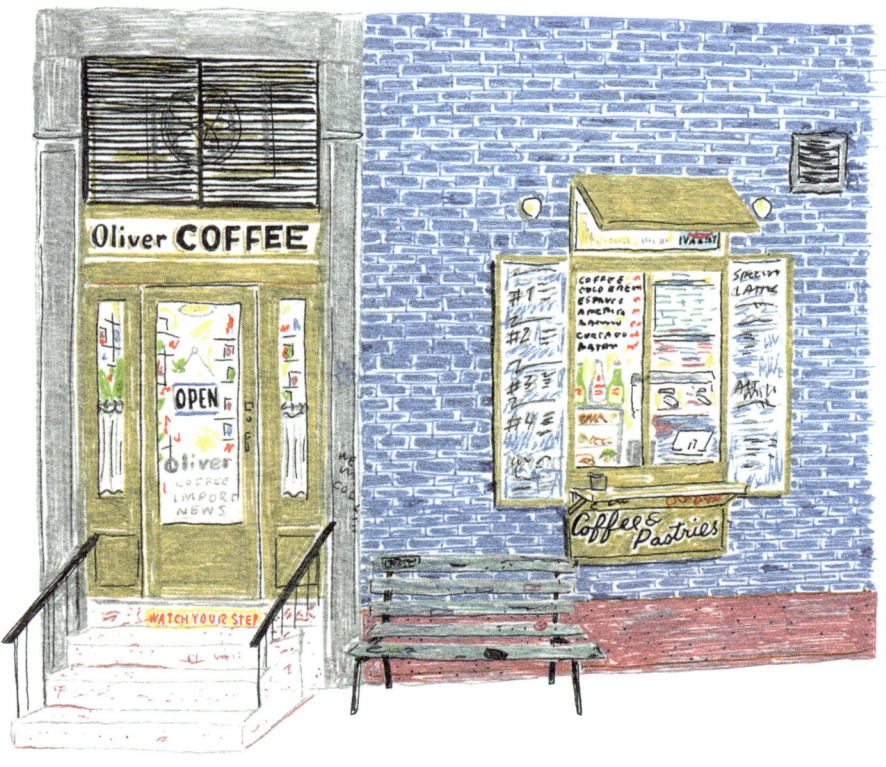

Bangkok Center Grocery

Anyone passionate about Thai cooking knows of this grocery store in Chinatown run by Yoottapong Pongsopon and his wife, Premjit Marks. Top chefs in the city—including the James Beard Award–winner Andy Ricker—have credited the tiny shop with their ability to find authentic ingredients for their Southeast Asian menus, including fresh kaffir lime leaves, a variety of palm sugars, and Laotian sausage.

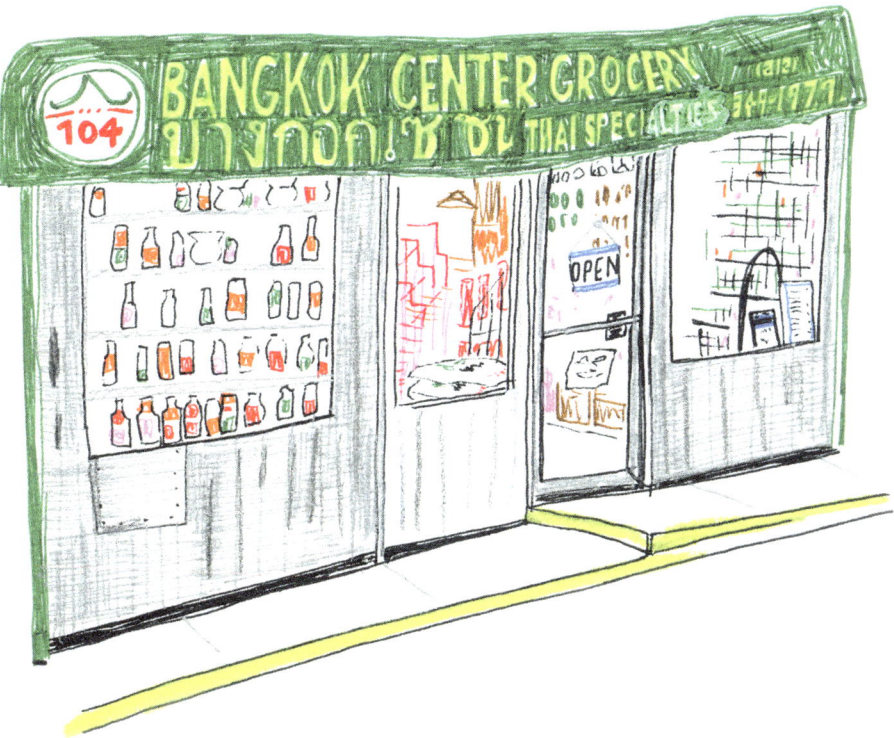

828 6th Ave.

between W. 28th and 29th Sts.

Superior Florists

A walk through Midtown's Flower District—where fresh-cut bouquets, towering fiddle-leaf figs, and rows of succulents compete with pedestrians for sidewalk space—provides a beautiful, brief reprieve from the concrete jungle that characterizes most of Manhattan's streets.

Superior Florists, opened in 1930, is among the area's many vendors. The year it opened, the district was much larger and mostly run by immigrants from Greece. As a result, Louis Rosenberg, the shop's Polish-born founder, learned to speak Greek fluently (and not English) to contend in the booming industry.

Today a lot of Superior Florists' competitors have been driven out of business with the rise of e-commerce flower delivery services, which take a large cut of profits from participating stores. In recent years, Rosenberg and many of his surviving neighbors have teamed up with Real Local Florists and other trade groups that urge customers to shop local and help stores conduct their businesses online.

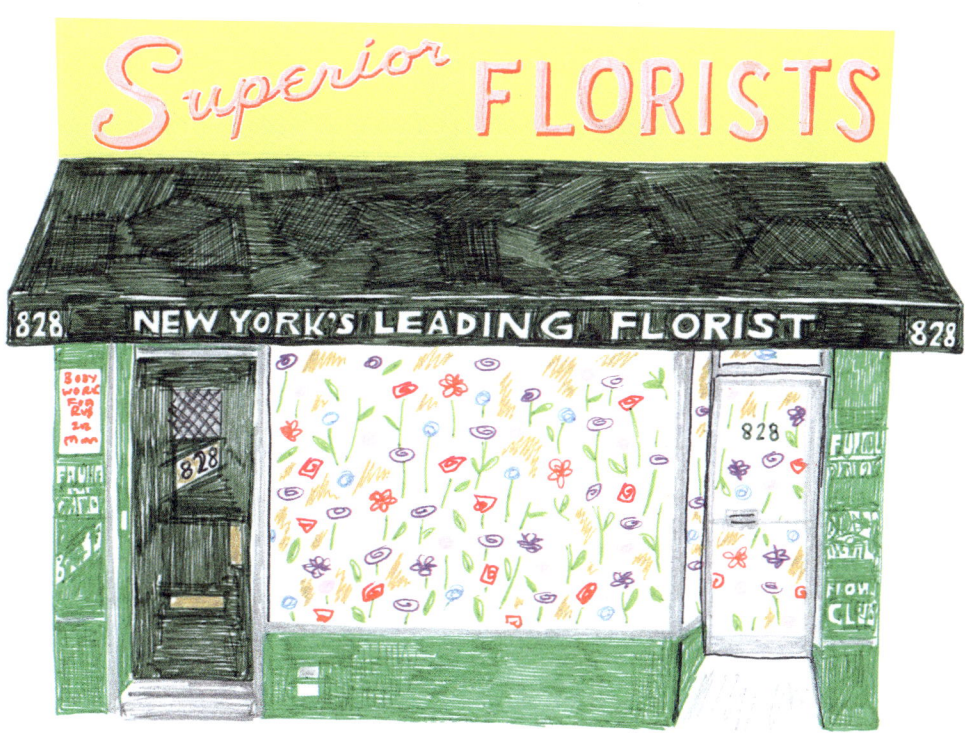

381 1st Ave.
between E. 22nd and 23rd Sts.

Sigfrido's Barber Shop

Andy Evangelista retired from this barber shop in 2016, where he worked for nearly fifty years. Today it continues under new owners, who have kept the name of the store, which Andy's older brother, Sigfrido, founded in 1961.

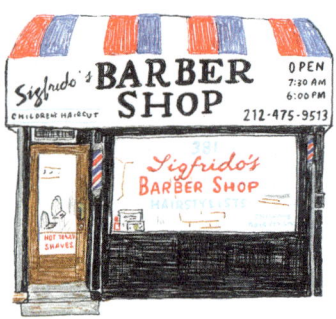

344 E. 11th St.
between 2nd and 1st Aves.

Russo's Mozzarella & Pasta

First opened on the Lower East Side in 1908 before moving to their current spot in the East Village, this Italian grocery also has two locations in Brooklyn—all of which sell some of the freshest mozzarella and homemade pasta in NYC.

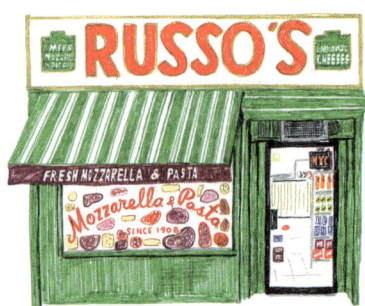

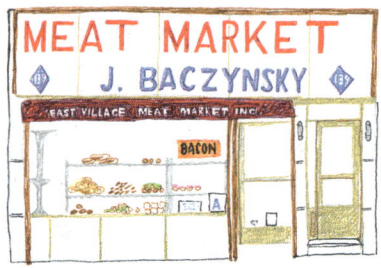

139 2nd Ave.
between St. Marks Pl. and E. 9th St.

J. Baczynsky East Village Meat Market

Julian Baczynsky opened this Ukrainian butcher shop in 1970. It specializes in kielbasa, a smoked sausage, which is prepared fresh every day.

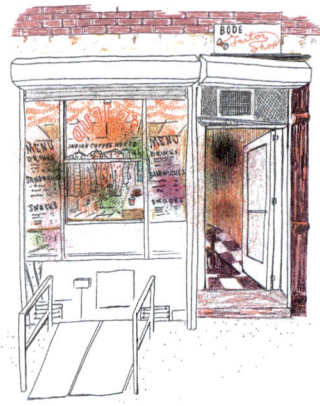

47 Canal St. #7
between Ludlow and Orchard Sts.

Bode Tailor Shop

This Chinatown spot formerly occupied the Hester Street location depicted here—and sold cardamom-infused coffee and Indian sweets, in honor of the coffee shop that had been in the space for forty years. Bode has since moved to Canal Street.

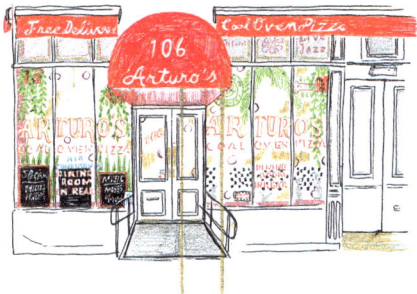

106 W. Houston St.
at Thompson St.

Arturo's Coal Oven Pizza

This beloved pizza spot, which has remained in the same location since 1957, combines three of the best elements of Greenwich Village into one: live jazz, pizza by the slice, and amazing people-watching.

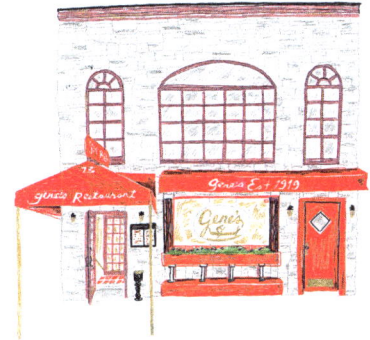

73 W. 11th St.
between 5th and 6th Aves.

Gene's Restaurant

Opened in 1919, this West Village Italian restaurant won't be found at the top of many trendy "best brunch" lists. But come dinnertime, in order to compete with Gene's regulars—which reportedly include Sarah Jessica Parker—you're going to need a reservation.

4140 Broadway
at W. 175th St.

United Palace

This Washington Heights theater is less known than many others in Manhattan but boasts a similar pedigree. Opened in 1930 as a home for vaudeville, United Palace was designed by Thomas Lamb, of Ziegfeld Theatre fame, and Harold Rambusch, who was responsible for the interiors of Radio City Music Hall.

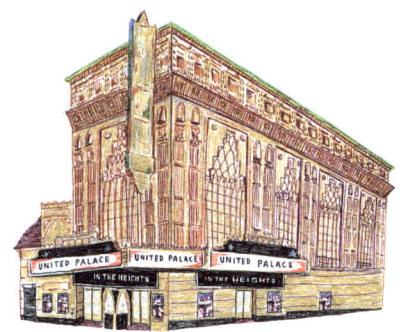

9 E. 47th St.
between 5th and Madison Aves.

Phil's Stationery

Billing itself as "thee pen shop with all your needs," this Midtown East stationery store sells everything from bound ledger books to vintage office supplies.

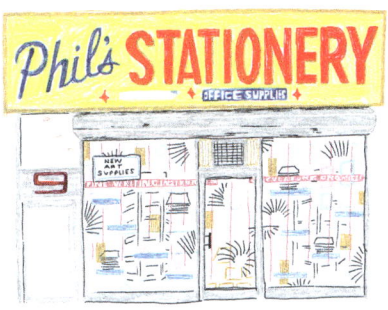

New York Replacement Parts

Need to fix a foreign toilet with hard-to-find plumbing parts? This hardware store is your best bet: they've built up a much-deserved reputation for tracking down and supplying parts that are impossible to locate in big box stores or even online. Think of yourself as "handy"? Speak to the staff for a humbling and entertaining experience—they're just as good for getting your Japanese dishwasher running again as they are with some easy banter.

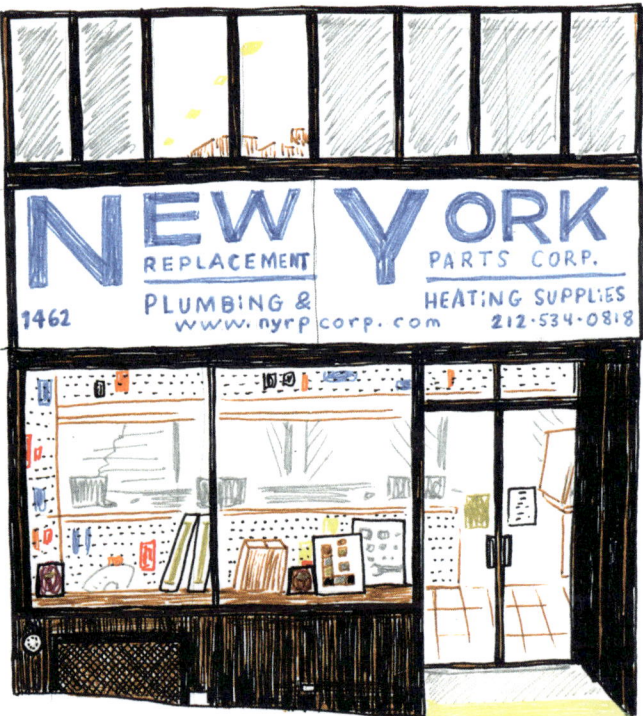

Old Town Bar

This bar and restaurant in the Flatiron District has been in business since 1892. During Prohibition it changed its name to Craig's Restaurant and began operating as a speakeasy. Over the years the owners have kept many of the space's original elements intact, including the marble-and-mahogany counter and the city's oldest still-operating dumbwaiter, which slings orders from the kitchen to the bar. If they have the soft pretzel available when you stop by, get it.

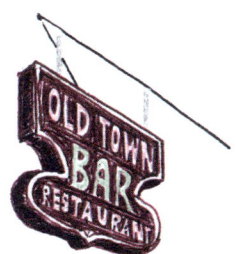

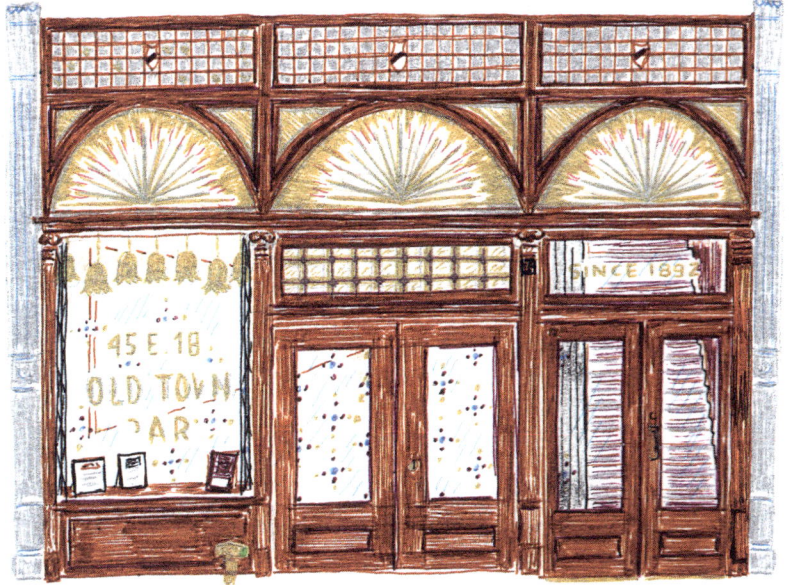

Murray's Bagels

Murray's cofounder Adam Pomerantz named this shop after his father, from whom he learned his love of bagels. And Adam's efforts have certainly lived up to this homage: in a city with no shortage of bagel shops, Murray's, which first opened in Greenwich Village in 1996, consistently ranks high on New York's "best of" lists.

The store is known for making its bagels the old-school way—hand rolled, boiled, and served fresh daily. Murray's began offering to toast their bagels in 2015, finally caving in to years of requests from tourists and regular customers. But traditionalists know that the bagels are best just as they come: crispy on the outside, warm and soft on the inside. (Speaking of which, arrive early to get them fresh out of the oven.)

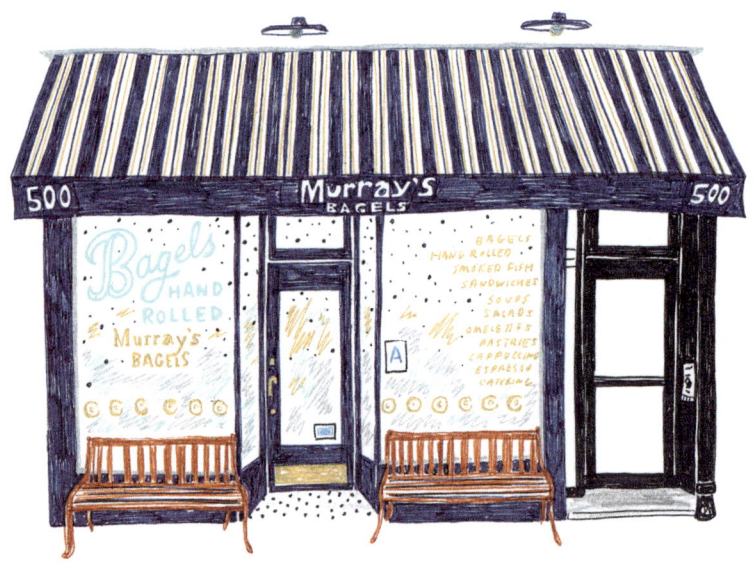

Fishs Eddy

Online reviewers variously describe the mugs, cups, and plates on offer at beloved home-goods purveyor Fishs Eddy as "eccentric," "sassy," and "not tacky." Upon opening the store in 1985, owners Julie Gaines and Dave Lenowitz initially stocked piles of unwanted vintage dinnerware they discovered in the basements of the Bowery's dwindling restaurant-supply district. With much of the original inventory long since snatched up, they now collaborate with designers such as Todd Oldham and Cynthia Rowley on antique-inspired housewares.

After making your purchases—which might include essentials like a coffee mug emblazoned with "Good Morning Asshole" or a tote bag proclaiming "Brunch Is Gay"—ask for a trip upstairs to the "secret" museum. Stocked with Fishs Eddy's remaining vintage cookware, the second floor provides a peek into the first version of the store, now forever preserved thanks to these antique dishware crusaders.

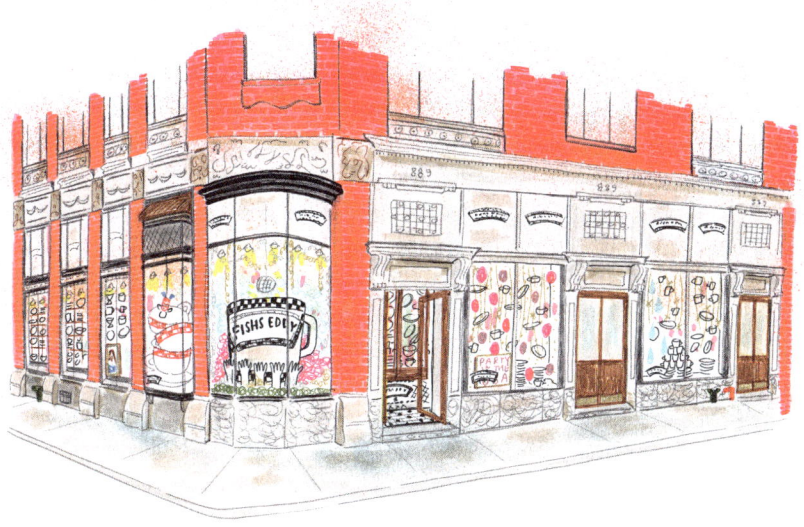

Scarr's Pizza

If you're ever starved for conversation with a group of New Yorkers, simply ask them which pizza parlor in the city is the best—then watch the sparks fly.

Though there's obviously no right answer to this question, in February 2021 Google released data on the most searched-for local pizza spots in each state. Scarr's, on the Lower East Side, was one of three pizzerias in New York to win this distinction, alongside Joe's Pizza (also in Manhattan, see page 60) and Uncle Mike's Hometown Pizza (in Camillus).

This honor may or may not have something to do with what *New York* magazine deems Scarr's "self-aware born-and-bred–New Yorker appeal": a photo of the city's skyline adorns the wall, as does a framed Mets flag, and you won't find any canned sauces here—all tomatoes are sourced from local farmers.

In 2023 Scarr's moved across the street from its original spot (which is illustrated here). Though the new space can accommodate a few more people, you wouldn't know it by the lines that still snake down the block during peak hours. Elbow your way into a back booth or snag a seat at the wraparound counter for a place to enjoy your slice.

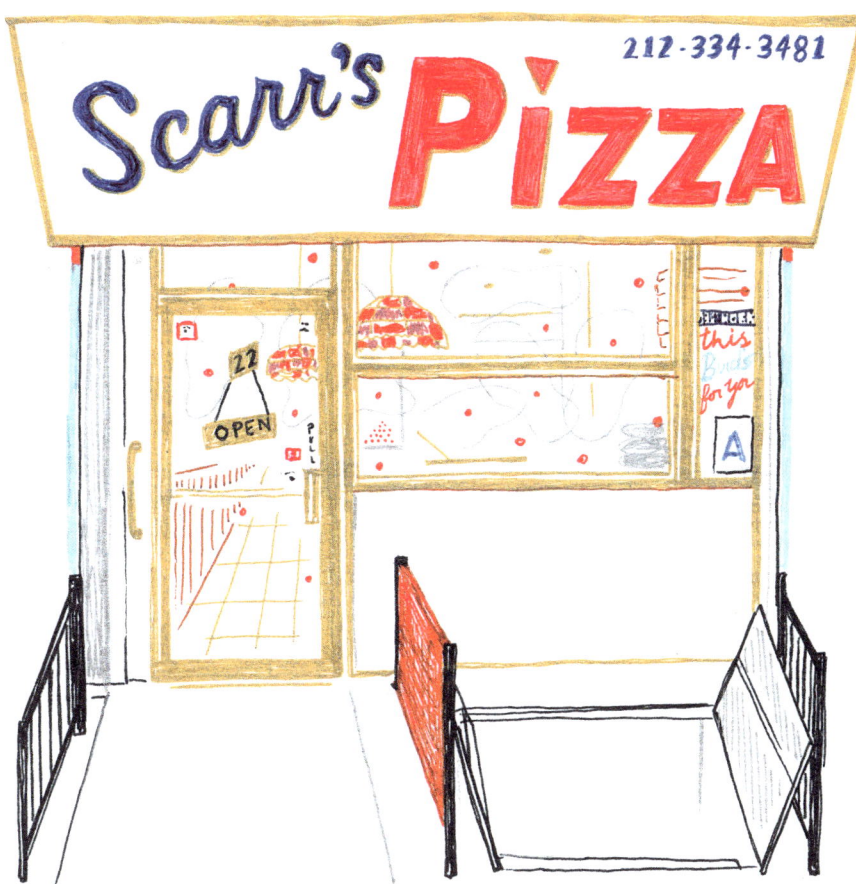

Takahachi

"Delicious sushi" and "reasonably priced" are rarely phrases you hear uttered in the same sentence in New York, but that's part of what's kept customers coming back to this East Village spot since 1990. The restaurant's owner, Hiroyuki Takahashi, recently sold the business to his longtime employee Jack Hlaing— but you wouldn't know it from the menu and decor, which have remained intact through the transition. Still, the lack of Hiroyuki's daily presence in the small space is enough to represent the end of an era— though he still drops in on occasion for some rolls and a chat with the regulars.

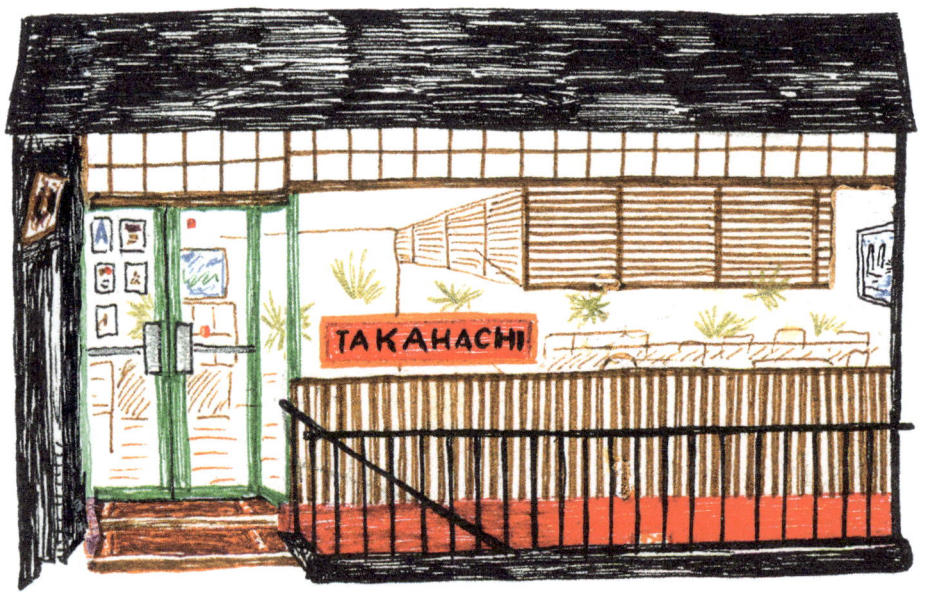

Shan Fu

Couple Dong Wang and Helen Chen have run this grocery store on the border of the Lower East Side and Chinatown since 2010, offering a wide variety of fruits and specialty foods. The shop is best known for serving up some of the freshest smoothies and juices in the area. The watermelon slushie is a crowd-pleaser, as is the massive snowperson Dong builds outside on the sidewalk following every major blizzard.

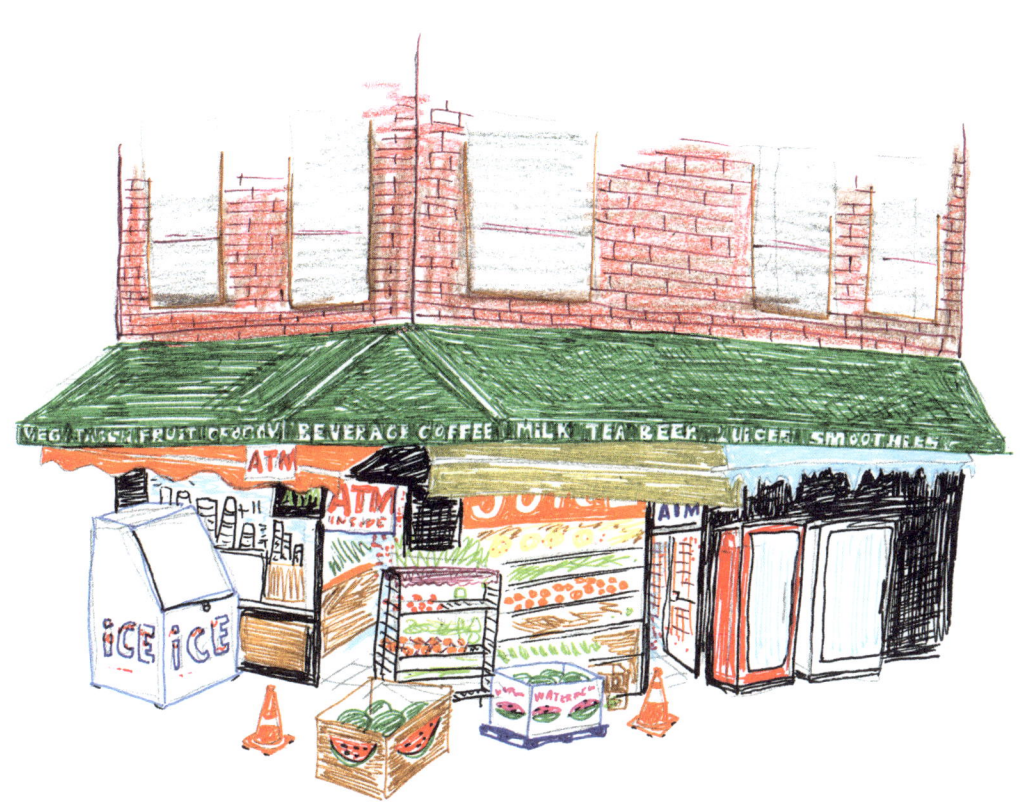

150 W. 4th St.
at 6th Ave.

Washington Square Diner

This diner sits in the same location as the former Pony Stable Inn, one of the city's first lesbian bars, which is also notable for its appearances in literary history. In her 1982 book *Zami: A New Spelling of My Name*, activist and author Audre Lorde wrote about being one of the few Black women to frequent the bar at the time. And beat poets Allen Ginsberg and Gregory Corso first met here in 1950.

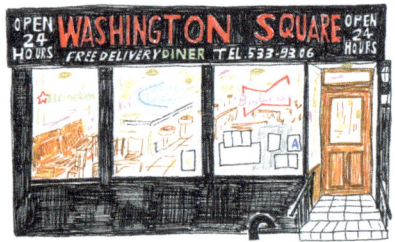

26 Pell St.
between Bowery and Mott St.

Mee Sum Cafe

Dedicated locals flock to this Chinatown diner thanks to its very low prices and quirky practices: there's no set opening time, the menu is completely in Chinese, and tipping isn't encouraged.

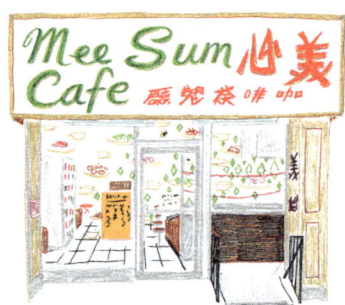

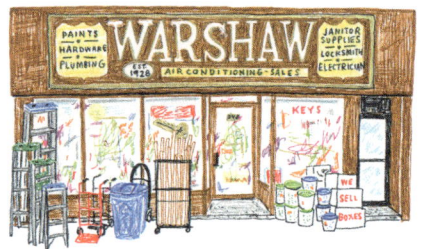

248 3rd Ave.
between E. 20th and 21st Sts.

Warshaw Hardware

Warshaw Hardware has been going strong for a century, even with the arrival of big-box stores and online retail, thanks to the dedication of four generations. Opened in the 1920s by Louis Warshaw, the shop is now run by his grandsons and great grandchildren.

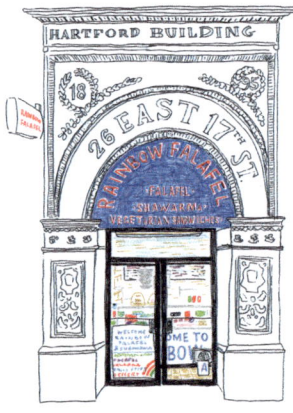

26 E. 17th St.
between 5th Ave. and Union Sq. W.

Rainbow Falafel

Easily noticeable from the street due to its arched entryway, this falafel spot commands a long line come lunchtime in the Flatiron District. But don't expect to enjoy your meal here, as Rainbow Falafel strictly sells its food to go.

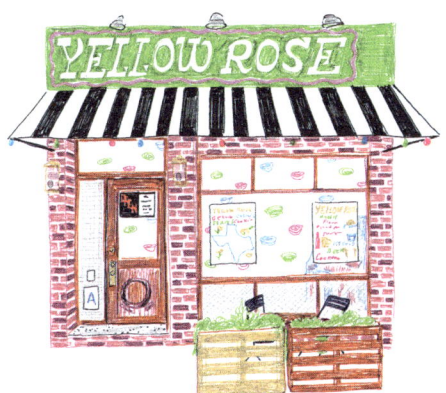

102 3rd Ave.
between E. 12th and 13th Sts.

Yellow Rose

The bean and cheese burrito may be the simplest menu item at this East Village Tex-Mex spot, which opened in 2020 as a pop-up before moving into a storefront, but it's also the runaway favorite.

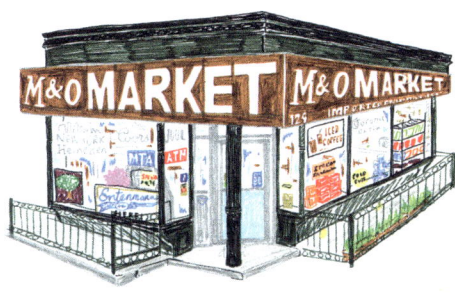

124 Thompson St.
at Prince St.

M&O Market

This Portuguese shop sells all the regular offerings you'd expect from a New York City market, plus an extensive deli menu of sandwiches. Don't leave without a *pastel de nata* (custard tart).

357 1st Ave.
at 21st St.

Tal Bagels

Though the awning here touts having the best bagels on the Upper East Side, this particular shop is actually in Gramercy—Tal has started something of a mini empire, with locations across the city.

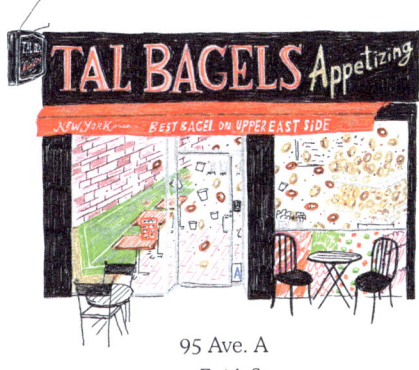

95 Ave. A
at E. 6th St.

Amor y Amargo

As its Spanish name (which means "love and bitter" in English) suggests, you'll find a wide selection of "bitters-forward" cocktails on the menu at this tiny East Village bar, opened in 2011—and no mixers or juices. Feeling frisky? Ask the bartender to create an off-menu concoction.

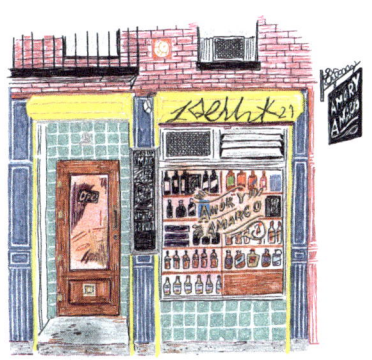

Mikey Likes It Ice Cream

Michael "Mikey" Cole started his ice cream business at this East Village shop and then expanded it into a mini empire, opening locations in Harlem and Hell's Kitchen. But in 2022, after struggling to keep his storefronts open during the Covid-19 pandemic, he decided to close his brick-and-mortar shops. Not to worry—he is far from done serving his community cold treats. In the years since, he's focused on selling his ice cream wholesale online and at private parties and events via his branded truck and cart.

Mikey is known for cooking up some killer ice cream, which began making a splash in the dessert world from nearly the first day he opened his doors back in 2014.

He's recognized for his creative flavors, many of which are named after cultural icons, such as Foxy Brown (mocha with crushed chocolate wafer cookies, swirled with caramel sea salt) and Brady Bunch (banana pudding with crushed vanilla wafers). He keeps his menu fresh and continues to roll out new flavors—some of which have even been custom-made with celebrities ranging from Jay-Z to Hillary Clinton.

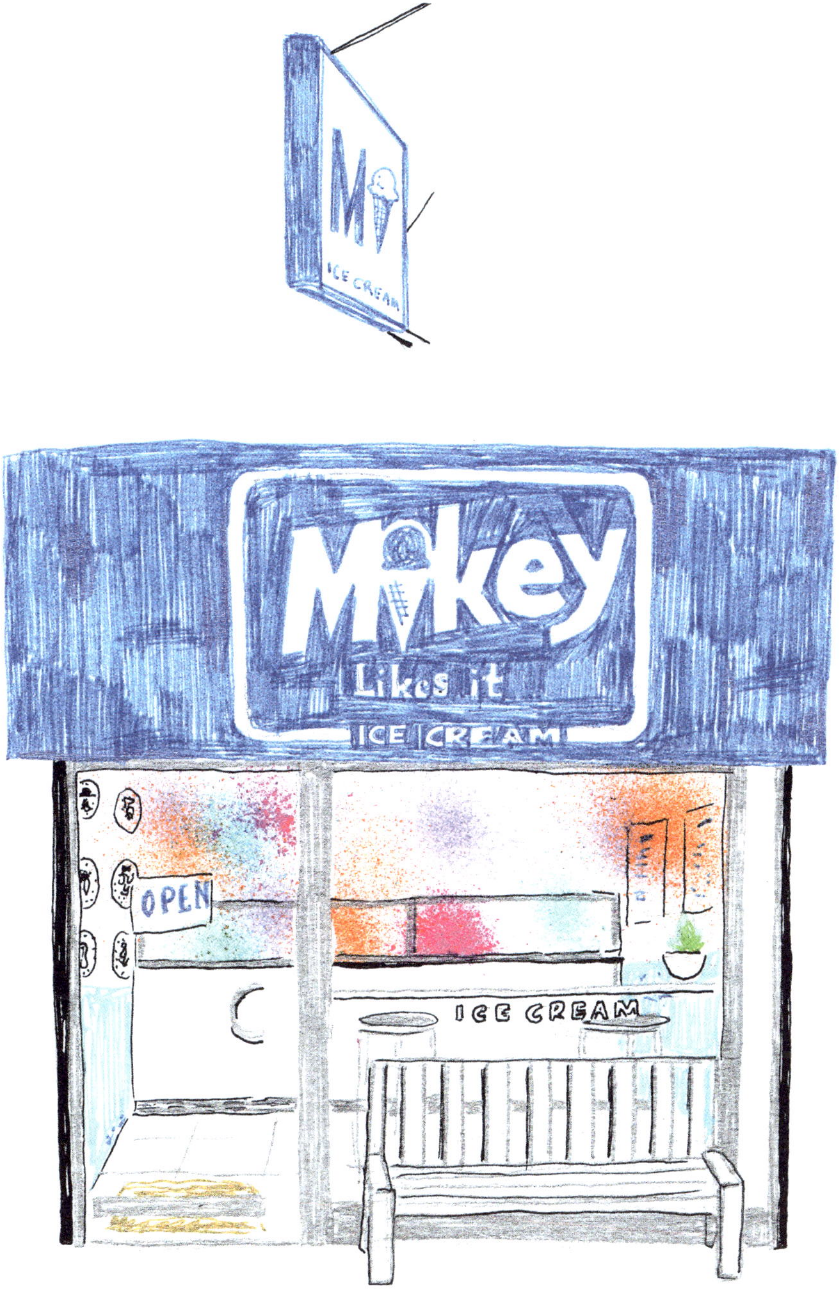

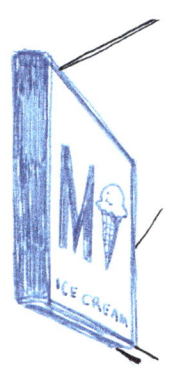

Ray's Candy Store

As a teenager in Iran, Asghar Ghahraman signed up to serve in the navy. When his ship pulled into Norfolk, Virginia, he jumped off in the middle of the night to make a new life for himself in the United States. From there, he took a train to Miami, where he became a window washer. After an FBI agent discovered his immigration status, he fled to New York with an old driver's license given to him by a friend with the name Ramon Alvarez. Under this new identity, Asghar found work as a dishwasher, country-club attendant, and valet porter. Eventually he saved up enough money to buy Andy's Candy Shop on Avenue A in the East Village in 1974, renaming it Ray's. Although Asghar became a US citizen in 2011, he continues to go by "Ray." But, as he told the *Villager*, "They can call me anything they want—I'm an American now." Make sure you try his fried Oreos.

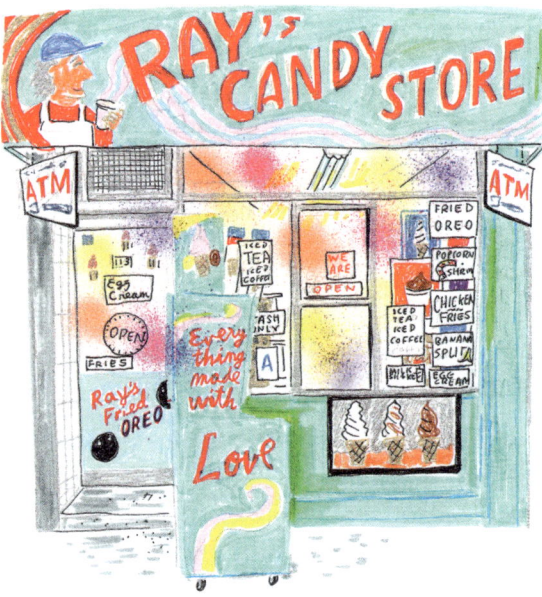

Bo Ky

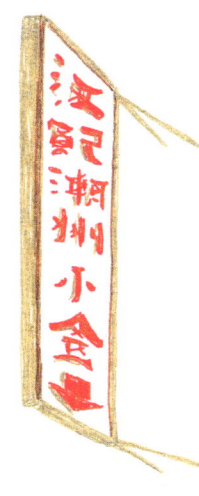

This Chinatown restaurant specializes in Teochew cuisine, which comes from Chaoshan, a region in China's southeastern Guangdong province. It was founded by Chi Vy Ngo, who originally hails from this region but grew up in South Vietnam. During the Vietnam War, he and his family were forced to flee on a boat, which tragically sank, killing many of the two hundred people crammed onboard. Fortunately, Chi Vy and his parents survived. After living for several years as refugees in Thailand, the family eventually immigrated to New York in 1979, where they began the task of integrating themselves into the Chinatown community. They opened Bo Ky at this spot on Bayard Street in 1986, and the shop, now run by Chi Vy's son Hung Ngo, has been serving Teochew food ever since.

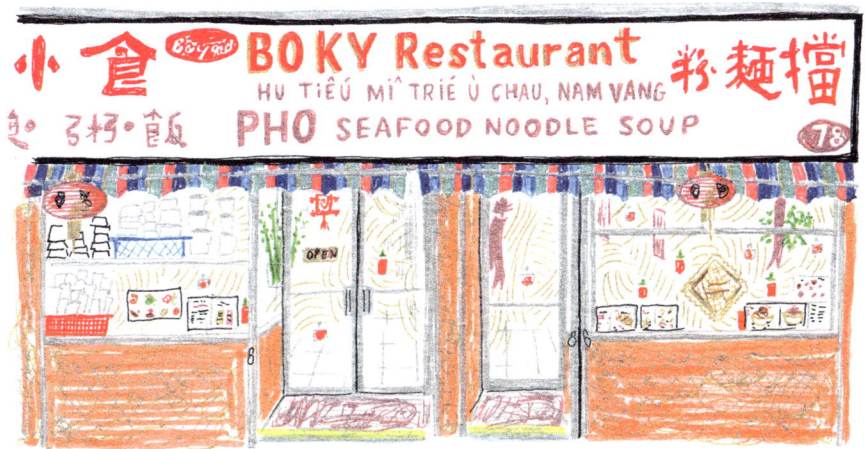

159 W. 10th St.
at Waverly Pl.

Julius'

———

The modern LGBTQ rights movement is most closely associated with the riots that took place at the Stonewall Inn (see page 131) in 1969, but a storefront around the corner, on Waverly Place, is also steeped in importance for the queer community. The building, which has hosted a bar in some form or another since 1864—and has been known as Julius' since the 1930s—became a hangout for gay men in the 1950s. It's often referred to as the city's oldest continually operating queer bar for that reason. (Stonewall, in fact, became a popular gay bar only three years before the riots there.)

Julius' was also home to a historic LGBTQ protest, which happened before the Stonewall riots, in 1966.

On April 21 several activists—who were part of the Mattachine Society, one of the first gay rights groups in the country—held a "sip-in" to challenge a law on the books at the time that effectively prohibited bars and restaurants from serving openly gay people (which Julius' then-owners adhered to, often harassing queer patrons). The protest was covered by many major media outlets, including the *New York Times*, which ran a story titled "3 Deviates Invite Exclusion by Bars" the following day. The demonstration helped prompt New York City's Commission on Human Rights to reverse the rule, allowing openly queer people to be served wherever they wished.

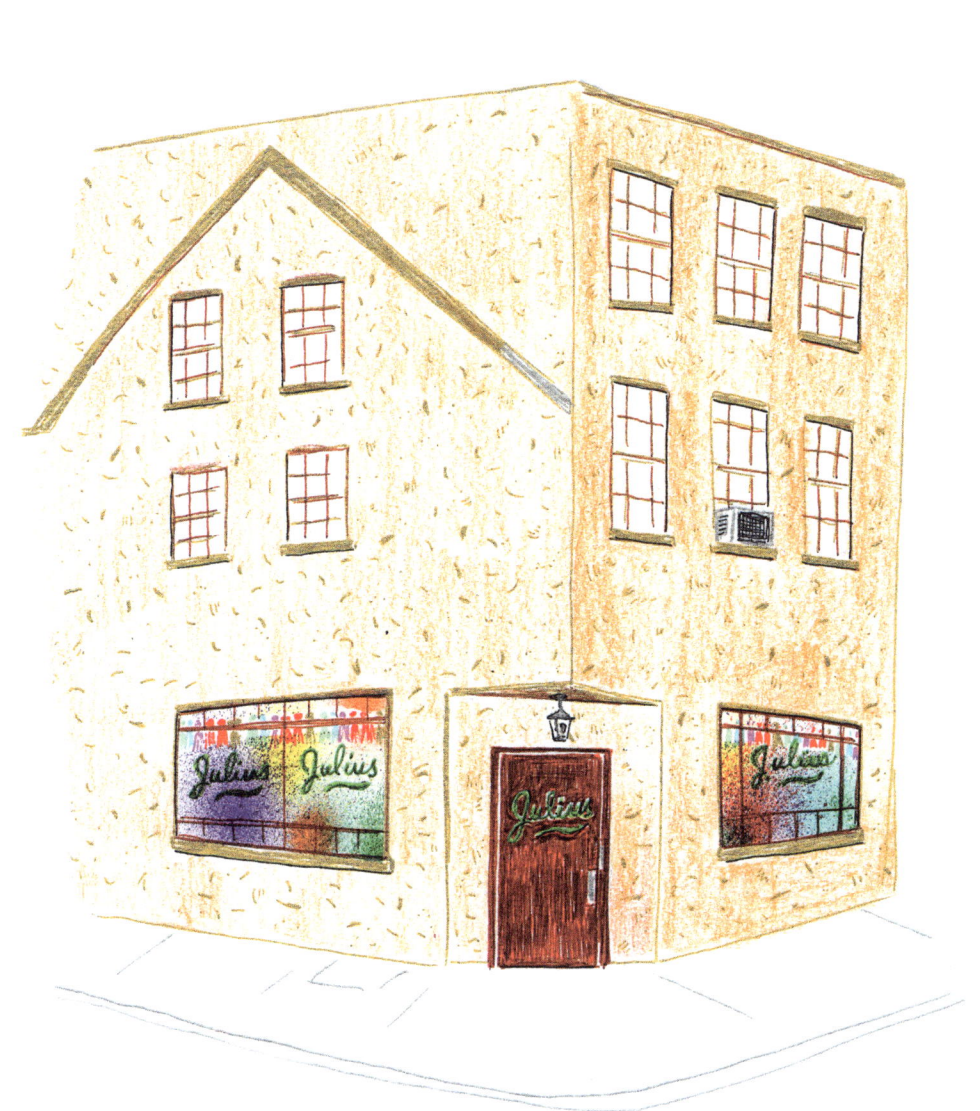

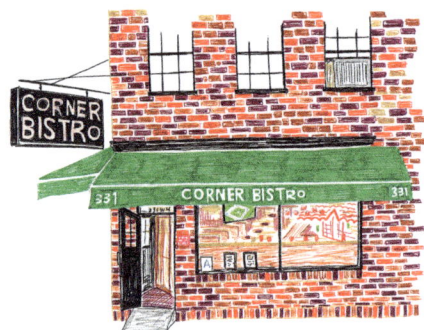

331 W. 4th St.
at Jane St.

Corner Bistro

This greasy spoon proclaims itself "the last of the bohemian bars" in the West Village, which is barely hyperbole. The bistro, with its tin ceilings and cheap burgers, has remained nearly unchanged since it opened in 1961.

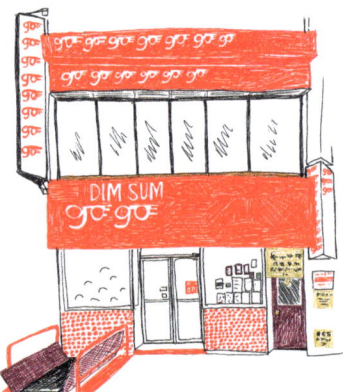

5 E. Broadway
between Chatham Sq. and Catherine St.

Dim Sum Go Go

Forgoing the massive-dining-parlor-with-carts style of some of its neighboring dim sum restaurants, this spot is home to off-the-menu ordering, lots of dumpling options, and a friendly staff.

946 1st Ave.
at E. 52nd St.

Sunshine Florist

This Midtown East florist prided itself on its wide offerings of floral arrangements, and before it closed down, the shop claimed to have the largest selection of clay pots east of Broadway.

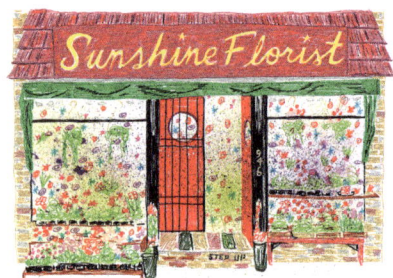

212 W. 44th St.
between 7th and 8th Aves.

Starlite Deli

Located just off Times Square, this deli ran from 1984 to 2022—outlasting "any Broadway show," as one online site wrote in a headline bemoaning the closure.

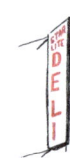

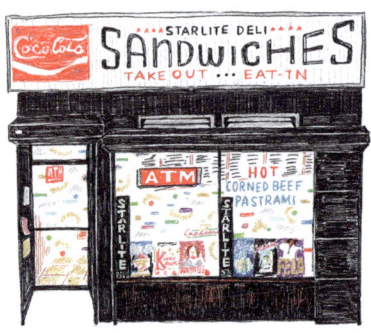

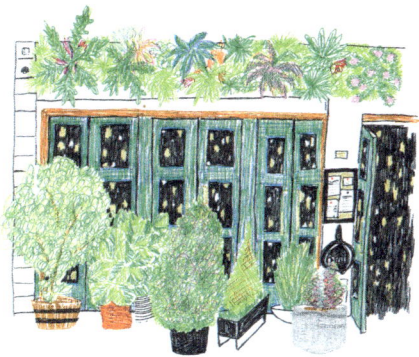

166 1st Ave.
between E. 10th and 11th Sts.

Ferns

As this restaurant's website says, "We're that East Village spot with all the plants outside." Try the donuts and the chicken sandwich—no gardening experience required.

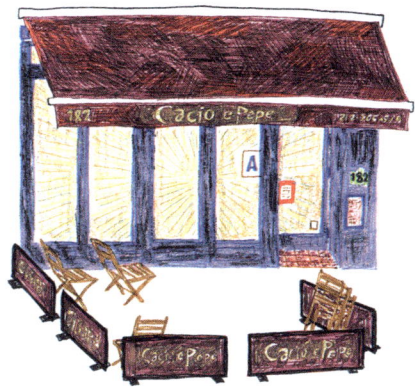

182 2nd Ave.
between E. 11th and 12th Sts.

Cacio e Pepe

Opened in 2014, this East Village Italian restaurant is named after its signature dish, created by tossing homemade pasta in a wheel of pecorino cheese.

71 Mulberry St.
between Bayard and Canal Sts.

Hai Cang Sea Food

This small seafood market (which is now closed) offered an impressive selection of fish, as well as a bit of peace and quiet compared to many of its large, bustling neighbors on Canal Street.

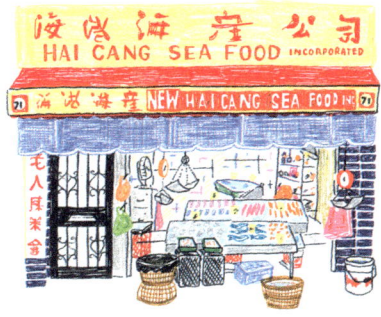

767 Washington St.
at W. 12th St.

Tortilla Flats

This West Village Mexican restaurant slung countless tequila shots down the throats of NYU students for thirty-five years before closing in 2018. Tortilla Flats, which counted Sarah Jessica Parker and Andy Cohen among its adoring fans, was known for its kitschy decor, trivia nights, and questionable (but hilarious) drunk Hula-Hoop competitions.

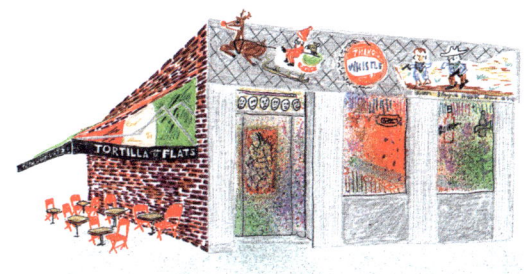

119 MacDougal St.
between Minetta Ln. and W. 3rd St.

Mamoun's Falafel

Mamoun's, the oldest falafel restaurant in New York (and one of the first US eateries to offer Middle Eastern food of any sort), took up residency on MacDougal Street in 1971.

Founded by Mamoun Chater, a Syrian immigrant, the shop is today run by his sons, two of whom even stopped practicing law to get in on the family business. Since taking over ownership, the sons have been busy turning Mamoun's into a mini empire: today stores exist in four states across the country, including one as far as Atlanta. Mamoun's now ships nationwide, too—and even to Canada. Still, the sons acknowledge the store's humble beginnings. In honor of its fiftieth anniversary in May 2021, they sold their signature falafel sandwich, still made with their father's original recipe, for seventy-five cents—which is what the meal cost back in 1971. Watch out: the hot sauce here is HOT!

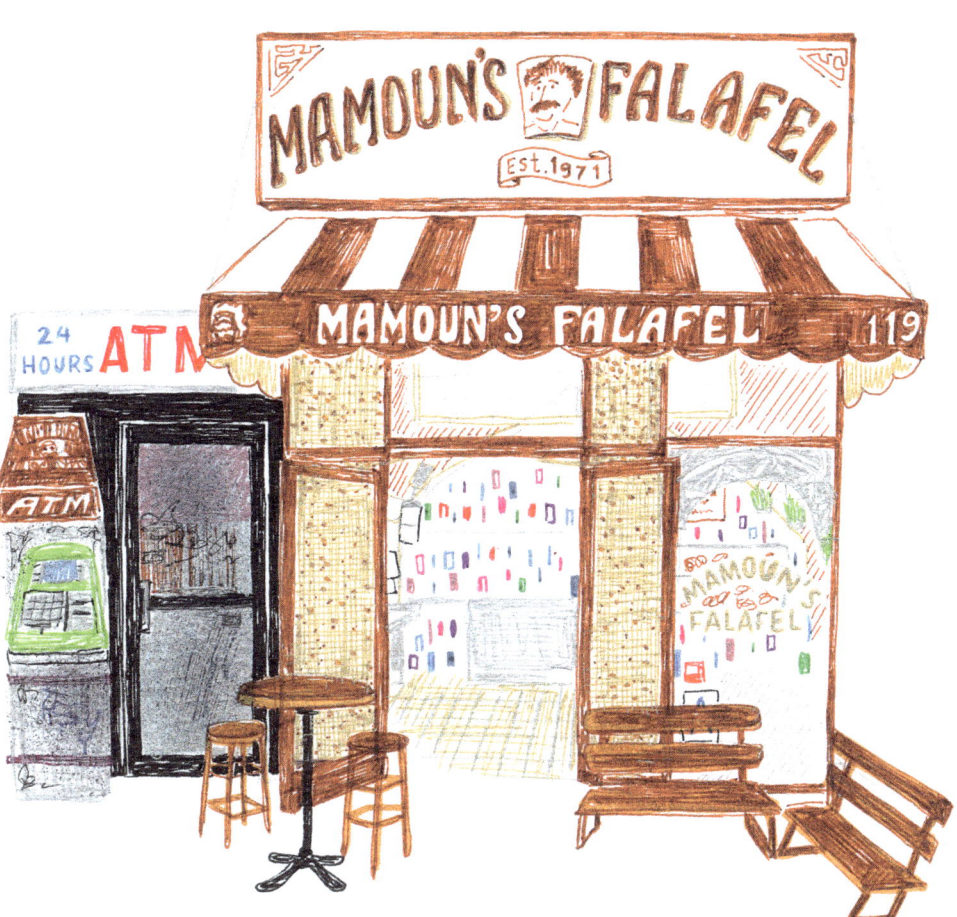

ABOVE 34TH ST.

—

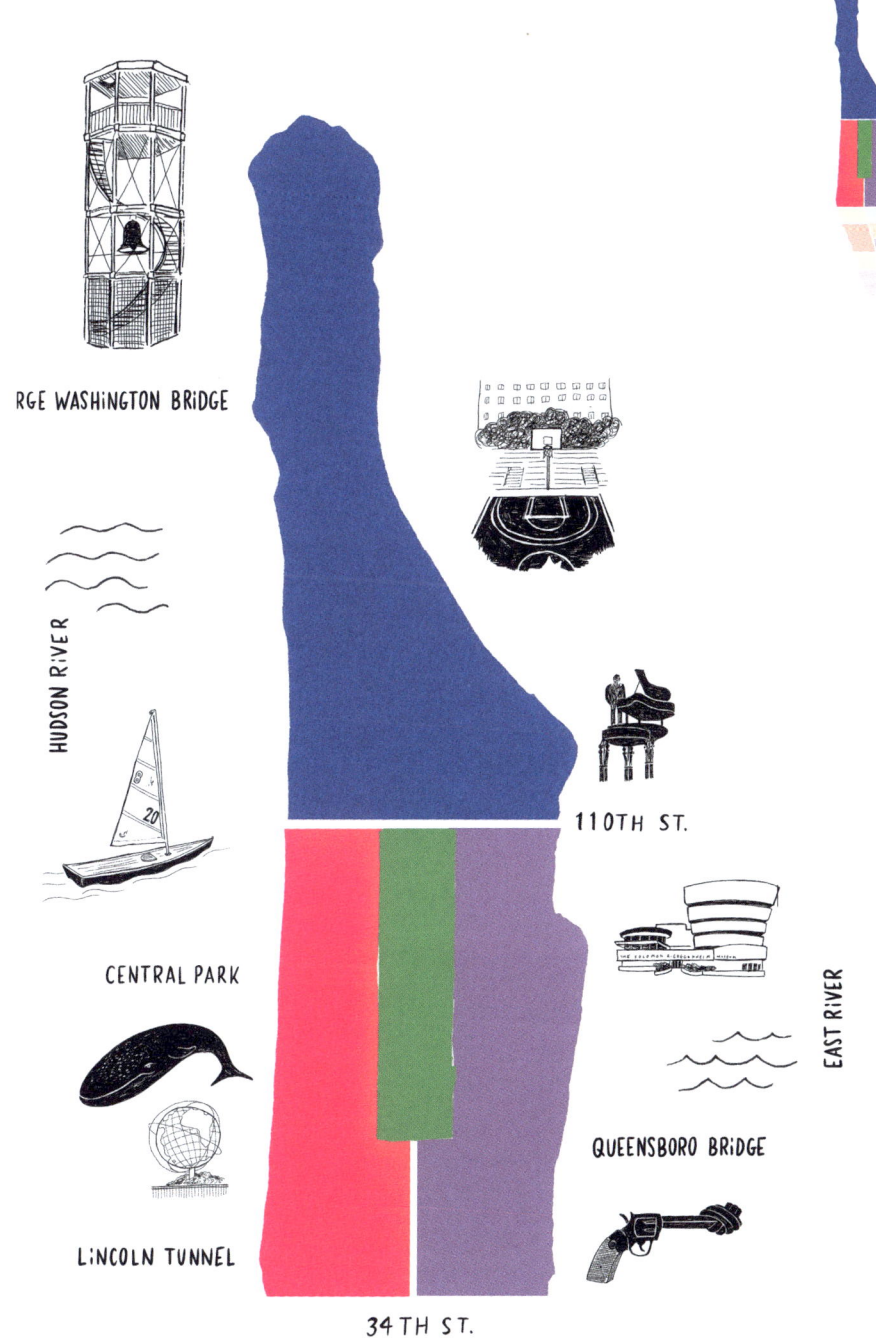

RGE WASHINGTON BRIDGE

HUDSON RIVER

CENTRAL PARK

LINCOLN TUNNEL

34TH ST.

110TH ST.

EAST RIVER

QUEENSBORO BRIDGE

ABOVE HOUSTON ST./ BELOW 34TH ST.

—

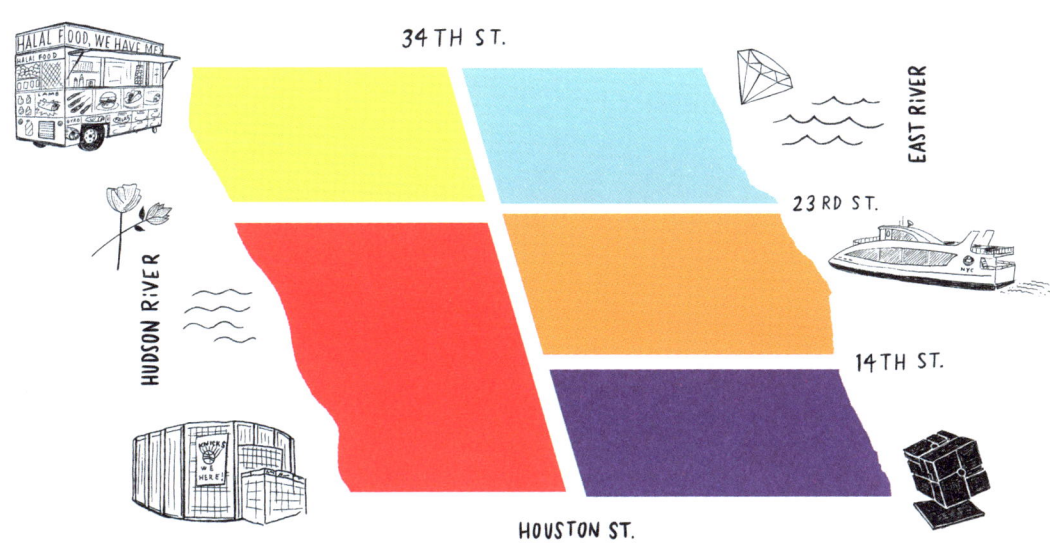

34TH ST.

EAST RIVER

23RD ST.

HUDSON RIVER

14TH ST.

HOUSTON ST.

BELOW HOUSTON ST.

—

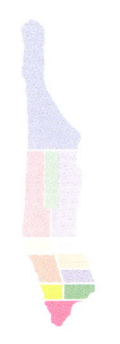

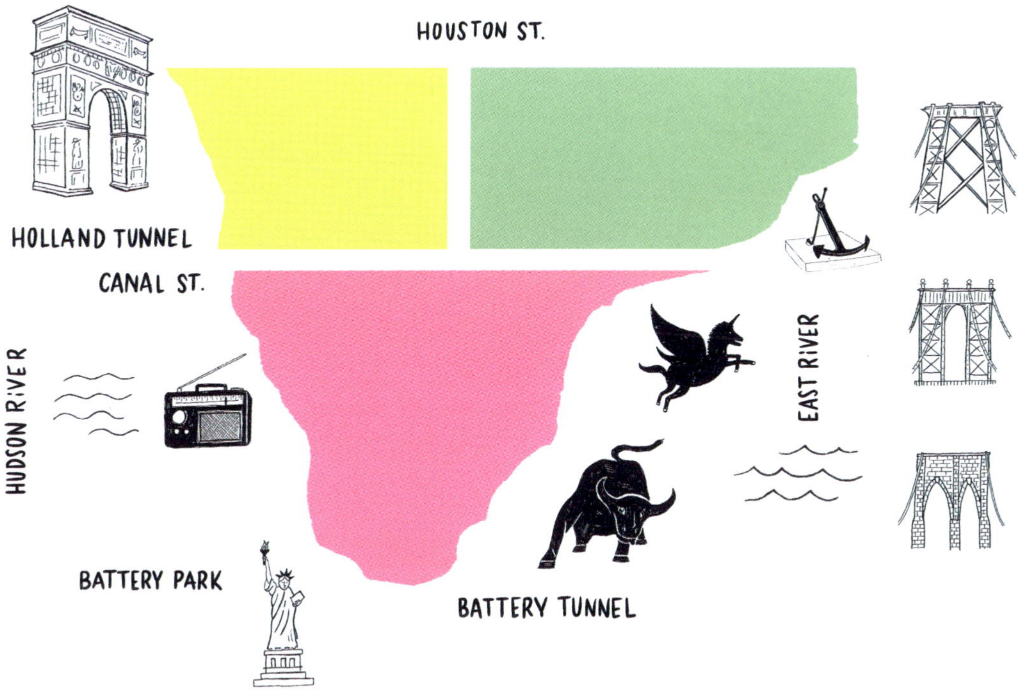

HOUSTON ST.

HOLLAND TUNNEL

CANAL ST.

HUDSON RIVER

EAST RIVER

BATTERY PARK

BATTERY TUNNEL

INDEX

BiOGRAPHiES

—

Joel Holland is an illustrator who has lived in New York City for over twenty years and who currently resides in Manhattan with his wife and two daughters. His illustrations have graced the *New York Times*, the *New Yorker*, *New York* magazine, Apple store windows across the world, and numerous book covers. He is also the author of *London Shopfronts*, *Brooklyn Storefronts*, and *Paris Shopfronts*, all published by Prestel. When not drawing, he can be found at the park with his family and friends or walking around the city taking it all in with a cup of coffee (a hot, twelve-ounce Americano with half-and-half).

David Dodge is a freelance writer living in New York City who covers travel, nontraditional families, LGBTQ stuff, politics, culture, and more. He is a frequent contributor to the *New York Times* and has had work appear in outlets including *CN Traveler*, *Travel + Leisure*, *Newsweek*, and the *Huffington Post*, among others. He is the coauthor of several other books published by Prestel, including *Brooklyn Storefronts* (alongside Joel), as well as *Sassy Planet* and *Category Is: Cocktails!* He lives in Gramercy with his two cactuses, but doesn't have a key to the park, so please stop asking.

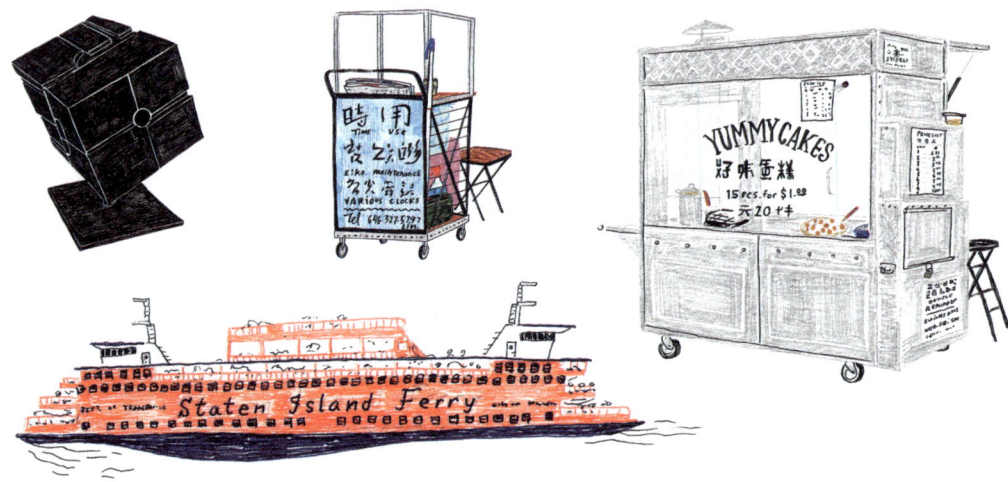

ACKNOWLEDGMENTS

—

JOEL HOLLAND

Big hugs and THANK YOU to my family. Thanks to my wife, Ploy Siripant, and our daughters, Ella Bee and Nina Sukri, for tolerating the constant pen-clicking and picture-taking. And thanks for always saying, "You should draw ___!" Or, "What about ___?!" To my parents for their love, and for joining Instagram just to follow what I am up to. You always support me in everything, and it means the world. To my friend Rodrigo Corral, for declaring that this collection of drawings should be a book very early on and making me agree. And a big thank you to Brian Rea for all of your time and wisdom in pursuing publication, not to mention your support during all these years. Thank you to Sara Bader and Christine Pride for your publishing insight. Thank you to James and Karla Murray for your guidance. Thank you to Nicolas Heller for your time; having you be a part of this is very special to me. What you do for the people of the city is incredibly generous and beautiful. Thank you to Ali Gitlow, editor of what's in your hands. Without you, there is no book. Thanks for your vision and direction. Thank you to David Dodge, writer of the words in this book. The energy of your writing connects with the images perfectly. Also, thank you to Michael Ferut for dotting our *i*'s and crossing our *t*'s. And finally thank you to Alex Stikeleather for your ingenious design. All of it, I love it! Thank you to all the owners and workers at the establishments featured here, for all that you do and have done. To all the NYC humans not pictured here, that make the sum of the city's parts so unforgettable. In memory of Leo. Everything reminds us of you.

DAViD DODGE

First, a huge thank you to Joel Holland for trusting me to give voice to his beautifully illustrated love letter to New York City, and to Ali Gitlow for having the foresight to know this would be such a fun and successful collaboration. Also, a preemptive apology to anyone unlucky enough to be stuck wandering Manhattan's streets with me—working on this project unearthed so many incredible anecdotes, personalities, bits of history, and lore about my adopted hometown that I now can't resist giving unsolicited walking tours wherever I go.

Thank you to the patrons of New York's small businesses who know they can buy pickles online, but instead choose to frequent that hundred-year-old spot on the Lower East Side that literally sells nothing else. Lastly, thank you to the owners and employees of the city's many storefronts, just a sliver of whom I had the opportunity to profile in these pages. It is your ingenuity and resilience that make New York the best city in the world, and what keeps us from turning into a giant Walmart. For that, I'll be eternally grateful.

© Prestel Verlag, Munich · London · New York, 2025
A member of Penguin Random House Verlagsgruppe GmbH
Neumarkter Strasse 28 · 81673 Munich
produktsicherheit@penguinrandomhouse.de

© for the illustrations by Joel Holland, 2022
© for the text by David Dodge, Nicolas Heller, and Joel Holland, 2025

A Library of Congress Control Number is available.
A CIP catalogue record for this book is available from the British Library.

Editorial direction: Ali Gitlow
Copyediting and proofreading: Michael Ferut
Design and layout: Alex Stikeleather
Production management: Luisa Klose
Separations: Reproline Mediateam, Munich
Printing and binding: DZS Grafik, d.o.o, Ljubljana

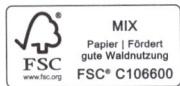

MIX
Papier | Fördert
gute Waldnutzung
FSC® C106600
FSC
www.fsc.org

Penguin Random House Verlagsgruppe FSC® N001967

Printed in Slovenia

ISBN 978-3-7913-9157-1

www.prestel.com

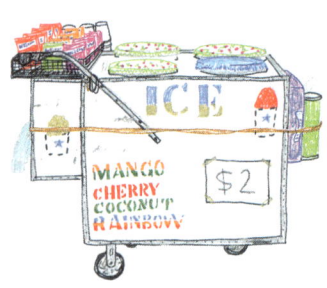

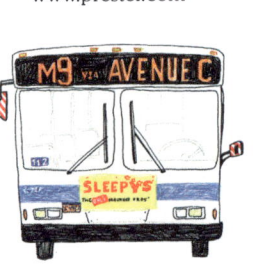

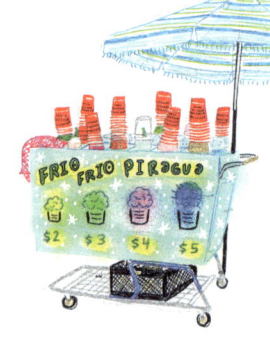

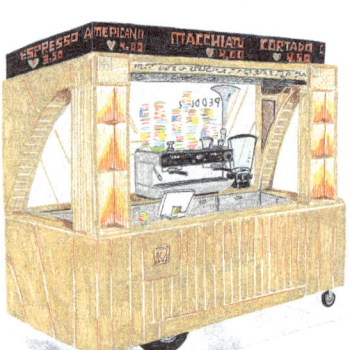

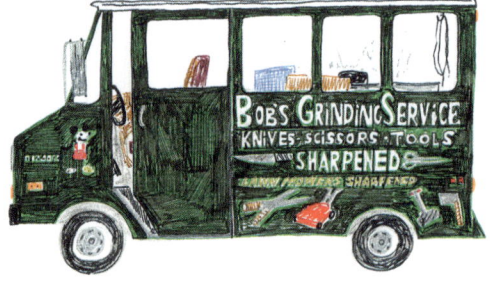